Greenhill Books

FIRE & STONE

CHRISTOPHER DUFFY

FIRE & STONE

THE SCIENCE OF
FORTRESS WARFARE, 1660–1860

Greenhill Books, London
Stackpole Books, Pennsylvania

Greenhill Books

This edition of *Fire & Stone*
first published 1996 by
Greenhill Books,
Lionel Leventhal Limited, Park House
1 Russell Gardens, London NW11 9NN
and
Stackpole Books,
5067 Ritter Road, Mechanicsburg, PA 17055, USA

British Library Cataloguing in Publication Data
Duffy, Christopher, 1936–
Fire and stone : the science of fortress warfare, 1660–1860. –
new ed.
1. Siege warfare – Europe – History
2. Sieges – History
I. Title
355.4'4'094
ISBN 1-85367-247-5

Library of Congress Cataloging in Publication Data
Duffy, Christopher, 1936–
Fire and stone : the science of fortress warfare, 1660–1860 /
Christopher Duffy. — [New ed.]
272 p. 24 cm. Includes bibliographical references and index.
ISBN 1-85367-247-5
1. Siege warfare—History. 2. Sieges—Case studies.
3. Fortification—Europe—History. I. Title.
UG444.D82 1996
355.4'4—dc20 96-32211

Publishing History
Fire and Stone was first published in 1975 (David & Charles).
This new edition incorporates revisions by the author.

Designed by DAG Publications Ltd.
Designed by David Gibbons; layout by Anthony A. Evans.
Printed and bound in Great Britain by Biddles Limited,
Guildford and King's Lynn.

Contents

INTRODUCTION TO THE SECOND EDITION, 7
PROLOGUE, 9

Chapter 1. Why Fortresses Were Built, 19
Chapter 2. Where Fortresses Were Built, 25
Strategic Considerations, 25
Local Considerations, 27
Chapter 3. How Fortresses Were Built, 37
Proposals and Plans, 37
Labour, 40
Building Materials, 41
Tracing the Site, 44
Excavations and Foundations, 46
The Building of the Rampart, 49
Chapter 4. The Parts of a Fortress, 53
The Fundamental Principles of Fortification, 53
The Ditch, 67
The Counterscarp, 69
The Covered Way, 69
The Glacis, 71
Detached Works, 72
The Citadel, 77
Detached Forts, 78
Auxiliary Defences, 80
Communications, 84
Interior Establishments, 91
Chapter 5. The Service of a Fortress, 97
The Composition and Size of the Garrison, 97
Provisions, 98
Armament and Ammunition, 99
Security, 103
Command and Administration, 105
6. The March of the Siege, 109
Plans and Preparations, 109

Investment, 112
Means of Reducing a Fortress Short of Formal Siege, 116
Formal Siege, 126
The Defence and Attack of Coastal Fortification, 191
7. The Great Sieges, 201
Namur 1692, 201
Namur 1695, 208
Antwerp 1832, 214
Algiers 1816, 218

APPENDICES
1. Glossary, 220
2. Schools and Systems of Fortification, 227
The Italian School, 227
The Netherlandish School, 227
The German School, 228
The French School, 228
3. Considerations in Fortress Wargaming, 230
Moves, 230
Cover, 231
Breaching the Scarp by Artillery, 231
Passage of the Scarp, 231
Mining, 231
4. Touring a Fortress, 233

NOTES, 236
SELECT BIBLIOGRAPHY, 243
THEMATIC INDEX, 249

Introduction
to the Second Edition

I have taken the opportunity to correct some mistakes and misprints which crept into the first edition of *Fire and Stone*, and update a number of details in the Bibliography and elsewhere. Likewise the typesetting and the presentation of the illustrations represent what is felt to be a more modern style. The substance of the original otherwise remains intact.

If *Fire and Stone* has worn reasonably well, it is because it set out to represent as accurately as possible the principles and practice of military engineers and their masters in the two centuries under consideration. In the twenty years which have elapsed since the first edition, the public has shown a much more lively awareness of the importance of artillery fortification, and the neglect and vandalism which were rife at the time of first writing have now become rare.

A less welcome trend has become manifest in the scholarly world. This is the interest shown in artillery fortification by people whose preoccupations might otherwise lie with the occult, and who read meanings into fortress design which extend well beyond any credible symbolism. In these circumstances I hope that the new edition of *Fire and Stone* will help to serve as a corrective.

In his review of one of my later books, a valued associate, the German professor Henning Eichberg, took me to task for having been less interested in the 'losers' than the 'winners', (i.e. sovereigns and governments which actually built fortresses), for having more consideration for fortress designs which were put into practice rather than remaining theoretical studies, and (a death-blow) for having the mentality of 'a second-ranking military architect of 1789' (*Ein Baumeister von 1789*). In the context of the present work, at least, I take the phrase as a compliment.

Prologue

One of the fundamental instincts of living creatures is to interpose some barrier between themselves and an unwelcome intruder. Whereas the deer had his speed and the lobster his armoured coat, it seemed to ancient and medieval man that his own best protection was a masonry wall which was tall enough to keep out the most nimble enemy, and hard enough to blunt or shatter all the bolts, stones, balls or rams that could be brought to bear against it.

We are all familiar with the kind of military architecture that was evolved to deal with these relatively homely threats – tall crenellated walls which are now in a state of picturesque decay, and reflected as often as not in the waters of some moat where swans cruise among the water lilies.

The arrival of gunpowder in fourteenth-century Europe wrought no essential change in the design of castle or town walls. The early cannon, after all, were heavy and obstinate beasts which put up a stubborn resistance if you wished to move them from one place to another. When, finally, you managed to plant them in front of their target, they rewarded you with a foul-smelling eructation which propelled a ball of stone or mis-shaped iron on a short and wobbly course.

Fortress architects were not compelled to revise their ideas until the fifteenth century, especially after Charles VIII of France descended upon Italy with a train of really mobile siege guns in 1494, taking a matter of days to wreck castle walls that had withstood sieges of months or years in medieval times.

This alarming experience gave new life and urgency to the age-old contest between the attack and the defence, engendering the lethal geometry of what is called 'artillery fortification' – a kind of fortification which has sunk into oblivion at the present time, yet one which contributed powerfully to the formation of modern Europe, and which still affects continental urban life in a profound way. The object of the present study is 'artillery fortification' in its most characteristic form.

The Italians, being ingenious folk, and the people who had been hit first and hardest by the new guns, succeeded by the 1530s in evolving a form of defence that was capable of both *mounting* and *resisting* the gunpowder artillery. The walls of the new Italian fortresses were built on a thick, low-lying profile which provided spacious and solid artillery platforms, and offered a good static defence against cannon shot. The trace, or ground-plan, was redesigned on strictly mathematical lines – most notably the old towers were trimmed into four-sided angular works called bastions, which were so shaped as to eliminate any dead ground by which the besiegers might have approached the foot of the wall unscathed.

The middle and later decades of the sixteenth century witnessed another important development – the evolution of the principle of defence in depth. The Italian engineer Tartaglia proposed in 1556 that a rim or ledge should be cut into the top of the counterscarp (the outer retaining wall of the ditch), so forming a walkway where masses of hand-gunners could be arrayed under partial cover. This *via coperta*, or covered way, was rapidly adopted all over Europe. The ravelin was another innovation which encouraged a forward defence. It was a free-standing, triangular work that was planted in the ditch between and in

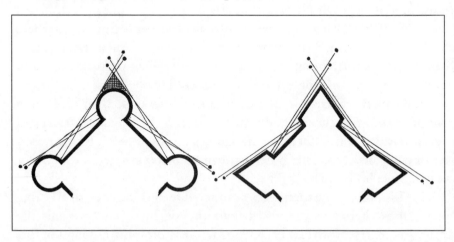

Comparison of (left) *ground plan of a medieval castle with circular towers, and* (right) *a bastioned plan, showing how the new design eliminated the dead ground* (shaded) *at the foot of the tower.*

front of the bastions, and which enabled the defending gunners to bring a cross-fire to bear on the ground around the fortress.

In cross-section, therefore, the artillery fortress presented a series of low-lying banks and walls, which were very difficult to knock down and gave the defenders plenty of space to deploy their musketry and artillery. The further edge of the ditch was rimmed by the covered way, and beyond that the fortifications tailed off towards the country in a long, bare slope called the 'glacis', where the attacker was totally exposed to fire from the fortress. Looking from above, the ground-plan resembled a star which was made up of a series of geometrically interrelated planes, the idea being to cover all the projecting parts of the fortifications by an effective cross-fire.

In their epic Eighty Years War (1566–1648) against the Spaniards, the Dutch took over the Italian ground-plan, complete with bastions, covered way and ravelins. They chose, however, to build their fortifications principally out of earth, instead of masonry. The Dutch-style earthen ramparts were cheap and easy to throw up, they offered almost unlimited resistance against artillery fire, and when suitably planted with palisades they were just as hard to climb as a masonry wall. The one fatal defect of earthworks was that they had to be kept up very carefully if they were always to be in a fit state to withstand a sudden siege. Most engineers agreed that works of masonry were a better long-term investment.

Thus the skill of the military architects placed the offensive at a relative disadvantage for the first two-thirds of the seventeenth century. During this period the 'trench attack' was a formless maze of saps and redoubts, by which dangerously exposed parties of workmen dug their way towards the fortress. The siege guns offered the men no very effective support, for the technology of artillery design had made no progress since the 1490s, and nobody was sure where the batteries should best be sited. The mortar, a short and stubby piece which fired an explosive bomb at high trajectory, had made its devastating debut in the 1540s, but this was essentially an 'area weapon', being aimed principally at the interior space of the town or fort.

It was left to Sébastien le Prestre de Vauban (1633–1707), the chief engineer of Louis XIV, to subsume all the previous notions of the attack and the defence into something that approached a coherent science of engineering.

11

On the defensive side, Vauban walled in France by constructing or rebuilding about sixty fortresses, planting them round the frontiers in double or triple rows in such a way that they could lend each other mutual support. Vauban was content to design the majority of these places according to the simple and elegant principles he inherited from another French engineer, Blaise François de Pagan (1604–65), though most people held that nobody was quite the equal of Vauban in the difficult art of adapting fortification to the irregularities of terrain.

Vauban's defensive achievement was more than counterbalanced by the new weight he gave to the siege attack. In place of the aimless meanderings of the old trenches he substituted a simple but exact scheme which was compounded of two elements – zigzag approach trenches (by which he won ground towards the fortress), and three or four transverse support trenches called parallels (where infantry could be arrayed in line of battle).

Vauban sited his first artillery batteries in or near the first two of these parallels and subjected the ramparts to a murderous enfilading fire. Then, after the garrison artillery had been dismounted and the trenches had reached the edge of the ditch, he arranged the heavy 24-pounder cannon in massed batteries behind the counterscarp and proceeded to knock holes in the ravelins and bastions. At this stage the fortress governor usually chose to capitulate.

No less importantly, Vauban trained up a corps of respected native engineers (280 of them by 1697), taking the place of the footloose and cosmopolitan masters who used to put their wits at the disposal of any prince who could be persuaded to employ them.

All this was made possible by the consolidation of state power by Vauban's master, the 'Sun King' Louis XIV (effective reign 1661–1715), who brilliantly harnessed the energies and resources of the French, the largest united population of Europe. Wars were now shaped by directions from the king, and became responsive instruments of state policy, and not, as they had tended to be in earlier times, modes of self-expression for great captains like Turenne or Condé. Campaigns could now be regarded as progressive steps towards the creation of coherent and defensible frontiers.

Vauban's near-contemporary Erik Dahlberg (1625–1703) was another energetic servant of the emerging seventeenth-century despotism, and he deserves the title of 'the Swedish Vauban' for his work on the defence of his chilly northern empire. The trio of the great seventeenth-century engineers was completed by Vauban's opponent Menno van Coehoorn (1641–1704), a Dutchman. Coehoorn's creative gifts were hardly inferior to Vauban's, but he laboured under the handicap of serving petty-minded masters who were contemptuous of his talents and believed that they could wage war on the cheap.

Vauban's work ushered in the classic century of military engineering, which lasted from the high tide of Louis XIV's conquests in the 1680s and 1690s to the break-up of the old political and military order at the time of the French Revolution. During this period the French engineers enjoyed an undisputed authority which was derived from the support of a centralised monarchy, from the continuity of direction that came from a large and well-organised engineer corps, and from the living tradition of Vauban, who had reduced siege warfare to an apparently infallible routine.

So it was that between 1744 and 1747 the French armies could sweep through the Austrian Netherlands and into Holland, taking fortress after fortress as easily as if the long-dead Vauban had still been in command of the engineers. Contemporaries were duly impressed, and the belief took root that once a fortress came under siege the date of its fall could be predicted to within a matter of days. A few engineers, like Marc-René Montalembert (1714–99), tried to devise alternatives to the bastioned system. Other souls despaired altogether, and Emperor Joseph II of Austria was so discouraged by the cost, inconvenience and apparent pointlessness of maintaining the Netherlands fortress barrier against the French that he had the whole system demolished in 1781.

That was going altogether too far, for history had shown that well-sited fortresses could serve a great variety of strategic ends. Their most spectacular performance as a frontier barrier was probably staged between 1706 and 1712, when the thick-set fortresses on France's northern border had closed about the advancing English, Dutch and Imperialists like an enveloping hedge. For offensive war, two or three well-found strongholds gave the best possible base for a move into enemy territory, as was proved by Louis XIV in the 1670s, 1680s and 1690s and by Frederick the Great of Prussia in his wars against the Austrians. Then there were energetic commanders, like Gustavus Adolphus or Marshal Villars, who maintained the speed of their advance by the

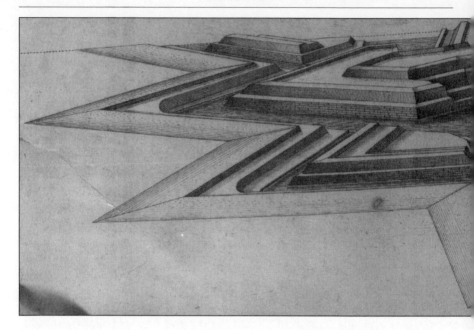

View of a front of fortification, with glacis, ravelins and bastions with cavaliers and retired casemented flanks (Heidemann 1673).

bold expedient of planting fortified depots across the actual theatre of war – the lesson was not lost upon Napoleon Bonaparte.

Fortresses, then, were extremely useful. What remained to be seen was whether they could maintain indefinitely the dominating position they had commanded in the seventeenth and eighteenth centuries, when roads were appalling, when armed forces were small but difficult to manoeuvre, and when a couple of energetically defended fortresses could dictate the course of an entire campaign.

Badly hit by the Revolution, the French engineer corps was regenerated by Napoleon, who in 1801 formed a united body of engineer officers and sapper troops – a formidable combination which performed brilliant services in the great conquests of 1805–7, in all the vicissitudes of the Peninsular War, and lastly in the defence of France in 1814 and 1815.

Foreign engineers admired the professionalism and devotion of their French counterparts, while harbouring reservations as to the obstinacy with which the Frenchmen clung to the 'modern corrected trace', which was simply a development of the bastioned system as enunciated

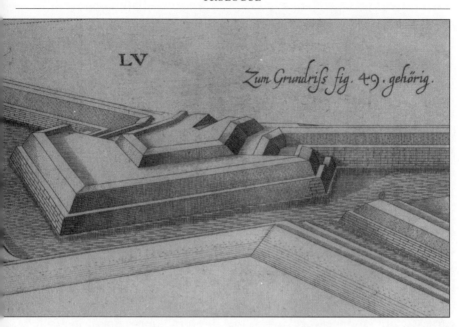

by the eighteenth-century pundit Fourcroy. Such, however, was the ascendancy of French ideas that the Austrian, Prussian, German, Russian and English engineers derived their inspiration from maverick Frenchmen whose doctrines had been rejected by the French engineering 'establishment'. For their ideas on passive defence the foreigners looked to Lazare Carnot's earthen ramparts and free-standing loopholed walls, while Montalembert *(La Fortification Perpendiculaire,* eleven vols, 1776–96) showed them how the artillery defence might be based on a new layout of the fortifications, dispensing with the bastion and arranging the guns in rampart casemates and in 'caponnières' – powerful batteries which projected perpendicularly across the ditch from the centre of each stretch of the rampart.

The debate became increasingly irrelevant, for influences were already at work in the first half of the nineteenth century that were inimical to any kind of permanent fortification. Geographical barriers were being opened up by railways, and by the driving of new roads and the metalling-over of old ones. Armies grew not just in size (thanks to conscription) but in flexibility as well, for the evolution of the system of semi-independent corps enabled generals to work round the flanks of fortresses that would have held them up for a whole season back in the old days, when an army used to move as an indivisible block.

15

Artillery, too, was comprehensively transformed (and any advance in artillery tended, on the whole, to the disadvantage of fortification). Gunpowder doubled in force, and guns and ammunition were manufactured more cheaply, more accurately and in far greater quantity than ever before. At the siege of Badajoz in 1812, for instance, the British fired away no less than 35,346 shot and shell, which was at least three times the quantity that we find in the greatest sieges of the time of Vauban.

Finally, towards 1860, the most advanced nations began to perfect rifled artillery, the deadliest of all enemies of fortification. The interior of gun barrels was now cut into spiral grooves, which imparted a spin to the projectile, giving it unprecedented range and accuracy, and allowing it to assume the characteristic elongated (cylindro-conoidal) shape of the modern shell – and hence a marked increase in weight in proportion to the calibre of the gun.

The race between the attack and the defence was now resumed in earnest, with engineers seeking to match every improvement in artillery (the rifled mortar, for example, or high explosives) with devices like concrete redoubts or armoured turrets. In purely technical terms the conflict was never resolved, for, contrary to the popular impression, fortifications continued to give a good account of themselves as late as World War II. In the process, however, the cost of permanent fortifications grew so exorbitantly that the main burden of the defensive came to rest upon trench lines, barbed wire and minefields – in other words, upon 'field fortification'.

But now we have stolen well ahead of our story. What is remarkable in the history of permanent fortification was not that it was changed so much by rifled artillery in the twenty years after 1860, but that it *changed so little* over the eight preceding generations. The masters of the early seventeenth century would have found nothing essentially unfamiliar in the enceinte of ninety-four bastioned fronts that was cast about Paris in the 1840s, or in the arguments that General Noizet put forward in his *Principes de Fortification* of 1859.

Undoubtedly the long reign of the old fortification was due in large part to the fact that artillery on the smooth-bore system failed to show any radical improvement for so long over the guns which Charles VIII had taken to Italy on his spectacular campaign of 1494. John Muller complained in 1757:

> Whoever consults the oldest authors, will find that guns are made at present nearly in the same form as they were at first; for since Dillich, a German, who wrote about a hundred years ago *(Hyperbologia,* Frankfurt-am-Main 1640), scarce any alterations have been made; and the French make their carriages exactly in the same manner at this day as he has delineated them in his work. [1]

Scientists were disappointed to discover that the crazy performance of the old artillery offered them no reliable foundation for their experiments, and they took their revenge on the whole race of gunfounders and artillerymen by presenting their researches in the form of indigestible mathematics and mechanics. The gunners, in their turn, clung to the traditions and mumbo-jumbo of the medieval trade guild. They had no interest in reducing the mysteries of their art to a mere science, which would be accessible to all. The consequent gap between the theoreticians and the practitioners did much to retard the development of an effective artillery, and gave all the greater validity to the elements of passive defence in fortification.

On the engineering side, the unique prestige of Vauban imposed a large measure of unity on his successors for well over a century after his death. In 1833 a captain in the British East India Company could state that 'it is a truth confessed by all engineers, that a thorough knowledge of Vauban's principles of defence and attack, and of the advantages and defects of his constructions will enable a right judgment to be made of every other method'.[2] Even the Prussians, so sensitive to national prestige in engineering matters, continued until 1860 to refer to Vauban for the best means of attacking a fortress.

By the nature of things the war of fortresses and sieges was the form of conflict which involved the 'respectable' settled population of a state most directly in the ambitions of kings and the calculations of engineers. Hence the direct human interest of artillery fortification.

The existence of fortifications converted the town into a military object, and so every now and then the citizens were subjected to the whole gamut of the experiences of a siege, beginning with the destruction of their villas and smallholdings outside the walls, and proceeding by way of bombardment and starvation to the final capitulation or massacre. Typhus, the bubonic plague and syphilis took root in Europe partly because of the squalid and static nature of siege warfare.

The implications were no less far-reaching in time of peace. Fortress towns were unable to expand through the deep and sterile zone of the defences, and lacking the space to build sideways the citizens were compelled to pile up floor upon floor of apartments. From this emerged the flat-dwellers of places like Paris or Vienna. But then there is the other side of the coin. If your home is not really your own, then in compensation you develop the habit of treating your city as a vast private ante-chamber. A favourite restaurant becomes your own dining-room, as in Vienna, or in a hotter climate you desert the narrow streets of the central city and stroll up and down some such avenue as the Ramblas in Barcelona.

What we have here is a life-style which made conditions in a crowded town tolerable, and even agreeable. Perhaps we could consider what lessons it might hold for us at the present day, now that the very purpose of the city is being called into question. As a habitat the old continental fortress town certainly had a great deal to recommend it. The place looked good from the outside. Its fortifications and glacis gave the people a pleasant green belt. It had an inner core where the places where people lived, worked and enjoyed themselves were all disposed within walking distance. And above all it evolved a way of living which enabled great masses of folk to get on together without encountering the eye-scratching doom that has been forecast for us by the scientists, with their experiments with caged rats. For city life, therefore, the siege cannon has turned out to be a creative force. Will we be able to say the same of the internal combustion engine?

Chapter 1
Why Fortresses Were Built

Military men and political philosophers had debated the utility of fortifications since at least the time of the ancient Greeks. In the sixth book
of his *Commonwealth* Plato commended the custom of the Spartans,
who built towns without walls, fearing that artificial defences would
make men effeminate, slothful and cowardly. In reply Aristotle sensibly
pointed out that you might as well say that you must always settle in the
open plain, so as to make it easier for the enemy to attack you.

The Classical debates were resumed with relish by the men of the
Renaissance, who plundered the Bible and recent history as well as the
ancient historians, in order to dredge up arguments to throw at their
antagonists.

This controversy was pursued with almost unabated passion until
the coming of World War II, but the credit for drawing up the most
complete and convincing statement on the purposes of fortification
belongs to Philippe Maigret, who in 1727 published his *Traité de la
Sûreté et Conservation des Etats par le Moyen des Forteresses*. Maigret then
occupied the comparatively lowly position of resident engineer at
Péronne, but he had known more exciting days as principal engineer to
Charles XII of Sweden on his fatal Norwegian campaign of 1718.

Maigret proceeded from the fundamental principle that fortification enabled a smaller force to hold its own against a stronger. A well-
sited individual fortress, or, better still, several fortresses acting in
concert were therefore capable of interposing a strategic barrier in the
path of a powerful aggressor.

In this respect the protagonists of fortification could draw the
attention of sceptics to the lessons of some of the great wars of modern
history. Mirabeau recalled later in the century that:

> without the help of the fortresses which studded the
> Netherlands, Louis XIV would never have escaped from the

consequences of all the mistakes which his age and weakness led him to commit in the War of the Spanish Succession. After seven years of endless blunders and misfortune this triple line of fortresses remained unpierced; it exhausted the patience and resources of the enemy, and by checking them at this final barrier it earned the monarchy . . . a more tolerable peace than you would have expected from the deplorable state of France. By reasoning and by the examination of facts we may establish that . . . a certain number of well-arranged fortresses are indispensable for the defence of a great state.[1]

As Vauban pointed out, the existence of its many fortresses rendered the tiny Netherlands more difficult to conquer than the whole of Asia.[2]

After the events of 1792–5, when the northern strongholds had saved the French Republic and his own neck, the war minister Lazare Carnot wrote in his most gushing and hypocritical vein that fortresses were the defensive arms of states, and the counterpart of the shield for the individual soldier. Shields do not inflict injuries on other people: they merely ward off hostile blows. Alone among the major weapons of war they may be justified in the eyes of humanity.[3]

A fortress system could reinforce the effort of the defensive in many useful ways. Most obviously, perhaps, the fortress offered a beaten army the opportunity for refuge, rest and recruitment, whereas 'if an enemy gets once the victory in a country that has no fortresses, he is at that instant master of the whole state'.[4] Some nations were thought to be more in need of this kind of support than others, and Maigret quotes an observation of Cardinal Richelieu regarding the character of the French, to the effect that the volatile spirits of our people require some stay or support against those impressions of terror they are capable of receiving from an unexpected attack, were they not perfectly well assured, that all the approaches to this Kingdom are barred by ramparts so strong, that no foreign violence can possibly force them at once, or till after much time is spent to make themselves masters of them.[5]

An inferior army could derive benefit from the properties of a fortress, without going so far as to lock itself inside. An individual stronghold could lend powerful tactical support to the flank of an army outside the walls, while a group of fortresses might enable a commander to hold

Discussion of fortress plans (Mallet 1673).

the field in an otherwise untenable province – the classic example being the Quadrilateral fortresses (Verona, Mantua, Peschiera and Legnago), which helped the Austrians to hang on in northern Italy until 1866.

Well-sited fortresses could endow natural obstacles with additional strength. In mountain valleys a single fortress could hermetically seal the only path of access, and secure the pasturelands from enemy foragers (Entrevaux in Provence, 1746–7). On rivers or narrow straits a fortress could deny a useful crossing to the enemy, and compel waterborne foreign trade to stop and pay dues (Frederiksborg, Gluckstädt). Where the gap was more than a couple of miles wide, a fair measure of control over traffic could still be exercised by a force of warships or privateers which roved from a fortified haven (Gibraltar, Malta, Dunkirk, Havana, Batavia).

Conversely the fortresses could be the guarantee of one's own military and commercial communications, by forming way-stations and bases on straits (the Danish islands), beyond mountain chains (Verona and Mantua for the Austrians), or on long and vulnerable communications that ran between neutral or hostile tracts of country (Fort Fuentes and Luxembourg for the Spanish in the Eighty Years War, Grosswardein for the Austrian communications with Transylvania, and West Point for the American rebels in the War of Independence). As a matter of principle it was well worth while to fortify rich cities lying within a hundred miles or so of the frontiers, since their wealth had to be protected against the enemy, and because these places nearly always stood on important avenues of access to the interior of the land.

Even when a prince was bent upon offensive action he knew that fortresses could lend powerful support to his designs. A well-stocked stronghold could effectively shorten his line of communications and act as a springboard for the attack over the border (in the second half of the seventeenth century the French used Arras in this way for operations in Artois, and Perpignan for their campaigns in the eastern Pyrenees). If he had fortresses on other frontiers, where he did not intend to stage major operations, he could safely entrust the guard to mediocre troops and concentrate his best forces on the decisive theatre.

The great Napoleon had firm opinions on these matters:

> In the last century [he wrote] there were people who asked whether fortifications were of any use, and there were even

22

WHY FORTRESSES WERE BUILT

some sovereigns who concluded that they served no purpose, and proceeded to dismantle their strongholds. As for
me, I would prefer to turn the question around and ask
whether it is possible to concert a war without fortresses,
and to this my answer is 'no'. Without depôt fortresses we
are unable to work out good plans of campaign, and without field fortresses (by which I mean posts that are proof
against hussars and raiding parties) we cannot wage offensive war. Hence those generals who, in their wisdom, have
rejected fortresses, are the very ones who are driven to the
conclusion that one cannot wage an offensive war.[6]

Political philosophers were apt to launch into long discourses whenever
the debate turned on the purpose of citadels, for these were the only
kind of fortification which could be turned equally against foreign enemies and fellow-citizens. Machiavelli claimed that an oppressive prince
would stir up such resentment that no citadel walls would afford him
protection against the wrath of the citizens.[7] This was rather too facile.
The town communities of the sixteenth century regarded the existence
of a citadel as a deadly threat to their freedom – that was why the good
people of Ghent, Utrecht, Valenciennes and Lille used to honour the
anniversaries of the demolition of their citadels as the second birthday
of their liberties.

The point of view of the authorities in those troubled times was
presented by the Sieur de Vieilleville, who in the 1550s begged Henry
II of France:

to consider that a town which lacks a castle or citadel, like
Metz, is never really safe. Without a secure place of refuge
it only takes something like a popular rebellion against the
troops, a violent mutiny in the garrison or a plot against the
governor in order to place that gentleman in danger of losing his life and his city.[8]

Henry II was won over by these arguments, and the citadel at Metz was
duly built.

The passage of time brought no accord between the three view-
points on citadels – the Machiavellian, the populist and the authoritar-

23

ian. Maigret concluded that kingdoms, aristocracies and newly established governments stood in clear need of citadels. He recalled the response of the Emperor Charles V, who came to Naples and noticed a mood of unrest – a rebelliousness that was symbolised in the unbridled, mad-looking horse represented on the city's coat of arms: ' "I intend," says he, "to have a good fort built on yonder hill, and that instantly; we shall perhaps by and by see the effects of it; for it is by no means proper that such a vicious horse should be without a bridle." '[9] The result was the building of Fort St Elmo.

In the later eighteenth century Frenchmen of advanced views were disinclined to accept Maigret's reasoning on citadels. Montesquieu and d'Arcon followed Machiavelli in arguing that citadels were actually dangerous to despotic states, because the tyrant could find no reliable people to guard them. Carnot, the populist, believed that citadels were a danger to liberties, and suggested to the National Assembly that the threat could be removed by the economical expedient of razing the fronts facing the town:

> since the fronts facing the countryside are incapable of harming the citizens, but only the enemy… A citadel is a monstrosity in a free country, a refuge of tyranny which should be the target of the indignation of every free people and every good citizen.[10]

Chapter 2
Where Fortresses Were Built

STRATEGIC CONSIDERATIONS

STATE DEFENCE

Princes arranged their systems of defence according to their judgement of their nation's geography, resources and potential enemies. Usually they found it enough to build or repair a couple of new fortresses, and knock down several old ones, in order to arrive at a system that was up with the times.

As far as national defence was ever discussed in general terms, most writers were profoundly influenced by Vauban's notion of barring the frontier by a double or triple line of strongpoints. Maigret[1] and C. F. Mandar[2] held that the frontier barrier should be supplemented, or in the case of small states largely replaced, by a powerful fortress in the centre of the land – this was the kind of thinking that led to the creation of the Belgian 'national redoubt' around Antwerp in the nineteenth century. Clausewitz adds that it was a good idea to fortify arsenals and provincial capitals as well; he said that the border was the more natural site for fortresses, but that the defence of the interior made for a more protracted resistance.[3]

RIVERS

Contrary to the protestations of ambitious statesmen, rivers rarely formed a satisfactory 'natural tier'. Thus for decades on end the French used to hold Philipsburg, Freiburg and other fortresses on the 'German' side of the Rhine, while the Empire maintained itself on the west bank at Mainz and the bridgeheads opposite Mannheim and Wesel. Any arrangement of forces for the defence of a river-line was inevitably a strung-out affair, and it was all too easy for the enemy to stage a feint at one point while making his real passage elsewhere.

All the same, a skilful defender could derive much profit by combining the peculiar properties of fortresses and river barriers. He could secure the best bridges and fords and intercept the roads which followed the bank, thereby endangering the flank and rear of the enemy who was rash enough to have passed the river at some other place. The variety of strategic opportunities was multiplied when there existed a bridgehead or fortified suburb on the far side of the river from the fortress. The situation became more interesting still if the fortress were placed astride the confluence of two rivers, for then the garrison could exploit three avenues of operations – namely up and down the main river and up the tributary (Namur on the Meuse and Sambre, Coblenz on the Rhine and Moselle, Mainz-Kastel on the Rhine and Main).

MOUNTAINS

For many powers, the maintenance of a fortress on the far, or 'enemy' side of a mountain chain was the only means of keeping a military presence in a distant province (Casale, Pinerolo and Exilles for the French; Verona for the Austrians). The defence of such isolated strategic footholds demanded a great deal of the garrisons, for the enemy were free to undertake the siege in spring or early summer when the path of relief over the mountains was still blocked by the snows. For that reason the prudent prince was careful to plant one or more major strongpoints on his own side of the watershed, to act as a rearward barrier and a base of operations (Briançon for the French, Palmanova for the Venetians). If the enemy came over the mountains to make a siege, they would have all the inconvenience of having to drag their guns and supplies over the passes.

One or two authors pointed out that it might be useful to plant forts in the actual necks of the passes.[4] Works of this kind might require a regular siege before they were reduced, and thus they could exercise a nuisance value that was out of all proportion to the modest costs of their construction.

The disruptive effect of a small mountain stronghold was demonstrated in a dramatic fashion in the early summer of 1800, when Napoleon was counting on sweeping into Austrian Italy unopposed by way of the Alpine valleys. Almost by accident the Austrians had left a garrison in Fort Bard, which stood far up the Val d'Aosta and directly in the way of the French horde which was spilling over the St Bernard passes. The little fort and its twenty-two guns threatened to upset the whole timetable of the French advance in a ridiculous fashion, for

Napoleon's reading of the maps had led him to believe that he could get his artillery past the fort without difficulty. In fact the fort stood on a conical mound just sixty or eighty yards from the road, which ran through the town below. Thus on 19 May 'the French army believed it had crossed every obstacle. It was following the course of a rather pretty valley, where the troops welcomed the sight once more of houses, grass and the springtime. Then the army came to a dead stop before the cannon of Fort Bard.'

Napoleon had to divert the march of the infantry over Monte Albaredo by 'a track known only to the goats'.[6] As for the guns, there was no alternative but to draw them along the road under the nose of the garrison. The French wrapped the wheels in cloth, then pulled the first pieces along the dung- and straw-covered street on the night of 24 May. The Austrians remained in ignorance of exactly what was happening, though they opened a blind fire which managed to blow up several ammunition waggons. Altogether 40 guns and 100 carts were got past the fort, enabling Napoleon to plant a depot at Ivrea and continue his advance into the Italian plain.

Fort Bard surrendered to Napoleon's rearguard on 5 June, but not before proving that it would have upset the plan of campaign of any army less resourceful than the French. As it was, Napoleon was deprived of most of his guns until 12 June. Nineteenth-century engineers and strategists were immensely impressed by the example,[7] and they invented a special kind of work called the *fort d'arrêt*, or *Sperrfort*, which was intended to reproduce the action of Fort Bard.

LOCAL CONSIDERATIONS

SIZE

The great French soldier the Marshal de Saxe was probably the only authority of any importance to argue that fortresses should on principle be purely military establishments, built in the country well away from the inconveniences of towns:

> The sieges which we conducted in Brabant (1744–7) would not have achieved such a rapid success if the term of the governors' resistance had not been fixed by the amount of

provisions they had in stock. They wished only to make an honourable capitulation, and they were just as keen as the besiegers to see a breach effected in their ramparts.[8]

Provisions were so short, he said, because they had to be shared with the civilians.

The weight of military opinion was firmly against Saxe. Major towns were nearly always important military objects, if only because they were sited almost by definition on nodal points of communication. As for the objection concerning the hungry and frightened populace, a hard-headed governor would not hesitate to expel the 'useless mouths', and requisition all the labour, materials and foodstuffs he needed for the defence.

Within certain bounds there was a good deal to be said for the view that the strength of a fortress town increased in almost geometrical proportion to its size. The roomy bastions could accommodate a large number of defenders, and the more the ground-plan approximated to a straight line the greater was the volume of flanking fire which could be brought to bear on the besieger. In addition the investing troops would be thrown out on a wide perimeter, and they might well find it impossible to seal off the fortress from relief.

> There are several other advantages in large fortified places, which cannot possibly be had in small ones; as that the sick and wounded may be lodged in a quarter remote from the attack, where they are pretty secure from the besiegers' shells and cannonshot; the several artificers necessary in a siege may do their business with less disturbance, and those troops which are not on duty may rest and refresh themselves, whereby they are better able to do their duty; and lastly, the powder may be lodged in several magazines at some distance from each other, so that it is not in the besiegers' power to destroy them, at least not all.[9]

There were, however, several restricting factors which had to be taken into account. The prince had first to consider how many troops could be spared to make up the garrison – few military men would have gone as far as Turenne in claiming that the only limitation should be the

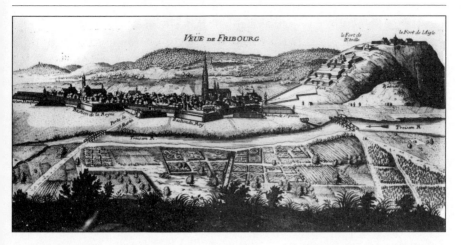

Freiburg. A fortress with detached works on an outlying hill (De Fer 1690).

quantity of provisions at hand. Then there was the question of expense. Even in the France of Louis XIV some of the more ambitious works of fortification were made practicable only by exceedingly large contributions from the cities. In 1701 alone Valenciennes paid up 31,250 livres, Lille 41,250 and Strasbourg no less than 60,000. The Scandinavian kingdoms were able to build and maintain such large establishments of fortifications by dint of resorting to cheap military labour, and by tapping such providential sources of revenue as the Sound and Elbe dues (in the case of Denmark) and generous subsidies from France (Sweden). Not many states were so fortunately placed.

The cost of a fortress was profoundly influenced by local factors like the availability of transport, labour and building materials. In general terms the bridges, gates, magazines and barracks were found to be the items most likely to involve the prince in unpredictable expenses. Good masonry works were costly to build, but represented an enduring investment: earthworks, on the other hand, were cheap to pile up and expensive to keep in good order.

GROUND

The healthiness of the site was one of the most important single considerations which determined the position of a fortress. Pestilential and swampy sites like those at Rochefort and Mantua were notorious throughout Europe for the rate at which they killed off their garrisons,

29

and the prospecting engineers tried to shun districts where they noticed that the inhabitants wore yellow or greyish complexions and died young, and where the livers of animals were pallid and corrupt.

If at all possible, the fortress was planted where there was a good depth of firm, well-drained soil. Sandy soil was apt to run like water, 'for which reason some naturalists have ranked it in the list of fluids'; it certainly hindered the besiegers from building firm-sided trenches, but 'when the wind is high, it blows that sandy surface about on all sides, ruffling it like the waves of the sea, filling up the ditches, and raising hillocks on the glacis, and beyond it almost as high as the parapets of the place'.[10]

It was expensive and difficult to blast and hack out foundations and ditches in rock, and no less inconvenient to build in a marsh, where the ramparts had to be supported on piling and the ditches were endlessly silting up. A loose, stony ground was probably the worst of all, for the earth was incapable of supporting itself, and every enemy cannon shot threw up a hail of stony splinters.

ADAPTATION TO EXISTING BUILDINGS

Architects seldom had the chance to give the same regularity and elaboration to their works in the real world as they did to the speculations they committed to their broad and empty sheets of paper. The existence of an important suburb, for example, might force them to describe an awkward salient which destroyed all symmetry in the design.

Most towns of Europe still possessed medieval enceintes which a skilful engineer could actually turn to good account in a number of ways. A long stretch of old wall could be left intact immediately behind the new fortifications to serve as a 'general retrenchment' or continuous rearward line of defence (as behind the Klein-Seite ramparts at Prague). In some places the medieval walls were already hidden behind a suburb, in which case the engineer would probably cast his new perimeter around the whole area, leaving the old wall embedded inside the town as another kind of 'general retrenchment'. If the medieval wall was in exceptionally good condition, the engineer could save a great deal of expense by surrounding the perimeter by ravelins (Vauban's re-fortification of Tournai, for instance, or Schall von Bell's project for Peking), or by grafting new bastions directly on to the old masonry (as at Evora).

30

MOUNTAIN SITES

The skill which an engineer required to adapt a design to man-made works was as nothing when compared with the ability to devise the various compromises that had to be made with the demands of nature. In 1861 General Prévost de Vernois proclaimed that

> the engineer should visualise his fortress as it will stand on the chosen plateau, mound, plain or rock very much as the sculptor sees his completed statue in his block of marble. But the engineer has to do still more – he must take advantage of all the resources of nature. Thus we know of twenty first-class sculptors, while all the labour of the ages has given birth to only one Vauban.[11]

In the seventeenth and eighteenth centuries opinion turned decidedly against the practice of fortifying sites on the summits of steep-sided hills or mountains. The two associated advantages – the difficulty of access and the facility of observation – were now considered to be counterbalanced by a host of inconveniences. In the first place a mountain fortress was exceedingly difficult to build, replenish and reinforce. Also the area for the accommodation of the men and stores was usually cramped, and the garrison was forced to depend for its water supply on rainwater cisterns which could be polluted beyond redemption by the fumes of a single exploding mortar bomb.

The efficacy of the garrison's own weapons was severely reduced. Sorties by infantry were difficult enough to launch and retrieve, and sallies by cavalry were almost out of the question. The musketeer had to lean over the side of the parapet to be able to aim at the enemy trenches, while the gunner lost most of the grazing effect he enjoyed on level sites. The Spanish veteran Diego Ufano observed that the shots from a highly-emplaced battery frequently bounced off the barrels of siege guns without causing any damage, whereas a well-aimed ball coming from below was likely to hit the gun carriage or the underside of the barrel with devastating effect. 'On entering many captured fortresses I have noticed that most of the fortress artillery has been dismounted by this means.'[12]

Height was in itself no sure guarantee against attack. At the great siege of Gibraltar (1779–83) the Franco-Spanish bombs from the *mortiers à plaque* soared a full 1,340 feet to wreck some works on the summit of the Rock. Crevices and faults in the rock sometimes laid a crag fortress as open to mining as one situated in a plain, as was proved at the Castle of Uovo at Naples in 1503, and at Alicante in 1709. At Gibraltar the miners managed to burrow some way into the north face of the limestone monolith.

The greatest argument against isolated hill fortresses, however, was the fact that they could so easily be left aside by the enemy main army and blockaded by a small force. That was why so many rock fortresses were abandoned in the course of the seventeenth century. Engineers came to see that a fortress might dominate an area without necessarily being perched on a mountain top. 'Such is Vieux-Brisach, standing not only on the border of the Rhine, but on an eminence which looks as if brought thither on purpose, and collected from a whole country as smooth as glass.[13]

The engineer was faced with many interesting problems when he had to plant a fortress on relatively low-lying ground within artillery range of surrounding hills. In some places an unaccountable lethargy held back the architects and garrisons from doing anything to improve their lot (thus Mont Feron was used as a site for enfilading batteries against Ath by Vauban in 1697 and again by Clermont in 1745). At the other extreme there were people like Frederick the Great of Prussia, who recommended the physical removal of dangerous crests, or the engineers of Genoa, who planted little forts on every hilltop within sight of the city enceinte. A common, and more moderate solution was to build detached works on one or two of the most threatening summits (Briançon, Freiburg).

A great deal could be done within the perimeter of the fortress itself. Traverses and parados (rearward parapets) offered good protection against plunging fire. As a specific precaution against enfilade the engineers tried to make sure that their works were built out of alignment with the likely sites of siege batteries. In the later eighteenth century and in the nineteenth the pedants went on to devise the feature of 'defilement', a kind of vertical safeguard against enfilade, by which the crest of the ramparts sloped upwards towards the country at such an angle that the imaginary prolongation reached *above* the summit of any dangerous ground, and not just to *the side*, as in the normal defilade.

There were two exceptionally difficult sites in the Pyrenees which displayed the ingenuity of Vauban to the fullest advantage. Mont-Louis was situated on a dome-shaped hill which at first sight offered no room for a fortress at all. Vauban solved the problem by crowning the summit with a continuous pentagonal rampart, and siting the corresponding five bastions a very short distance down the hillside. As a precaution against enfilade, he aligned the bastion faces in such a way that the imaginary prolongations fell clear of the surrounding heights. Immediately to the south of the main fortress a large crownwork enclosed the village of Mont-Louis, which was built on a spur that happened to be the sunniest dwelling-site in the whole of France. The long branches of the crownwork ran directly towards the wide valley of the Tet, and were thus safeguarded against ricochet fire.

Further down the valley of the Tet, the long and narrow town of Villefranche was hemmed between two walls of mountains. Here Vauban adopted a different solution. He added bastions to the medieval wall, then covered the circuit of the ramparts with a stout timber roof, calculating that the enemy could get their miquelet snipers (but not their artillery) up the mountain slopes. He sited a small fort on a nearby hill to serve as a citadel.

The principle of overhead protection was taken over in the middle of the eighteenth century by the Piedmontese engineer Colonel Pinto, who converted Exilles and other places into box-like *maisons fortes*. He began to do the same at Glatz in Silesia in 1768, but Frederick of Prussia did not like his designs and took him off the job.

Unfortunately most of the engineers based their plans on the very limited capabilities of contemporary artillery, and believed that it was safe to ignore any heights which stood more than about 1,000 yards from the fortress. With the introduction of rifled artillery this one oversight was enough to detract from the value of many otherwise excellent works (Würzburg in the siege of 1866, and many of the French fortresses in the Franco-Prussian War).

MARSH AND LAKE SITES

The essential virtues of swamp fortresses were summed up by Ville: 'These places enjoy the advantage that they can be attacked only at a few points. For that reason they require smaller garrisons... and the few accessible sectors can be built up so strongly that it will be almost impossible for the enemy to force them.'[14]

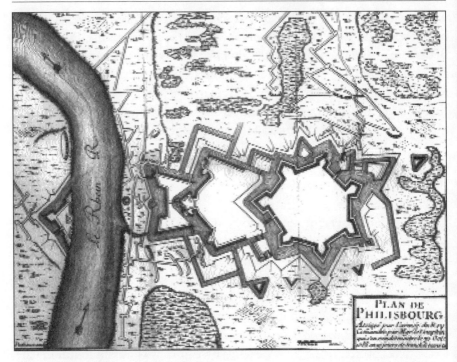

Philippsburg. A riverine fortress. The works are extended towards the Rhine by means of a crownwork and a hornwork. The siege trenches are those of 1688 (De Fer 1790).

Some of the most famous fortresses of the world derived their reputation principally from their marshy or aquatic situation (Coevorden and other Dutch fortresses, Philippsburg, La Fere, Péronne, Mantua, and Ayut'ia in Siam). The strength of the marsh fortresses increased with every yard of swampy ground that the besieger had to cross, and for that reason the main enceintes were characteristically simple, while the detached works were usually of earthen construction.

Like a mountain-top stronghold, a swamp fortress suffered from the disadvantage of being unsuited to sorties and easy for the enemy to blockade. Engineers also had to reckon with the inconvenience of the place being deprived of its watery protection by summer drought or winter frost. The worst feature of all was the prevalence of malaria and dysentery in 'these colonies of death and depopulation', to use the phrase of the *émigré* engineer Bousmard.[15] Without knowing precisely why, contemporaries learnt to associate these distempers with standing water. 'If there is any stagnated marshy water adjacent to the place, the heat of the sun draws up the corrupted particles, which fall in the cool of the night, and infect the air.[16] In 1732 a current was introduced into the wet ditches at Neuf-Brisach, and an improvement in the health of the garrison became immediately apparent. In the following year the Austrians in Pizzighettone prospered on their well-water until a French mortar bomb smashed the pump, compelling the defenders to drink the foul waters of the ditch. The 'Kaiserlicks' were soon stricken with disease, and they had to capitulate on 29 December.

RIVERSIDE SITES

Engineers had a variety of solutions at their disposal when they had to adapt their fortifications to flowing water. In the case of a smallish river, such as the Saar at Sarrelouis, the water could simply be led round the perimeter of the town by way of the fortress ditches; larger rivers were not so amenable, and they either drove past one side of the town or ran straight through the middle, dividing the town into two approximately equal parts. In the latter case the river frontages were left unguarded, or at the most were protected by a simple parapet with obtuse-angled bastions. Such was the inaccessibility of river frontages within the town that it was advisable to make them as long as possible, so that the landward fronts could be flattened out into something which approached the straight-line trace, with its power to deliver heavy flanking fire. In low-lying sites, some of the river water could usually be diverted by sluices into the ditches of the land sides (Strasbourg, Landau, Maubeuge, Valenciennes, Condé, Tournai, Menin).

The points where the river intersected the enceinte on entering and leaving the place were protected by bastions or half-bastions on either bank, and the stream itself was sometimes obstructed by ravelin-like islands (Geneva, Bayonne). At Strasbourg, and in his project for the fortification of Paris, Vauban went so far as to carry the enceinte across the water on arches.

Riverside fortresses were influenced by the seasons in much the same way as their cousins among the marshes. A hard winter or a burning summer could place the stronghold in grave peril. On the other hand there were times when the whole neighbourhood would be under water. The surroundings of Philippsburg were submerged every spring, when the Rhine was swollen by the melting snows of the Alps. For places in the Mediterranean lowlands, the season of winter rains was the time when they were usually least accessible (Perpignan, Cremona). Nevertheless there were striking local variations within the larger regions. The Piedmontese fortress of Cuneo was best left alone in high summer, for then the torrents on either side were liable to 'flash floods' caused by cloudbursts and snow-water from the tallest peaks. Only a reading of local history and a persistent questioning of the natives could make an engineer acquainted with all these peculiarities.

Chapter 3
How Fortresses Were Built

PROPOSALS AND PLANS

THE PROJECT

Once the building of a new fortress or the extension of an existing
work had been settled in principle, the initiative lay with the senior
engineer on the spot, who drew up a memorandum to explain the
shape, cost and properties of his projected fortification. The document
was accompanied by several sheets of plans, which displayed the individual works in some detail, and made clear their relation to the fortress
as a whole and the countryside up to the distance of about a cannon
shot.

Vauban used to get through this stage of the proceedings with
remarkable speed. Thus he entered the fortress city of Strasbourg with
the first of the occupying French troops on 30 September 1681, and
already on 16 November he was able to send the war minister a large
portfolio of memoranda and seventeen sheets of plans, giving the details
necessary for the improvement of the existing enceinte and the building
of a new citadel of five bastions.

In drawing their plans for a new fortress, engineers always began
by determining the centre point of the projected place, and the general
alignment of the fronts. The next step, and the foundation of even the
most elaborate schemes, was to devise the geometrical construction of
the individual fronts. This was executed in one of two ways.

In the older, and more complicated process of designing from
the *interior* side, the engineer chose the line of the curtain as the basis
of the front of fortification, and built up the corresponding two bastions as diamond-shaped figures around the angles formed by the
meeting with the curtains of the adjacent fronts. This construction
went out of use in the second half of the seventeenth century, although
it was still employed when some feature of the terrain, such as an old

wall, made it imperative to fix the position of the curtain in advance to within a few feet.

The design from the *exterior* side was made popular by Pagan and Vauban. In this case the draughtsman first settled on the salient points of his two bastions (A and B), and joined them by an imaginary line (A–B), which in Vauban's 'first system' would be about 180 toises (360 yards) long. He then built up the outline of his bastions and the curtain on the *inner* side of this base-line. At the centre (C) of the line he erected a perpendicular (C–D) thirty toises long. He connected the points A and D, and B and D to determine the alignment of the faces of the bastions, and fixed the shoulder angles at points (E and H) fifty toises from the respective salients. It only remained to find the re-entrant angles (i.e., where the bastion flanks met the curtain). With one point of the compass at the shoulder point E, and the other extended with the radius E–H, an arc was drawn inwards until it intersected the imaginary prolongation of the line A–D at G; the same operation was performed from the shoulder point H, with the radius H–E and the arc intersecting the imaginary prolongation of B–D at F. The points E, F, G and H were joined by a heavy line to indicate the completed outline of the front. Even when the terrain dictated some departure from per-fect symmetry, the engineer strove as far as possible to make his fronts correspond with this geometrical ideal.

According to the accepted convention, the outlines of most works were drawn in black Indian ink, although all masonry construction was represented in carmine red. Dry ditches and the profiles of earthworks were washed with a light, flat tint of burnt umber, burnt sienna or tobacco juice, while turfed surfaces like parapets usually appeared in green. Wet ditches, rivers and the sea were coloured with a wash of verdigris (sea-green) or light blue. Projected or incomplete works were traced in gamboge yellow. For the purposes of shading the light was supposed to enter from the top left-hand corner of the plan, and most people followed Vauban's practice of taking 'left' and 'right' to mean those directions as they were seen from the fortress, not the country. The toise, or fathom of six feet, was the most widely accepted unit of measurement. [1]

In the fortification or engineering ministries of many states it was the practice to build elaborate and realistic models of the nation's fortresses. These delightful constructions served for the instruction of

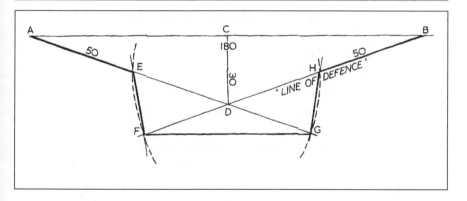

Geometrical construction of a front of fortification.

officers and cadets, as three-dimensional records, and as the means of explaining projects to monarchs who, like Philip II of Spain, were not very good at understanding two-dimensional plans. Given the limitations of contemporary cartography, a model was frequently the only practicable means of representing a sharply accidented terrain. Such galleries of models represented one of the most jealously guarded of state secrets, the most renowned of all being the splendid *Galerie des Plans Reliefs* in Paris.

The initial plans as drawn up by the chief engineer on the site were forwarded to the capital for detailed examination by a committee of officials, senior commanders and technical experts. These gentlemen's suggestions and criticisms were then incorporated into the definitive 'fair plan' which formed the basis of the work. Even engineering overlords like Vauban, Coehoorn or Dahlberg were ultimately responsible to some higher authority, whether the sovereign or a bureaucratic committee.

THE CONTRACT

The work of construction was usually entrusted to civilian builders. However, the responsibility of carrying out an all-embracing 'general contract' was beyond the powers of most of the building concerns of the time, and the work was therefore farmed out among several builders, each contracting for a particular fortification.

In France the contracts were settled and signed in the presence of the builder, the head of the municipality, a representative of the ministry of fortifications, and the military engineer in overall charge of construction. Among the papers that made up this document the most important was undoubtedly the *devis,* which set out in detail the method and order of building, and the stipulated cost of each work.

The opportunities for fraud and deception were manifold. Even a relatively honest contractor might seduce the government by putting in a low tender, and then find that he did not have the resources to carry on the job. The best safeguard against this kind of misfortune was to devote plenty of time to the assembling of materials and labour, and afterwards press ahead with the work with all speed. Skulduggery of some kind was almost inevitable when, as sometimes happened, the engineer himself acted as contractor.

LABOUR

The labour force comprised one or more of three categories of workmen: paid troops, hired civilian labourers, or forced labour of various kinds – whether convicted criminals, or the victims of the *corvée* or *rabot* (the labour that was exacted from the populace by official order). Of the three kinds, the hired workmen were reckoned to be the most willing and skilful.

The chief engineer of the fortress exercised a close supervision over the progress of the work, and when military labour was being employed the officers of the regiments were expected to keep their men up to the mark. The French war minister Louvois wrote coldly on 25 October 1682:

> If any officer does not apply himself sufficiently to this work, His Majesty's intention is that the offender should be placed under arrest and his name forwarded to me. According to the report which I shall send to His Majesty, the King will punish him in such a way as to teach the officers that they ought to carry out their orders more effectively.[2]

As for the labourers, Vauban was convinced that the way to exact the most work was to pay the men by piece rates, 'for once a workman is sure of his wage he invariably takes his time about things, whereas a man whose pay is proportionate to his work needs no other spur than his own interest.'[3]

These men were subject to quasi-military discipline. Vauban was the soul of humanity, but at Lille in 1669 he appointed two mounted guards to swoop down every morning on the houses of absentee workmen and haul them back to the site by their ears. Twelve years later he reported how he had established a satisfactory routine for the soldiers who were at work on the citadel of Strasbourg.

> This is what happens. In the morning the bell is rung as the signal for the town gates to be opened and the soldiers to walk to their work; once they have left the gates not a single man is allowed to return before evening. At lunchtime the drum is beaten to mark the beginning and the end of the meal-break. At three in the afternoon eight or ten cavalrymen of the watch come out and place the citadel under a tactful investment, and keep a watch on every path by which the soldiers might escape. Ignoring all the curses and jeering they detain the soldiers around the citadel . . . until the drum beats the retreat, upon which everyone returns without delay to the city.[4]

The engineer had to calculate the excavation of the earth very precisely if the progress of the work was not to be subject to constant interruptions. Here he had to take into account the local habits of work, as well as the hardness of the ground. At Antibes in 1691, for instance, the progress was exceptionally slow because the earth had to be transported by the basketful on the heads of women and children. It was also important to ensure that the labourers' pay arrived regularly, otherwise 'the best workmen would quit . . . [and] the bad only stay because [they were] not sure like the others to find employment elsewhere'. [5]

BUILDING MATERIALS

To mobilise the resources for the building of a fortress involved hardly less effort and expense than the launching of an army on campaign.

Stone-cutting (Mallet 1673).

Between 1667 and 1670, for example, the construction of the citadel of Lille consumed 60 million bricks and 3,300,000 of the long, square-sectioned foundation stones called *parpaings*. Since it was established that a single barge could carry as much material as a hundred waggons, Vauban actually found it economical to cut a canal from the upper Dyle in order to carry stones from a nearby quarry to the site. He pulled down country houses to provide further masonry, and had whole forests laid waste for the sake of their timber.

The same sort of thing went on at Antibes in 1691, where the ancient Roman theatre was treated as a quarry for building-stone. The lawyer Jean Arazy makes the fawning comment: 'The Theatre of Antibes never served more gloriously than on this occasion, when it managed to be of some little use for the service of the king.'[6]

The quality of the local stone was the subject of much musing and speculation on the part of the masons, engineers and contractors. At Belfort the builders were fortunate enough to have at hand the sandstone of the Jura, which was easy to cut but hardened very satisfactorily on contact with the air. In general an extremely hard stone was considered to be a poor material, for it shattered under the impact of a cannon shot rather more easily than did a softer stone or brickwork, in which the ball would drill a small, neat hole. The stone from boulders and exposed rock did not bind well with mortar, for it had lost its 'seminal spirit', though on account of its durability it was occasionally used for facings, foundations and sections of masonry that were exposed to water.

Some masons believed that a wall gradually became firmer over the first century of its existence, remained in a strong condition for the next two centuries, and thereafter slowly weakened. Others held that the influence of time was less important than that of climate, for a wall exposed to the north was accounted the weakest in a cold country, whereas a south-facing wall was the feeblest in a hot land.[3] It seemed an ascertainable fact that moonbeams were the enemy of masonry, a pernicious influence which contemporaries attributed to some 'humid quality' in the moonlight, rather than to the effect of a freezing starlit night on damp stonework and mortar.

In many places brickwork offered by far the cheaper medium for construction in masonry. Not only was brickwork inexpensive in itself, but it was much easier to repair or extend than work of stone. Where durable and dense material was required, as in foundations, or the angles of bastions, the builder could still resort to stone, or he could use the adamantine, semi-glazed 'clinker bricks' that were formed by the intense heat at the heart of the kiln or clamp.

When it came to the making of mortar, the prescriptions of Vitruvius were still held in high regard by seventeenth- and eighteenth-century builders. In Spain the masons actually preserved the traditions of Roman cement manufacture – that was why in the Peninsular War it was found that the battering of a breach in such material required the expending of twice as much ammunition as in the sieges of the brick-built fortresses of Flanders and northern France.

The waterproof cement for cisterns, foundations and underground chambers was usually composed of a mixture of two parts unslaked lime, one part sand, and one part pulverised tarass, a stone of volcanic origin which was quarried in the Rhineland. When no tarass was to be had, a passable substitute was provided by burning and pulverising tiles.

The length of the building season was strictly determined by the nature of the local climate, for it was equally dangerous for newly laid mortar to be seared by the sun as for it to be assailed by the frost. In the Baltic lands Dahlberg arranged his working year in two sections, one of which was made up of a seven-month building season which ran from 15 March until 15 October, while the other was devoted to the drawing up of reports and accounts. In places that were subject to extremes of temperature the building season could be very much shorter still. At Château-Queyras in the Savoy Alps Vauban stipulated that work should go ahead only between the middle of April and the middle of June. At Louisbourg, set amid the swirling mists of Cape Breton, there was no real building season at all, and the place fell down as quickly as it could be built.

TRACING THE SITE

Once all the trees and scrub had been cleared out of the way, the engineer in charge of construction determined the central point of his intended work. Here he set up his plane-table, which bore a large-scale and very carefully drawn plan, and had a horizontal sighting arm which pivoted about a pin set in the centre of the plan.

The engineer orientated the table by compass, and swung the sighting arm round until it coincided with the capital (centre) line of one of the bastions on his plan. He directed his assistants on to the required line, and they walked along it with their measuring chains and rods until they reached the point that was assigned for the salient, where they planted a picket. The process was repeated for each bastion in turn. After that the plane-table was carried to the salient angles, and thence to the shoulders and re-entrants, until every change of direction in the trace was marked by a picket and the whole connected by cords. Vauban once wrote about the

> great difference which exists between the qualifications of an engineer who knows how to build fortresses, and one who knows only how to besiege them . . . it takes fifteen or twenty years of hard work to make a good fortress-builder . . . and

Pegging out the site for a fortress (Guinard 1725).

45

even then he must have been extraordinarily industrious, and he must have been employed on a variety of tasks.[8]

The engineer certainly had to summon up all his skill and experience in order to make a good job of the final process of surveying – this was to determine the best 'ground level' round the perimeter of the enceinte. Here he had two ends in view: firstly, in the case of a new fortress, he wished to make sure that there would be a slope of at least six feet from the centre of the fortress to the ditch, so that the sewage and rainwater would drain freely away; secondly, he hoped that on any given sector of the fortress the volume of the *déblai* (the earth excavated from the ditch) would approximately equal the *remblai* (the material which built up the body of the rampart). He would run into great additional expense if he had to transport earth from any distance.

EXCAVATIONS AND FOUNDATIONS

The work of construction began when the labourers dug the ditch and foundations, and piled up the spoil *(déblai)* on the site of the intended ramparts behind. The space for the foundation of the revetment (masonry facing) of the rampart appeared as a continuous trench or slot which was sunk along the inner or 'rampart' side of the ditch. In good firm earth this trench reached down to four or five feet below the level of the floor of the rest of the ditch, though in Vauban's experience 'a mason cannot really dig his foundations too deep'.[9] The foundation itself was made up of two or three courses of large stones, which were tilted slightly towards the inner side of the fortress so as to counteract the pressure exerted by the mass of the rampart.

It took Vauban many years to learn all the secrets of the art of lay-ing foundations in waterlogged ground. Where the excavation was liable to rapid flooding, the masons of Flanders taught him to dig one short section of the foundation trench at a time, and build up the masonry above the water level in the course of the same day. When the whole foundation climbed safely above the water table, it was best to lay down the rest of the masonry in continuous courses all round the perimeter of the fortress, so that the pressure on the boggy ground would be evenly spread, and the revetment would everywhere subside into the earth at

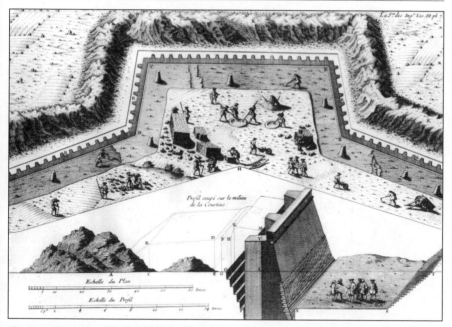

Excavating the ditch (Belidor 1729).

an equal rate, without the risk of cracking. If there was any danger that this stately downward progress might continue too far, the revetment and the whole rampart would have to be supported on a raft made of a planked-over timber grating. In very bad ground, piles were driven into the quagmire first, and the crossings of the grating were positioned over their heads. Vauban writes proudly of the success of this technique at Ath, where 'the curtain subsided imperceptibly, without cracking or losing any of its levels or slopes. It is now stable and laden with earth, and gives no sign of ever having moved.'[10]

There was little likelihood that the supports would rot, as long as the timberwork was embedded in waterlogged ground – oak and fir actually became harder with long soaking. In the tropics, however, timber foundations provided a delectable feast for white ants. At Fort St George at Madras the British solved the problem by turning to the native practice of resting the walls on well-shafts.

A rock foundation presented the engineer with as firm a foundation as he could wish, but in revenge it forced him to adapt his walls to perhaps as many as fourteen pronounced changes of level in a single work. By the eighteenth century the French had learnt to meet the chal-

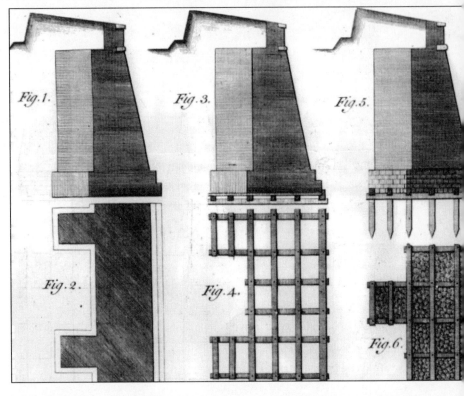

lenge in a very effective and 'modern' manner, by setting up two parallel walls of wooden shuttering along the line of the intended foundation and pouring cement into the middle. The hardened cement offered a perfectly level surface at the top of the shuttering, while conforming exactly to the surface of the rock at the bottom.

The casemates and other underground chambers were dug out at the same time as the ditch and the foundations. The masonry was left to dry over several months, and then covered with waterproof cement and several layers of gravel and earth. Five or eight feet of earth, lying on top of an arch three or four feet thick, was enough to keep out almost any mortar bomb. If a permanent countermine system was to be constructed, the lines were marked out on the surface with pickets and cords, and shafts were sunk at intervals. The galleries and branches were extended from the bottom of the shafts, in much the same fashion as in offensive mines, although the dimensions were rather greater than in the latter. The extra room allowed tunnels of masonry to be built within the timber framework, and as the continuous masonry arch advanced

Left: *Rampart sections and foundations (Muller 1746): Figs 1–2 show a revetment resting on firm ground; in Figs 3–4 the masonry rests on a timber framework, to prevent it sinking into soft ground; Figs 5–6 show the piling which was necessary in marshy ground (e.g. at Ypres); in Figs 7–8 the earthen mass of the rampart is interlaced with branches.*

down the tunnel, so the wooden supports were removed and the space was filled with earth and stones. Shallow galleries were more conveniently built by the 'cut-and-cover' technique.

THE BUILDING OF THE RAMPART

The lower part of the revetment sprouted from the foundation in the guise of a wall (usually of stone) which sometimes reached to a height of eight or a dozen feet. Where the rising revetment coincided with the level of the floor of the ditch, the outer face was withdrawn for a foot or two, leaving the fore-part projecting like a step or ledge. According to the availability of materials, the work was continued to the full height of the scarp in either stone or brick.

Vauban's revetments usually reached for about thirty or thirty-five feet from the floor of the ditch. The thickness at the base was the equivalent of between one-third and one-half of the height of the revetment, in other words about twelve feet, but the revetment narrowed to only about five feet at the coping stone, or cordon, which crowned the summit. The marked difference in width between the bottom and top was produced by the pronounced slope, or batter, which was given to the outer face of the revetment for the sake of stability. Vauban built his revetments with a batter equivalent to one-fifth of the height, a slope which was found by later engineers to render the masonry vulnerable to the ravages of vegetation and the elements. Cormontaigne reduced the batter to one-sixth, and nineteenth-century engineers attained the near-vertical slopes of one-tenth or even one-twentieth. It was easy enough

Rearward view of masonry rampart, showing counterforts and tablette (De Ville 1629).

to cut stones to conform with the required batter. Bricks were less amenable, and in masonry of this material the slope had to be produced by building the whole face at a tilt.

As if the massive revetment were not already stable enough, the engineers used to prolong the masonry into the earthen mass of the rampart by means of tapering counterforts, or interior buttresses. In the case of Vauban's thirty-foot-high walls the counterforts were eight feet long, five feet wide at the roots and three feet four inches at the tail, and disposed at intervals of fifteen feet between centres. A few engineers liked to join the summits of the counterforts by arches, which gave a solid foundation to the rampart walks and braced the revetment very firmly indeed.

In some fortresses the revetment was prolonged above the cordon in the form of the tablette, which was a masonry wall four feet high and three feet thick. The purpose of the tablette was to enable the revetment to support a slightly greater height of parapet, but this little wall went out of fashion in the eighteenth century, for it was found to be costly and flimsy, and it interfered with the cutting of embrasures through the parapet.

Some authors held that it was best to build the revetment as a free-standing wall, and then allow the masonry to dry out before you

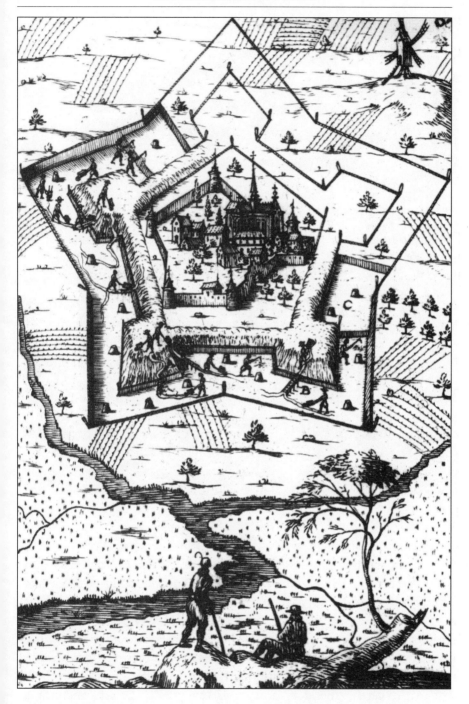

Piling up the body of the rampart (Guignard, 1725).

Building a bastion salient (Rüsensteen 1668).

formed the earthen body of the rampart behind. Rüsensteen and Belidor were among the people who preferred to build up rampart and
revetment together, so that the masons had a spacious platform for
their work. In either event the earthen mass of the rampart was heaped
up in layers between nine inches and one foot deep, each of which was
firmly rammed before the next was deposited on top. Vauban liked to
use troops of cavalry for the purpose. Small branches could be embedded in the earth, giving greater consistency to the work, and doing
something to reduce the pressure on the masonry revetment.

Chapter 4
The Parts of a Fortress

THE FUNDAMENTAL PRINCIPLES OF FORTIFICATION

Confronted with the self-indulgent fantasies of many of the writers on fortification, Maigret made the wise remark:

> There is nothing easier than to propose and give the dimensions of works, and even to execute them; but it is evident
> . . . that to apply them properly is a matter of great consideration, and it is this last kind of knowledge which constitutes an engineer. From which we may likewise conclude that no one general system, to make use of a modish phrase, will serve for all kinds of fortress . . . and that an engineer must have several [systems] at command, and know how to vary them according to the various circumstances of the places to be fortified.[1]

In effect, this facility of the engineer came down to the observance of a few simple and well-tried principles that were common to most of the projected 'systems' of fortification.

In adapting a 'system' to a site, one of the most needful things was to make the intended fortress equally strong on all sides. Since a fortress was only as strong as its weakest 'front', all the monies spent on the other sides went to waste until the vulnerable sector was brought up to the required strength. By observing this principle of the equilibrium of defence, the engineer was almost invariably forced to introduce some irregularity in his trace. Along a well-protected side of the fortress, where, for instance, the perimeter fronted on to a wide river or a steep slope, the curtain would probably be long, and the bastions small and far apart. Conversely, the engineer would take care to protect a vulnerable salient by building powerful bastions and detached works.

The great inherent virtue of the bastioned system was the fact that the component parts were designed to lend mutual support, each flank sweeping the ground in front of the face of the adjacent bastion, each face in turn commanding the ditch in front of the ravelin, and so on.

By the eighteenth century almost all engineers had been converted to the doctrine that the fortifications should be spaced in such a way that every part was capable of being swept by musketry, and not just by cannon-fire, as some had held in earlier times. The history

Ideal fortress, with a proliferation of almost every device known to military engineers (Guignard, 1725).

of sieges had shown that once the defending artillery was knocked out, some 'dead ground' was bound to appear around the works, if the fortress had been designed solely with the range of artillery in mind.

Human nature was also taken into account. Since most infantry-men fired blindly straight in front of them, without bothering to seek out targets to either side, it was found that the greatest effect could be attained from musketry by arranging the parapet at right-angles to the front of the work that was going to be swept by fire. In a well-designed fortress the flanks of the bastions were therefore placed perpendicularly to, and within easy musketry range of the face of the next bastion. For the same reason the ditches in front of the ravelins were designed to be subjected to fire coming at right-angles, or nearly so, from the faces of the bastions behind. Because the effective range of the smooth-bore musket amounted to two hundred yards at the very most, a front of two bastions violated an important principle of fortification if the exterior side, or imaginary line between the bastion salients, greatly exceeded 375 yards in length.

Commonsense considerations such as these helped to determine the general shape and proportions of the bastion. The length of the bastion face was the equivalent of about two-sevenths of the length of the exterior side of its front, which gave a good length of parapet for the command of the open country and the ditch of the ravelin. The length of the bastion flank, in its turn, approximated to rather more than half that of the face. The two faces of the bastion met at a salient angle of between sixty and ninety degrees, which enabled the engineer to sweep the ditches by reasonably 'perpendicular' fire, and gave the bastions a comfortably wide gorge, or neck.

THE PROFILE OF THE RAMPART

The heart of every fortification, whether ancient or modern, consists of some formidable obstacle to the progress of the enemy infantry. In the age of smooth-bore artillery fortification, this obstacle most commonly comprised a continuous enceinte, or ring-wall, which was formed of a masonry revetment, and a thick backing of earth which supported the troops and guns. In its trace, or ground plan, the rampart was broken into straight sections called curtains and angular projections called bastions. It was the projection of the bastions which enabled the defenders to direct

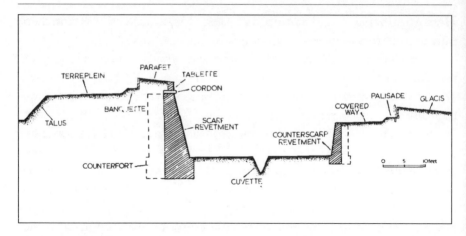

Profile of fortification.

a cross-fire along the ditch, which added immensely to the value of the rampart as an obstacle.

The construction of the revetment has already been discussed in some detail. It did not withstand artillery fire for a great length of time, as Vauban was the first to avow, but it served very well its primary purpose of preventing the enemy infantry from breaking into the fortress by any means except escalade or breach. The height, which was preferably of at least thirty feet in the case of a full revetment, was calculated to force the enemy to employ scaling ladders which would be so long and heavy as to be almost beyond the capacity of human beings to carry.

In its profile, or cross-section, the earthen massif of the rampart described a number of slopes and platforms. At the rear, facing the town, a grass slope rose from ground level for about a dozen feet to the wide terreplein, the main artillery fighting-platform. The terreplein was terminated along its outer side by a small bank called the banquette, which served as an infantry firing-step. The terreplein and the banquette were screened from enemy view and fire by a stout earthen parapet, which sloped gently down to the top of the revetment. We shall now examine these features in more detail.

'Talus' was the technical name for the rearward slope towards the town. It ascended at an angle of forty-five degrees, which was considered to be the natural slope of most ground – the inclination eventually assumed by the subsidence of an unsupported vertical bank of earth.

Here and there a ramp ran up the talus to give access to the earthen fighting-platforms above.

In keeping with the rationality which determined every feature of the design of artillery fortification, the width of the terreplein was usually fixed at about forty-four feet, a figure which was reached by allowing fourteen feet for the space taken up by a 24-pounder cannon, a further twelve feet for its recoil and service, and eighteen feet for two ammunition carts to pass abreast on the rearward part of the terreplein. In order to allow rainwater to run freely away to the rear, the gravel floor of the terreplein sank by anything between six and eighteen inches between the foot of the banquette and the lip of the talus. The slope also helped to afford some protection against plunging fire.

From the terreplein a slope two or three feet long rose at an angle of about forty-five degrees to the banquette. This firing-step was between four and five feet wide, which was enough to accommodate two ranks of musketeers, yet sufficiently short to permit a man to

Profiles of ramparts and ditches (Muller 1746).

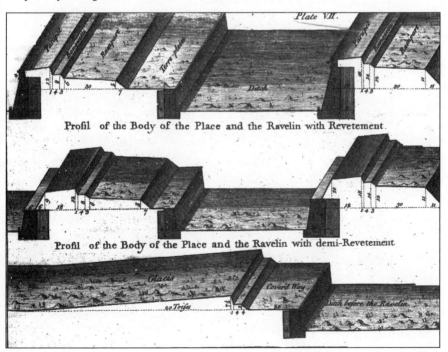

Plate VII.

Profil of the Body of the Place and the Ravelin with Revetement.

Profil of the Body of the Place and the Ravelin with demi-Revetement

descend in one or two strides to the terreplein, where he could re-load in relative safety. The banquette was razed at intervals, to permit the cannon to be trundled right up to the parapet.

The banquette gave immediately on to the rearward face (usually revetted in masonry) of the parapet. The parapet, the most vital and exposed part of the rampart, was usually formed of soft, stoneless and well-beaten earth. Vauban, and all other engineers after him, prescribed that the rearward face of the parapet should rise four-and-a-half feet above the floor of the banquette, thus affording the musketeer a convenient rest for his weapon, while shielding most of his body. The terreplein, the next step downwards, was therefore situated above seven feet below the crest, or edge of the parapet.

If the cannon were mounted on high carriages of the 'Gribeauval' type, they were aimed *en barbette* over the crest of the parapet. Failing

Forms of guérites: masonry guérites on the top row; wooden, movable guérites along the bottom (Belidor 1729).

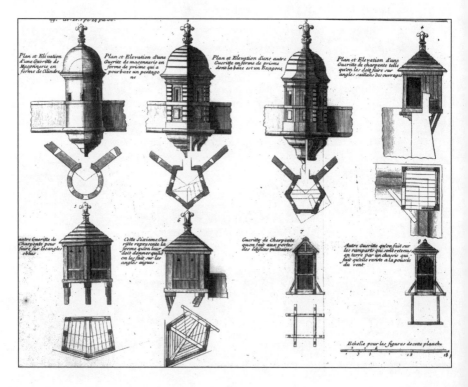

that the barrels poked through embrasures (gun ports) that were cut through the thickness of the parapet. The inner side of the embrasure was narrow, so as to give protection to the crew and the gun carriage, but it splayed out markedly towards the exterior, affording a wide field of fire. The embrasure was open on top, though the cheeks (sides) were revetted in masonry or gabions.

The parapet was about eighteen feet thick between the crest and the top of the revetment or the tablette. This quantity of earth was proof against all the weapons of the time, for the shot of the 24-pounder siege gun would penetrate only about fifteen feet in light earth, and twelve in more resistant soil (musket balls had a greatest penetration of about thirty inches). The upper surface of the parapet inclined downwards at a slope of about two feet in the total thickness of eighteen, so that the imaginary prolongation coincided roughly with the crest of the covered way on the far (outer) side of the ditch. As a precaution against erosion and flying splinters the whole surface of the parapet was carpeted with turf.

In most fortresses the great thickness of the parapet succeeded in blanketing long stretches of the ditch from the view of the sentries who paced the banquette. The ordinary rounds were therefore supplemented by a number of standing sentinels, who took up their positions in round or angular masonry sentry-boxes which were built on to the cordon at the angles of the bastions. These 'guérites' were pierced with four or five observation slits, and were capped with small domes. The sentries gained access to the box along a narrow, slot-like corridor that was cut through the parapet.

The guérite looked like some misplaced summer-house or gazebo, and lent an elegant, almost fanciful note to the otherwise sombre and heavy architecture of artillery fortification. Its very distinctiveness unfortunately helped the besieger to determine the position of the salients, and in the later eighteenth century the engineers preferred to employ light wooden sentry-boxes which could be planted on any section of the rampart.

In 1685 the Irish engineer Jacob Richards remarked on the quantity of vegetation on the walls of Maastricht:

I observe that throughout Holland as well as here they take great care to plant their works with trees, and in bringing up their earth or turf works (be the soil never so good) they interlaced every floor of earth with willow boughs and grass seed which extremely binds and secures their works, which practice we have wanted in England and has been the greatest reason of many of our earth works falling and giving way.[2]

This was the time when the terrepleins of newly completed French fortresses were being planted with the finest Flanders elms on the orders of Louis XIV. In other lands, Antwerp, Padua and Lucca were among the many fortresses which were famous for the beauty of their leafy rampart walks. As well as binding the fabric of the rampart more closely together, the trees gave shade to the garrison, and in time of siege they were cut down as a source of timber for such commodities as gun-carriages, gun-platforms, bridges, boats, pit-props, fascines, gabions, barricades, storm-poles and palisades. From the end of the eighteenth century it became fashionable to plant trees and bushes on the glacis as well; they too yielded timber and brushwood, and their root systems remained in the earth to present the enemy with an infuriating obstacle to the progress of his trenches. In some places it was also found expedient to encourage the growth of thorny bushes as a kind of natural barbed wire.

There existed several important variations on the 'standard' profile in full revetment which has just been described. Among these one of the most frequent was the profile in demi-revetment, in which the masonry rose for only a dozen feet above the floor of the ditch. In order to give the rampart as a whole an adequate profile, the earthen parapet made up the deficiency by ascending another twelve feet or more.

Instead of following the single, gentle slope to the crest above the banquette, as in full revetment, the surface of the parapet climbed steeply from the top of the masonry to a height of ten feet or so, then 'broke' into a more restrained angle which it followed to the crest. To allow for a certain amount of subsidence, the first, steep slope of the parapet sprang from the inner edge of the cordon, leaving the surface of the cordon as an open ledge which could receive and retain the débris. Very often this space was utilised as a narrow sentry walk, the 'chemin des rondes'. The tablette was retained at the outer edge of the cordon under the name of the 'garde-fou', and prevented the patrolling sentries from falling over the side in the dark.

The rampart in demi-revetment presented the engineer with a nice association of advantages and disadvantages. It was undeniably more vulnerable to escalade than was the version in full revetment. On the other hand, it was considerably cheaper, and allowed the engineer to conceal all his masonry from the fire of the enemy batteries standing on the glacis. Coehoorn built his entire fortress of Bergen-op-Zoom in demi-revetment. Other engineers liked to retain the enceinte in full revetment, and carry out the ravelins, hornworks and the like in demi-revetment. In any case the detached works were almost always of more modest dimensions than the main rampart behind. This was partly because there was no need to make space on the outworks for the circulation of military traffic. Then again the detached works were usually low-lying, for the whole system of defence was generally arranged in a step-like conformation which allowed the rearward fortifications to engage the enemy from the beginning of the siege. Thus the ravelin was usually lower than the enceinte, the hornwork lower than the ravelin, and so on down to the outworks lying beyond the glacis.

In northern lands, where there was a high water table and a good thickness of earth, many engineers dispensed with the masonry revetment altogether. Their ramparts formed a single homogeneous earthen massif, in which the parapet gave directly on to a grassy outer slope which led down to the floor of the ditch. The ditch (usually wet) gave some degree of protection against infantry assault, and as a further deterrent against storm the rampart was planted with one or more rows of storm-poles (French *fraises*), which were stakes which projected horizontally from the earthen scarp, or inclined slightly downwards so as to give less purchase to groping hands and persuade the enemy bombs and grenades to roll off them into the ditch.

At the foot of these earthen ramparts the soil was sometimes piled into a ledge or bank called the berm, a first cousin to the chemin des rondes, which served to retain and support any débris subsiding from the slope above. In many of the older fortresses the outline of the enceinte was duplicated in the ditch by a narrow and low-lying bank which went by the name of 'fausse-braye', and hugged the berm or the foot of the rampart. Fausse-brayes went out of fashion in the seventeenth century, for experience showed that they were 'exceedingly costly and almost useless for the defence of towns, on account of the great volume of earth required for their construction, and because the soldiers suffer from the rubble and splinters which rain down on them from the surface of the rampart'.[3] We have already become familiar with the peculiar virtues and vices of earthen fortresses. Earthworks were easy and fairly cheap to build, but very hard to keep in good order: they offered an almost unlimited resistance to solid shot, and yet of all fortifications they were the most vulnerable to a sudden rush of infantry.

In striking contrast stood the all-masonry fortress – which was often the most practicable type of stronghold in rocky, coastal or colonial sites where there was little space or earth to spare, or where the place was unlikely to come under regular siege by heavy artillery. The detached works (if any) were few and simple, and the glacis was often lacking altogether. The body of the enceinte was usually hollow, and provided precious room for accommodation, magazines, commercial stores or even shops. On top there was a stone-flagged terreplein, and a six- or nine-foot-thick masonry parapet which was pierced by splayed artillery embrasures. All masonry work, however, was exceedingly expensive, and parapets of this material had the notorious habit of throwing off showers of deadly splinters when they were hit by a cannon shot. These considerations deterred engineers from building masonry parapets unless they were presented with no reasonable alternative.

It was sometimes desirable to throw up cheap, serviceable defences against infantry attack along the communications between

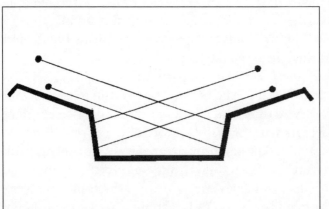

Alternative conformations of bastion fronts.
Left: *Flanking on the 'razing system'.*
Right: *Flanking by lignes fichantes.*

works, or round the perimeter of establishments like dockyards and arsenals. For this purpose it was enough to build a simple wall something like two feet thick and six-and-a-half feet high, and pierce it with small loopholes. In the nineteenth century this free-standing wall was often placed by English, Austrian and German engineers at the foot of earthen ramparts, and glorified under the name of the 'Carnot scarp'.

THE FORM OF THE BASTION

By the beginning of the seventeenth century engineers were in broad agreement as to the interrelated proportions of the bastions and curtain – in other words the approximate outline of the main body of the fortress. It took a little longer, however, to resolve the more detailed problems of the shape of the bastion flank, and the precise angle at which it should meet the curtain.

Until about 1680 many architects continued to house the flanking artillery of their bastions in a 'retired flank', a recessed sector of the flank which was largely screened from fire by the orillon (literally 'ear-work'), which was a projecting massif of masonry at the shoulder of the bastion. The corners of the orillon were squared off or rounded, according to the fancy of the engineer. There were several possible arrangements of the retired flank itself. The cannon could be arrayed behind one, two or even three levels of parapets, each of which was disposed either along a straight line, or in a concave curve with the idea of gaining a little extra space.

Orillons and retired flanks are prominent in some of Vauban's earlier fortresses, and Coehoorn continued to employ them until the

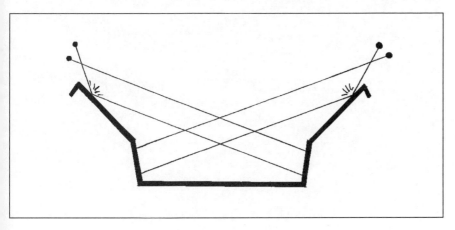

end of his building career. Nearly all the later engineers, however, chose to follow the example of Vauban and abandon these works in favour of a single, straight flank which ran in a direct line from the shoulder angle to the curtain. Their reasons are not far to seek: retired flanks were complicated and expensive, they cramped the gorge of the bastion, and they severely limited the arc of defensive fire while offering in return only the inert obstacle of the orillon; also it was decidedly uncomfortable to serve the guns on one of the lower levels of a multiple flank while the enemy cannon shot were filling the confined space with ricochetting splinters, and all the time your own guns on the upper levels were showering you with sparks and flaming wads and lifting you off your feet with the blast; at the same time the billowing smoke from the lower level effectively blinded the gunners on the upper storey.

View of a bastion from the gorge, showing a cavalier (Heidemann 1673).

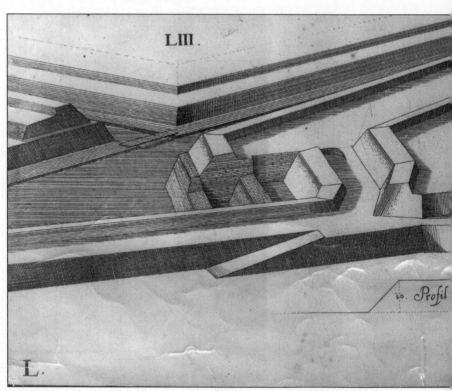

Whatever the form of the flank, it was vital that it should be spacious enough to accommodate at least two cannon, otherwise an enemy escalading force would be up and over the face of the adjacent bastion before the crew of a single gun had time to re-load.

The length of tbe flank was a matter of some debate. Pagan, Vauban and Cormontaigne and almost all later engineers were devotees of the 'Spanish', or 'razing system' of flanking, by which the line of defence (the direction followed by the imaginary inward prolongation of the bastion face) of one bastion intersected the re-entrant angle of the adjacent flank. This arrangement produced the maximum length of flank consonant with the need to give every foot of the flank a view along the face of the adjacent bastion.

Some architects of earlier times – the Dutch school, Errard and de Ville – based their flanking on the system of 'lignes fichantes', a disposition by which the line of defence met the curtain short of the re-entrant angle. Bastions built on this principle were almost too well swept, for the shot from the flanks were apt to strike the faces *en bricole,*

in other words gouging furrows by oblique blows. The faces of such bastions were very long, and they described acute salient angles which were vulnerable to enfilade fire.

At the other extreme there were some old fortresses on the Italian system (eg, Berwick-upon-Tweed) which possessed bastions that were so blunt that some of the flanking gunners commanded no view of the adjacent faces at all.

CAVALIERS

The 'cavalier' was a raised battery, usually sited in the middle of a bastion, which shielded the rampart walks from enfilade, and enabled the defenders to overlook the enemy siegeworks. Cormontaigne writes feelingly about his sieges in the 1740s that 'these cavaliers invariably made it difficult for us to defilade our approaches, and greatly inconvenienced us in our trenches by their plunging fire'.[4]

Cavaliers rose to a height of between ten and fifteen feet, and usually conformed in their outline to the shape of the surrounding bastion. Few authors ventured to lay down precise rules as to the design of these works, though Vauban insisted that they must be endowed with a revetted scarp and a ditch which cut them off from the rest of the rampart.

Despite its utility, the cavalier was seldom built unless the bastion lay hard under some 'dangerous' high ground outside the fortress.

RETRENCHMENTS

At Hesdin in 1637 the heroic Spanish governor managed to build interior defences, or retrenchments, behind every one of the five breaches which the French had blasted in the fortress. This feat was remembered as something of a prodigy – indeed at the defences of Luxembourg in 1684, Charleroi in 1693 and Ath in 1697 the Spanish proved incapable of throwing up adequate retrenchments of any kind. From these and similar experiences, Vauban and other authorities concluded that if you wished to build a retrenchment at all, it was best to do so in time of peace, when you had the leisure to give the work solid revetments, and endow it with countermines, fougasses and all the other marvels of the engineering art.

The retrenchment was almost invariably sited in the bastion, for by the second half of the seventeenth century this work had become the invariable target of the attack in preference to the curtain. In its simplest form the retrenchment consisted of an ordinary breastwork which ran from one side of the bastion to the other. The elaborate versions resembled miniature bastions or even an entire bastioned front. The safest line for a retrenchment was across the gorge, for a more advanced position – from shoulder to shoulder, say, or from face to face – exposed the defenders to the danger of being cut off from the rear.

Very occasionally we encounter a general retrenchment, a rearward defence that was designed to isolate not just a single bastion, but one or more fronts at a time. The Dutch had a general retrenchment at Ostend at the end of their great defence of 1601–4; the Piedmontese had another in the citadel of Turin in 1706. From these examples we may conclude that the building of a general retrenchment was a sign of very great determination. The simple bastion retrenchment was itself something of a rarity, for it cluttered up the gorge, and few governors seriously intended to hold out once the enemy had opened a breach in the enceinte.

THE DITCH

We have it on the authority of Vauban that 'a good ditch is always the best element in a work of fortification'.[5] This great gash in the earth extended from the foot of the ramparts to the covered way (which was the outer perimeter of the fortress proper) and embraced all the intervening detached works – tenailles, ravelins, hornworks and the like.

Oddly enough the engineer did not have a great deal of freedom in the design of his ditch. The depth and the width were determined not so much by immediate tactical purposes as by the need to find the requisite volume of spoil (*déblai*) for building the ramparts. In rocky terrain the ditch was almost invariably narrow: in ground with a high water table it was inevitably wet.

Montecuculi states rather unhelpfully that a good ditch should be deeper than the height of a tall man, and wider than the length of a high tree.[6] Most of what the authorities have to say about ditches is couched in similarly vague terms. At least the pundits were generally agreed that the best wet ditches were fairly wide and the best dry ditches moderately narrow.

Once the water of a wet ditch had reached a certain depth, say six or eight feet, the engineer had to extend the excavation horizontally, if he wished to endow the obstacle with any greater value. The capacity for passive resistance was, indeed, almost the only favourable feature of a wet ditch. This one advantage was offset by a host of inconveniences – the danger of water-borne disease, the hindrance to the defenders' own communications, and the fact that the garrison was denied the use of the floor of the ditch for such varied purposes as shelter, the assembling of troops for 'exterior' sorties, the launching of 'interior' sorties, and the grazing of cattle and horses. In hard winters the wet ditch stood in danger of losing even its worth as an obstacle if the garrison did not break the crust of ice at least twice in every twenty-four hours. Imaginative governors took the opportunity to heap up the fragments of ice on the inner side of the ditch to make a breastwork, or they poured water over the main ramparts until the fortifications were covered with continuous sheets of unscalable ice (like General Roth at Neisse in 1741).

An excessively wide dry ditch, on the other hand, actually weakened the fortress, for the extra width added nothing to the strength of the place, and the enemy needed only to depress his battering cannon slightly in order to be able to breach the ramparts along their base, which was the most telling target for this kind of fire. It was much more difficult to effect a breach across a narrow, slot-like ditch of the kind favoured by Frederick the Great.

The draining of rainwater from a dry ditch could be effected by tilting the floor gently downwards in the direction of the enceinte, and leading the water away by a small ditch which followed the curve of the revetment. A common alternative was to cut a cuvette, a V-sectioned trench which ran round the fortress in the centre of the ditch. The cuvette also served as a useful deterrent against enemy miners, particularly if it were cut down to the level of the water table.

Probably the best ditches of all were those that combined the advantages of wet and dry. Coehoorn razed the floor of some of his ditches to within a few inches of the water table, so that the garrison could move freely over the surface, while the besiegers could not attempt to make a trench 'passage of the ditch' without being at once flooded out. Many ditches could be filled and drained at will by 'water manoeuvres'. These were effected by sluices, the function of which will be discussed shortly. Water could be retained in an isolated section of an otherwise dry ditch by a dam called the 'batardeau' (of which there is an excellent example at Berwick-upon-Tweed).

THE COUNTERSCARP

The outer side of the ditch was retained by a continuous wall, the counterscarp, which described a zigzag course conforming with the salients and re-entrants of the bastions and any detached works that stood in the ditch. In construction and form the counterscarp wall is best described as a scaled-down rampart (scarp) revetment. It reached a height of twelve or fifteen feet, which was enough to deter enemy infantrymen from jumping too gaily to the floor of the ditch. The besieger was therefore compelled to devote some time to breaking through the counterscarp revetment from a mine tunnel, or planting charges to blow it bodily into the ditch.

THE COVERED WAY

The covered way was an outer infantry position which ran round the top of the counterscarp in the form of a rim or ledge set into the earthen glacis – the cleared and sculptured stretch of country immediately surrounding the fortress. Ten yards was a reasonable breadth for the terreplein of the covered way – wide enough for the movement of the defending troops, but too narrow to permit the besiegers to plant their breaching batteries without having to carve out some of the glacis as well.

Towards the country the covered way had a banquette and covering parapet of the same kind which crowned the top of the ramparts. Strictly speaking the term 'parapet' is a misnomer for this earthen screen, for the full height of seven or eight feet from the floor of the terreplein to the crest was usually formed half by excavating below ground level, and half from the artificially raised mass of the glacis.

The covered way was protected against infantry assault by the palisade, a fence of close-set, pointed wooden stakes. In the sixteenth and seventeenth centuries the Spanish and Austrians used to set their palisades on the crest of the covered way, in which position the stakes were almost immediately smashed by the enemy artillery. From Vauban's time onwards the stakes were planted two-and-a-half to three feet deep in the banquette at the foot of the interior slope of the parapet. They rose for the full height of the parapet, but left only nine inches or a foot of the pointed end to project above the level of the crest.

The stakes were triangular in section, and measured between twenty and twenty-two inches around the three sides. One of the flat surfaces faced inwards towards the terreplein, and the individual stakes were joined together by a timber cross-piece which was fastened by pegs about a foot below the point. There remained an interval of three inches between the stakes, which was just wide enough to permit a musket-barrel to be inserted and traversed. As a final touch of pure malice, the cross-piece was sometimes set with spikes, so as to discourage the enemy infantryman from planting his shoe between the points of the stakes.

Palisades were so expensive, and so liable to decay, that they were planted only round fortresses which stood in imminent danger of attack. The approach or outbreak of war was therefore the signal for furious activity in the most vulnerable of the frontier fortresses. Once the siege had begun and the enemy had declared his fronts of attack, it was the custom to plant a rearward palisade two feet behind the first on the threatened sectors (Mainz 1688, Lille 1708). Vauban argued in vain that double palisades were an unnecessary extravagance.

Opposite the salients of the bastions and ravelins the corresponding branches of the counterscarp wall met in a curve. This gave additional space to the terreplein of the covered way in front, which was termed the salient place of arms.

Where the zigzag course of the covered way described a re-entrant angle, between a bastion and a ravelin, the engineer sited his 're-entrant place of arms'. The parapet of the re-entrant place of arms jutted into the country in the form of a redan (a V-shaped work of two branches, open to the rear), the two arms of which projected from the parapet of the covered way at angles of a hundred degrees. Thus the musketeers who were stationed in the re-entrant place of arms could blast away in the usual manner of infantrymen, straight ahead, with no great danger to their comrades elsewhere along the covered way, which slanted away at a safe ten degrees from the perpendicular.

The places of arms formed screened-off areas where infantry, cavalry, or even light artillery could be assembled for a sortie. Up to 1,000 men at a time could gather in a single one of the re-entrant places of arms in Vauban's larger fortresses. A small ramp gave access to the salient of the redan, where there was a movable barricade in the palisade.

As the enemy siege works came nearer, the salient place of arms and much of the covered way became untenable. However, it was still possible to put up a prolonged resistance in the re-entrant place of arms, if this work happened to be furnished with a 'redoubt of the re-entrant place of arms'. Coehoorn, Cormontaigne and some other engineers liked to equip their places of arms with strong permanent redoubts, complete with masonry revetment and ditch, but most redoubts were improvised in the course of the siege and consisted variously of a simple breastwork, earth-filled wooden coffers, or the palisaded enclosure that went by the name of palanka or tambour.

The defence of the covered way against enfilading artillery fire presented something of a problem. One solution was to cut the parapet into a saw-tooth trace *(en crémaillère)*, which afforded a small sheltered space behind each of the indentations. More frequently the engineer adopted the more positive measure of intercepting the cannon shot by a number of traverses, which were twelve-foot-thick earthen banks running perpendicularly across the terreplein from the parapet to the counterscarp. Especially thick palisaded traverses were built on either side of the re-entrant place of arms, provided that work was not already equipped with a redoubt. Traverses served the secondary purpose of enabling resolute defenders to dispute the covered way foot by foot, as happened at the great siege of Lille in 1708.

Two disadvantages were associated with a covered way which was interrupted by traverses: in the earlier stages of the defence these massive earthen banks obstructed movement up and down the covered way, for the troops had to squeeze past them by way of narrow passages which were cut into the parapet; later on in the siege, when the enemy had lodged on the salients, the traverses interfered with the sweeping of the covered way by defensive enfilading fire from the re-entrant places of arms and the ravelins.

THE GLACIS

The glacis was a fire-swept zone of cleared ground which extended round the entire perimeter of the fortress. Beginning at a distance of about eighty yards from the crest of the covered way, it rose gradually towards the place at a slope of between 1:16 and 1:40. The gradient was rarely steeper than 1:10, for it was believed that no cannon mounted on an ordinary carriage was capable of being fired under a greater depression.

The ground was shaped in such a way that it presented an even slope falling away at right-angles from each branch of the covered way. The adjacent planes met along the capital lines of the bastions and ravelins, which gave an attractive pleated effect to the glacis of a well-maintained fortress.

The glacis played an important part in compelling the enemy to attack the fortress by the lengthy and laborious process of regular siege. First of all it forced the besiegers to dig trenches, if they wished to escape being massacred on the grassy slopes by the unobstructed fire from the ramparts and covered way. Secondly, as it rose towards the crest of the covered way the glacis screened the revetments from view, leaving the besiegers with no alternative but to bring their breaching guns all the way to the edge of the ditch.

Beyond the glacis there extended a tract of land called the zone of servitude, where building was prohibited altogether, or the populace were at the most allowed to throw up sheds and small villas on the understanding that they would have to be cleared away in the event of siege.

DETACHED WORKS

THE RAVELIN AND RELATED FORTIFICATIONS

In their wilder excursions of fancy, military authors and engineers loved to populate the ditches of their imaginary fortresses with a variety of extravagant detached works. All the best-known kinds will be treated here, for the sake of completeness, but the ravelin remained the one essential adjunct to the continuous enceinte in the comparatively few projects and 'systems' which survived to the stage of being carried out on the ground. As Vauban put it, 'ravelins are beyond doubt the best and most excellent of all outworks'.[3]

The lineal descendant of the medieval barbican, the ravelin was a triangular work which was sited between the bastions and directly in front of the curtain. In the early years of its existence the ravelin was content to remain a more or less passive block of earth and masonry,

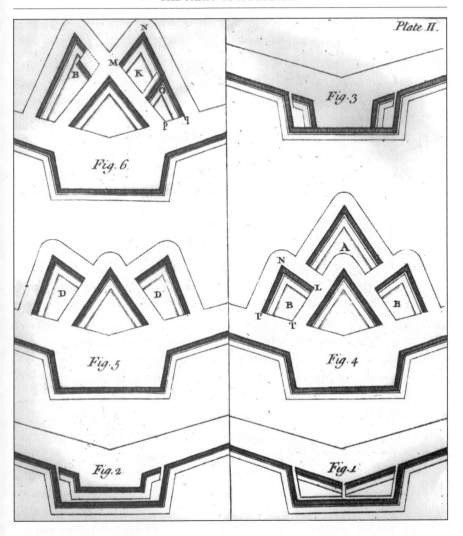

Types of outworks (Muller 1746): Figs 1, 2, 3 – forms of tenailles; Figs 5, 6 – ravelin with tenaillons or lunettes; Fig 4 – ravelin with tenaillons (B) and bonnet (A).

sheltering the curtain and the gate from the anger of the enemy. After this it grew gradually in size and confidence until Vauban placed it in the first rank of defensive works, shoulder-to-shoulder with the bastions on either side. It could pour a close-range and deadly fire along the ditches and covered ways in front of the adjacent bastions, and it exercised a measure of command over the glacis and the open country beyond.

In form the ravelin was essentially a redan, which presented a scarp revetment and a parapet along the two branches facing the enemy, and a simple scarp without parapet (or even an unrevetted bank) on the gorge face towards the enceinte.

Vauban's ravelin finally attained a width of about sixty-five yards and a length from salient to gorge of about sixty. It was frequently furnished with a redoubt, which was built either as a loopholed redan, or as a miniature interior ravelin complete with revetment and parapet. Vauban was given to squaring off the ends of the two ravelin branches into flanks, which certainly gave an increased volume of fire along the ditch but at the same time, however, exposed certain sections of the curtain to view from the crest of the covered way. At their recapture of Landau in 1703 the French utilised this defect in order to breach the curtains.

The French school of the eighteenth and early nineteenth centuries distorted the ravelin into more and more extreme forms, in an attempt to secure ever greater depth of defence. Fourcroy made the ravelin the central point of the 'Cormontaigne' system, and teased the unoffending work out to a length of about 150 yards. By the middle of the nineteenth century the salient had crept forward a further fifty yards, and assumed the extremely acute angle of sixty degrees. After that, the engineers gave up the struggle and came to see that detached forts were the most effective and economical means of dominating the country beyond the main fortress.

The ravelin owned a number of close relations, which were distinguished from the parent less by shape than by the position which they occupied in the trace of the fortress. The demi-lune, or half-moon, is best described as a ravelin which was sited in front of a bastion, and not, as in the case of the true ravelin, in front of the curtain. Much misunderstanding on this point springs from a difference in terminology. The present work follows the English and northern European usage, whereas Vauban and the later French authors call our ravelin the 'demi-lune'. The ravelin was sometimes flanked by a pair of works called 'tenaillons' (and sometimes also 'lunettes'). Each tenaillon was made up of a long face running parallel with the adjacent branch of the ravelin, and of a short return which 'broke' towards the ravelin from the salient. The 'bonnet' was a redan which stood directly in front of the salient of the ravelin, and covered it in much the same way as the demi-lune protected the bastion. Lunettes were redans that were planted on or even beyond the glacis. They came into vogue in the 1690s.

THE COUNTERGUARD

The counterguard, or couvreface, was a detached bastion which stood in the ditch a few yards in front of a bastion proper. Vauban's counter-guards at Landau and Neuf-Brisach were massive works on their own account, and dwarfed the casemated 'bastion towers' which lurked behind. In Coehoorn's 'first system', on the other hand, the counter-guard was little more than a narrow breastwork which formed a passive screen for the masonry of the enceinte.

In some fortresses the counterguard was prolonged into a contin-uous outer enceinte variously called the envelope or *couvreface générale*. Such perimeters were carried out in semi-permanent style at Ostend before the great siege of 1601–4, at Augsburg by the Swedes and by the Royalists at Oxford in the Civil War. Mesgrigny's powerful citadel at Tournai offers probably the most impressive example of one of these envelopes executed as a permanent work in masonry.

THE TENAILLE

Floriani *(Difesa et Offesa della Piaze,* Venice, 1630) and Vauban sup-pressed most of the continuous fausse-braye of the old Dutch school, but found it useful to retain the section which lay in front of the cur-tain and behind the ravelin. Under the name of 'tenaille', this trun-cated remnant sheltered the troops when they were assembling for sorties across the ditch, commanded the ditch by close-range fire, and concealed the base of the main rampart from artillery fire. The trace of the tenaille usually conformed with the direction of the 'lines of defence' of the adjacent bastions, which gave it the shape of a shal-low 'V'. Sometimes, however, the trace was broken in such a way as to represent a diminutive bastioned front of two half-bastions and a curtain.

The tenaille was positioned at least ten yards in front of the cur-tain and eight yards clear of the bastion flanks on either side, lest it should facilitate the escalade of the main enceinte. Since the tenaille served only for close-range defence, it was important to make sure that it in no way masked the fire from the curtain and the flanks. For that reason the crest of the parapet was allowed to rise no more than two or three feet above the level of the terreplein of the ravelin in front.

THE HORNWORK AND RELATED FORTIFICATIONS

The hornwork was a most spectacular piece of architecture. It took the form of two long branches that ran into the country on parallel or slightly divergent courses, and terminated and joined in a 'head front' of two half-bastions, a curtain and a ravelin. Vauban employed the

Hornworks and other outworks (Muller 1746): Figs 1, 2 – ravelin and bastion with counter guards; Figs 3, 4 – hornworks.

hornwork with prodigality at Ypres, Lille and Tournai, and seems to have been delighted with the device: 'These works are really excellent when they are well-revetted, and possess a deep revetted ditch with good ravelins and a well-traversed covered way. We may employ artillery and mines to defend them just as readily as in the main fortress.'[8]

The hornwork offered a relatively simple means of adding strength to a weak side of the fortress. Most of the earlier engineers liked their hornworks to spring from the curtain, whereas Vauban preferred to position the hornwork in front of the bastion, which thereby acted as a powerful retrenchment.

The cautious enemy had to devote a special siege operation to the reduction of a hornwork before he could so much as begin to approach the enceinte. The bloody siege of Lille in 1708 demonstrated that the besieger would come under murderous enfilade fire if he was misguided enough to leave the hornworks to either side, and try to drive between them directly towards the main enceinte.

The large and boxy interior space of the hornwork rendered it an eminently suitable fortification for enclosing a bridgehead, a suburb, or a dangerous piece of ground like an outlying hillock. A still greater area could be taken in if you built a 'crownwork', a kind of hornwork which possessed an expanded 'head' made up of two half-bastions, two curtains and a full central bastion. A double crownwork was a still grander affair boasting two full bastions, three curtains and two half-bastions.

THE CITADEL

The citadel was an independent and immensely strong work of four or five bastions, which was built on an advantageous site adjoining the main fortress. It was usually built with one (or both) of two purposes in mind – to hold the townspeople in awe, or to give the garrison a place where they could stage a last-ditch stand after the main fortress had fallen.

Bastioned citadels originated in the sixteenth century, and they were a concrete expression of those troubled times when sovereigns held down restive subject cities, or tried to secure a newly acquired territory without going to the expense of building a new town wall. One of the earliest, and certainly the most famous works of this kind was the five-bastioned citadel which Pacciotto of Urbino built for his Spanish masters at Antwerp in 1567.

Pacciotto rejected the notion of a square stronghold, for this would have scarcely accommodated the force of four or five thousand men that would be needed to put up a respectable defence and hold the city in awe. A pentagon, on the other hand, gave a useful increment of space, without demanding too large a garrison for its defence. Furthermore the geometrical properties of a pentagon guaranteed that the besieger would be confronted by the fire of three bastions, from whatever direction he approached.

Pacciotto embedded the Antwerp citadel in the town enceinte in such a way that the citadel could derive protection from the town walls if the place came under external attack, and yet could maintain an independent defence in the event of a popular revolt. Counting off the 'fronts' in a clockwise direction, beginning with the south-eastern, the first two fronts looked on to the open country, the third faced the Scheldt, and the fourth commanded the city. The fifth, or eastern front was artfully sited to have views over both city and country, and to enfilade the rampart of the city enceinte, which met the curtain at right-angles. Gateways were pierced in both the country and townward sides of the citadel, and a broad open space, or esplanade, separated the citadel from the houses of the town.

Thereafter the Antwerp citadel served as a model for almost every work of the kind.

DETACHED FORTS

Engineers came to recognise that a good defence in depth was one of the most important properties of a strong fortress. Unfortunately the limitations of manpower and finance imposed a severe curb on the kinds of fortification which could be organically incorporated with the enceinte and the main ditch. By the second quarter of the nineteenth century, therefore, engineers settled on the solution of surrounding the fortress town with a ring of detached forts – independent works which stood well into the country, while forming a coherent zone of defence. Detached forts had been known since almost the earliest days of fortification, as a means of holding an important locality, like a hilltop,

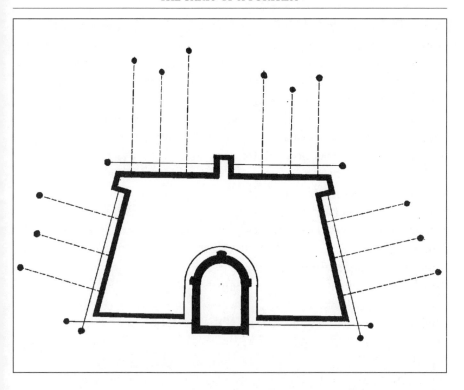

Simplified plan to illustrate yhe principles of a typical nineteenth-century detached fort on the 'polygonal' system. Long-range fire (dotted lines) is delivered from the upper ramparts, while the ditch is swept by caponnières – a conventional central caponnière is at the centre of the head front, and cat's ear caponnières on the lateral fronts. On the gorge front there is a strong defensible barrack block.

which lay outside the perimeter of the main fortress. However, the most direct ancestors of the nineteenth-century detached forts were probably the ring of nineteen lunettes which Vauban cast about Namur in the three years from 1692. The example was imitated at Landau in 1702, Turin in 1706, Le Quesnoy and Bouchain in 1712, and at Freiburg in 1713.

At Schweidnitz, from 1747, Frederick the Great took the development an important step further by placing the main weight of the defence on a girdle of detached forts and lunettes: the town enceinte was a feeble affair by comparison. The Austrians found the scheme incomprehensible, when they captured Schweidnitz in the Seven Years

War, and they proceeded to join up the works by a continuous entrenchment.

Napoleon's engineer Chasseloup de Laubat built seven enor-
mous lunettes round Alessandria by 1813, but the detached fort first
came into general favour only in the post-Napoleonic period, when
Prussia, Austria and the German Confederation were rebuilding the
defences of Central Europe. The French followed suit, and in the
mighty defence works around Paris in the 1840s the government of
Louis-Philippe built a ring of detached forts as well as a continuous
enceinte. The detached fort came in three main forms: the miniature
bastioned fortress (like the forts at Paris), the star fort (as at Schweidnitz), and most commonly the original lunette, which Henri de Brialmont and other engineers skilfully adapted to the exigencies of rifled
artillery in the later nineteenth century.

AUXILIARY DEFENCES

OBSTRUCTIONS

The strength of the fortress proper could be greatly enhanced by the
cunning and malicious employment of a variety of obstacles.

You could render the ground dangerous for unwary enemy
infantry and almost impassable for cavalry by the simple expedient of
sowing caltrops. These were small iron tetrahedrons which were
obliging enough to come to rest with one of the points uppermost
no matter which way they fell – a property which has given the caltrop the distinction of being the one item of military equipment
which has remained unchanged from ancient times until the present
day.

A belt of forest or scrub could be made into a most formidable
barrier by judicious felling and shaping. The trees were cut down in
such a way that they fell towards the enemy. The base of the trunk was
then secured to the ground with pickets, the leaves and twigs were
stripped off, and the remaining branches trimmed into sharp points.
These 'abatis' came into their own in heavily-wooded country, where
they could supplement regular fortifications, as at Fort Carillon (Ticonderoga), or form important components of frontier lines like the ones
in Bavaria and Russia.

Breaches and other gaps in fortifications could be obstructed by the planting of spears or stakes through the faces of a squared-off timber beam to form a *cheval de frise*. On the Hungarian theatre in the seventeenth and early eighteenth centuries the Austrian infantry was actually equipped with boar spears (Swedish feathers, *Schweinsfeder*) for this purpose. The stakes or spears could also be bound together round their middles, making up a globular 'star' which had points sticking out in all directions.

'WATER MANOEUVRES'
Probably no other branch of military engineering demanded so much of practical, theoretical and local knowledge at the same time as did the effective arranging of water defences. An 'inundation' was the flooding of an area round a fortress by means of the damming of a river, or the release of a pent-up body of water further upstream. In both cases the necessary control was usually achieved by funnelling the flow of the water through a narrow neck, where it could be freed or detained at will by a Dutch sluice – a stout shutter sliding up and down in grooves.

In 1757 the Austrians sought to smash the Prussian bridges above and below the beleaguered city of Prague by throwing timber on to a lake close by the river Moldau and breaking the retaining dyke. The operation of 'water manoeuvres' was not usually so spectacular. In 1677, while the French were being besieged in Oudenarde, they signalled to Marshal d'Humières to release the Scheldt upstream at Tournai; the river ran for only about twenty-five miles between the two fortresses, yet in this flat country it took five or six days for the artificial tide to flood the meadows all the way to Oudenarde. Still more patience was required when an inundation was spread by the alternative technique – stopping up the river. It was reckoned that anything between fifteen and twenty days was needed for the river Lave to effect the great inundation of La Brette to the south-west of Béthune.

Around Bergen-op-Zoom and many other places the country was not flooded except 'on the greatest emergencies, for a very good reason: which is, that it is not so easily cleared again of that load of water, which penetrating into a spongy spewy ground maintains its position till dried up by the sun, and then there is a dreadful danger remaining, upon that supposition, which is, that it casts up many gross and noxious vapours, which may, and doubtless do, carry a dreadful and noxious quality about them, and subject the adjacent inhabitants to many disorders'.[9]

'Water manoeuvres' of an unusually speedy kind could be effected when the fortress ditch itself was capable of being flooded from a river. Three barrages of sluices were required if you wished to take full advantage of this happy circumstance: firstly an entry sluice (*écluse de chasse*) at the upstream end of the fortress, so as to admit water to the ditch; secondly a barrier and a sluice positioned in the river a short distance below the entry sluice, in order to shut off the stream from its old course; and last of all an exit sluice (*écluse de fuite*) which was sited at the point where the ditch rejoined the river downstream of the enceinte.

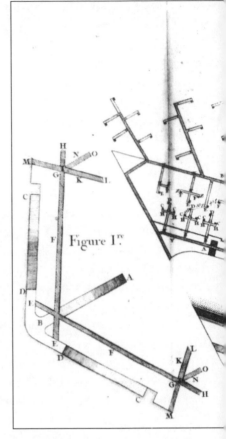

Figure I.re

Beginning with a full ditch, you could produce a satisfactory rush of water by closing the river sluice and opening the entry and exit sluices simultaneously, which had the effect of diverting the river through the ditch. If this failed to tear away the causeways or bridges which the enemy were building across the ditch, you could conjure up a mighty deluge by shutting the entry sluice, letting the ditch water drain away through the open exit sluice, and winding the entry sluice up again; at this the full force of the river, which was pent up against the closed river sluice, swept along the almost empty ditch in a veritable wall of water.

COUNTERMINE SYSTEMS

A system of permanent countermines was one of the most expensive but effective adjuncts of fortification, enabling the governor to offer a foot-by-foot three-dimensional defence of the ground from the tail of the glacis all the way back to the counterscarp.

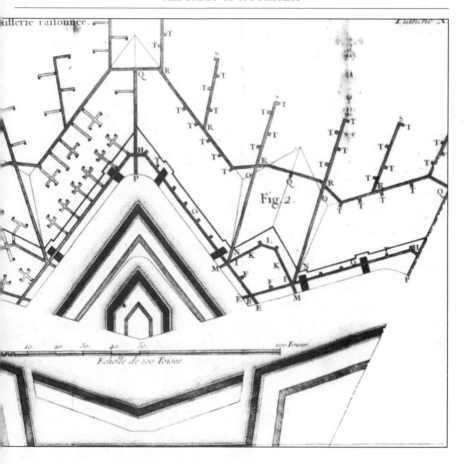

Plan of a countermine system.

The basis of most countermine systems was a six-foot-high and three-foot-wide main gallery (magistral gallery, counterscarp gallery) which ran round the perimeter of the fortress immediately behind the counterscarp. Since the counterscarp formed a ready-made rearward wall, the main gallery may be regarded as one of the cheaper components of the system. The access from the floor of the ditch was gained by means of doors which were cut through the counterscarp at the salient and re-entrant angles. Occasionally (as in the citadel of Turin) there was a communication gallery running beneath the ditch from the rearward works. From the main gallery, a number of galleries or half-galleries (four-and-a-half feet by three) radiated underneath the glacis along the imaginary prolongations of the capital (central) lines of the bastions and ravelins. From these again there was a further proliferation in the form of major branches (rameaux, three by two-and-a-half) and simple branches or listeners (écoutes, two-and-a-half by two) which sprouted off at right-angles. These stuffy masonry tubes gave the counterminers the means of detecting the approach of the enemy, and offered a variety of sites where they could plant their charges of gunpowder. The branches and listeners were built of such small dimensions, not for the sake of economy (in fact it was very awkward to excavate them), but because small tunnels were easy to tamp (stop up) when a charge was about to be exploded.

The Piedmontese at Turin and the Dutch at Bergen-op-Zoom possessed probably the most famous permanent countermine systems in the world. The French excelled at the theoretical investigation of the science of countermining, but by the end of the *ancien régime* not a single one of their fortresses owned a defence of this kind. In 1792 the King of Prussia amused himself by touring the impressive demonstration galleries at the mining school near Verdun, while his engineers set about the siege of the actual fortress, which was devoid of any means of underground defence.

COMMUNICATIONS

The individual works of a fortress might be ever so fine, but all the skill of the engineer would go for nothing if (as sometimes happened) he forgot to provide adequate means of getting men, artillery and materials to the fortifications and back again. Nothing was better calculated to undermine the morale of the defenders than the knowledge that there existed no secure path of reinforcement or retreat.

The main gateways were usually sited in the centre of the curtains, for this place was 'sheltered from the enemy fire, yet is commanded by the flanks of the two adjacent bastions. Also a gateway in the centre of the curtain enhances the beauty and symmetry of the town, for then the streets can be aligned directly on the gates'.[10]

The passageway was a tunnel through the rampart which was usually spacious enough to allow two highly laden carts to pass abreast,

Opposite page: Design for a fortress gate (Belidor 1729).

Right: *Plan of a bastioned front with cavaliers* (centre), *with front* (bottom) *and rear* (top) *elevations of gateways (Belidor 1729).*

indicating a width and a height of at least twelve feet each. If a gateway had to accommodate heavy traffic, small arches would be pierced on either side of the main opening, giving access to pavements which bordered the road inside the tunnel. Guard houses were often let into the tunnel on one or both sides.

There were many reminders of the medieval past. The passageway might describe a sharp bend, or the roof might be pierced with holes through which bullets or flaming liquids could be poured on unwelcome intruders. At either side there could well be grooves in which a portcullis travelled up and down. Almost inevitably there was a pair of stout, iron-studded doors, and a massive drawbridge and an associated counterweight.

As well as its purely utilitarian elements the gateway possessed an impressive façade, which was the one feature of the fortress on which the engineer felt free to lavish his architectural instincts. The vehicular and pedestrian entrances were usually carried out as soaring archways, which were separated by heavily rusticated columns rising to the pediment which crowned the whole confection. The idea came from the triumphal arches of ancient Rome.

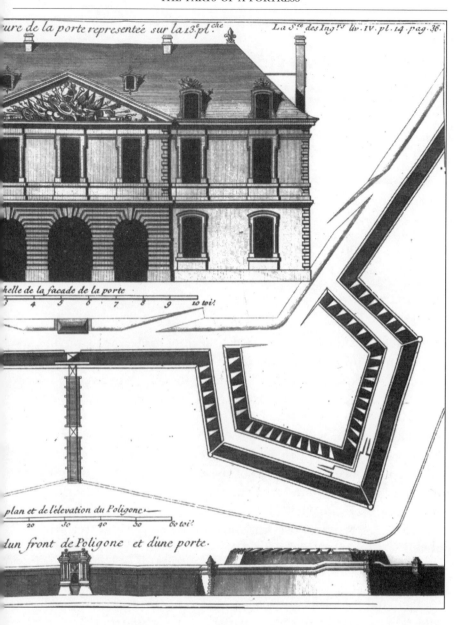

The façade might render forty feet of the curtain useless as a gun-platform and show the enemy the exact position of the bridge, but engineers could not bring themselves to forego the wonderful opportunity offered to them of displaying their sovereign's power and their own taste. Hué de Caligny wrote in the early eighteenth century that 'the

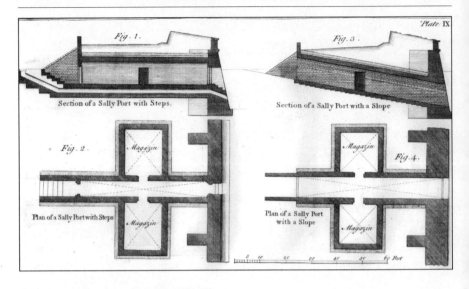

Plate IX

Fig. 1.

Section of a Sally Port with Steps.

Fig. 3.

Section of a Sally Port with a Slope

Fig. 2.

Magazin

Fig. 4.

Plan of a Sally Port with Steps

Magazin

Plan of a Sally Port
with a Slope

Magazin

Magazin

Types of sally-port (Muller 1746).

gate façades should be executed in the doric order, with ornaments appropriate to the town within. The whole design should possess a certain virility, as befits a fortress, though we should be as careful to shun the gothick influence as that which savours of the trumpery and effeminate.'[11]

The road pursued a tortuous path from the gateway to the open country. It passed from the drawbridge on to a stretch of standing bridge, and thence to the gorge of the ravelin in front. It then snaked to right or left in the interior of the ravelin, and cut through the parapet of one of the branches. Finally a small unroofed gateway and a second bridge led the road over the ditch of the ravelin and so across the covered way to the glacis.

The width of the standing bridges corresponded roughly to that of the main arch of the gateway, in other words about twelve or fourteen feet, and the plank surface was covered with stones or gravel as a protection against cart wheels. If the defenders did not destroy the bridges of their own accord at the beginning of the siege, they would nearly always be wrecked anyway by the enemy gunfire in the course of the struggle.

The main gateways and the permanent bridges were frequently of less immediate military importance than were the various devices by which the defenders climbed, scrambled, dropped or rowed from one work to another.

The talus, or interior slope of the rampart, was bordered by a continuous military road at ground level by which artillery and carts could reach the rear of any part of the enceinte. The carts and guns were hauled to the level of the terreplein up twelve-foot-wide earthen ramps which ascended the talus diagonally at a gradient of about 1:6. Here and there along the talus gaped the entrance to a downward-sloping tunnel which ran through the rampart to a postern, or sally-port which was pierced in the revetment of the curtain. The corridor itself might be as much as ten feet wide and might offer useful space for accommodation and stores in time of siege, but the postern was a diminutive five or six feet wide by nine feet high, for the engineers lived in fear that the enemy might rush the door and gain entrance to the interior of the fortress. For the same reason the postern was usually left walled up until the defenders wished to use it for their communications or to carry out a sortie. In a fortress with wet ditches the floor of the postern corresponded with the water level, but in the case of dry ditches the floor was sited six or eight feet above the bottom of the ditch, and the men had to descend by means of a movable wooden ramp. Bastions with retired flanks possessed similar but much shorter corridors or stairways, and the corresponding posterns were sited on the inner side of the orillons.

The gorges of the ravelins and other detached works were ascended by flights of steps, or by earthen ramps of the same kind that were cut in the talus of the enceinte. In dry ditches it was possible to effect a sheltered communication with the detached works along the caponnière, a sunken roadway or trench which was screened by parapets on one or both sides.

Wet ditches were crossed by bridges, or by boats or rafts which plied between the enceinte and tiny harbours which were built in the gorges of the outworks. Vauban recommended the use of a flotilla of ferry boats, each twenty feet long, four feet wide and two-and-a-half feet deep, and capable of carrying up to forty men at a time. At the brilliant defence of Grave in 1677 Chamilly housed seventy troops and two light cannon in a floating redoubt, with the ambition of engaging in miniature naval warfare in the ditches.

In order to reach the covered way from the bottom of the ditch the troops had to ascend the counterscarp by the aptly-named 'pas de souris' ('mouse steps'). Vauban's pas de souris were very steep and only three feet wide. It was recognised that these were an unsatisfactory and even perilous means of communication, but no one could devise another arrangement which would not make it easy for the enemy to descend the counterscarp in a large body. Everything considered, it was a wise precaution to transport all the necessary artillery, ammunition and heavy equipment to the outworks before the fortress came under actual siege.

Vauban's powder magazines (Muller 1746).

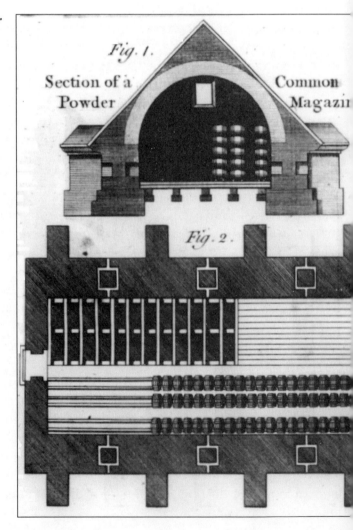

INTERIOR ESTABLISHMENTS

POWDER MAGAZINES

One of the least accountable habits of later medieval engineers was their storing of gunpowder in the ordinary towers of the enceinte. Erasmus has a telling description of the effects of an accidental explosion of one of these towers at Basle. Not surprisingly, the 'powder towers' were supplanted in the course of the sixteenth and seventeenth centuries by specialised powder magazines, standing free of the enceinte. The correct design of these buildings was a matter of crucial importance, for the

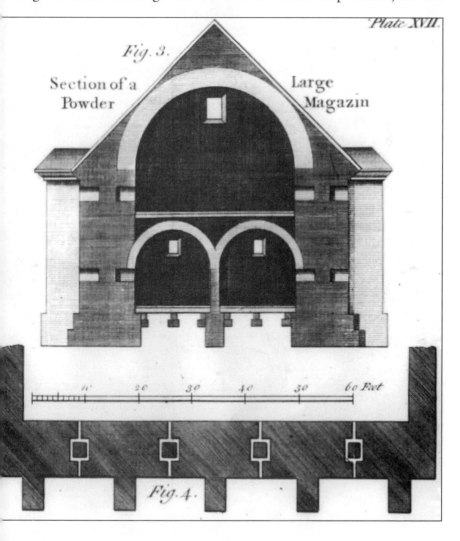

powder had to be kept dry (and therefore above ground level) as well as protected from enemy fire.

The first true powder magazines were massive and expensive constructions which housed the powder on two levels, each consisting of a floor, a number of heavy arches and a covering. This design gave way to a single-storeyed building, in which the roof was supported on gothic arches. The single-storey magazine was less liable to collapse under its own weight than its predecessors, but Vauban believed that the architecture was weak and inelegant, and he substituted a magazine type which became one of the most widely admired of all his designs.

In Vauban's magazine the steeply pitched roof rested on extremely strong round arches which were carried down nearly to ground level, leaving the greater part of the side 'walls' embedded in the earth like foundations. The floor was inserted at the spring of the arches, and was covered with planks and beams which rested on a bed of stones and chippings for the sake of dryness. At Bombay in 1756 an inspecting engineer was horrified to discover that the powder barrels were resting directly on the stone flags, 'for if a barrel should fall down upon the floor it may force a grain of sand to take fire, and blow up the magazine'.[12]

The air gained entrance to Vauban's magazine through perforated iron plates fixed in the walls, and it circulated round a rectangular masonry 'dice' set in a space inside the wall before it could reach the interior of the magazine. This circuitous path effectively intercepted all sparks and flaming embers. In fine weather a draught could be induced by opening the shuttered windows that were let into the walls at either end.

By the middle of the eighteenth century not a single one of Vauban's magazines was known to have exploded, even though they had been the targets of thousands of mortar bombs in the course of the various wars. This was just as well, for each of these buildings could house between 90,000 and 120,000 pounds of gunpowder – enough to wreck the town and kill half the people if it had gone up.

In time of siege the powder from one or more magazines of the type already described would be distributed little by little to a number of improvised expense magazines of timber and earth construction, which were built to serve individual sectors of the works.

ARSENALS

Most of the material of the artillery was stored and serviced in arsenal buildings. The forges, workshops and the heavier items of ordnance – cannon-barrels, gun-carriages, shot and bombs and the like – were arranged on the ground floor or in an open courtyard. The stands of muskets, the cordage, iron fittings, tools and pontoons were housed on the upper story, on the assumption that this equipment was unlikely to crash through the floor.

BARRACKS

The 'militarisation' of armies made a considerable stride in the late seventeenth century and in the eighteenth century, for that was when the authorities began to remove the troops from their billets in inns and private houses and concentrate them instead in specialised barracks.

The fortress barracks were sited parallel to the ramparts, but far enough away to leave a space where the troops could parade and

Plans and elevations of barrack blocks (Belidor 1729).

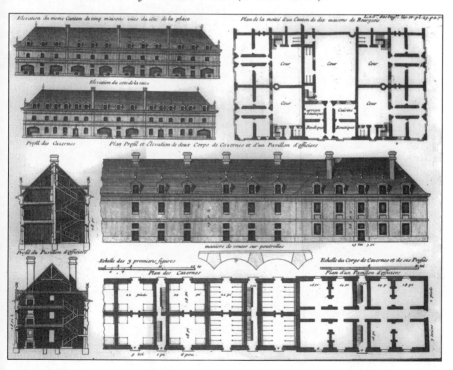

Forms of waterworks (Belidor 1729). Four plans and elevations of cisterns, and (bottom right-hand corner) *plan and elevation of a rampart latrine.*

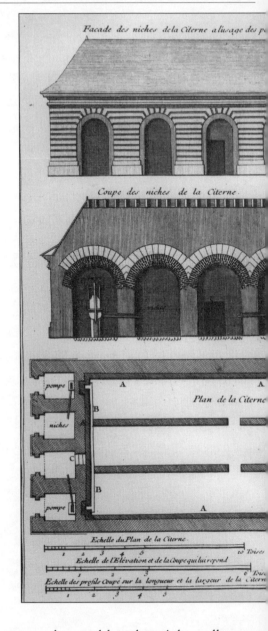

Facade des niches de la Citerne a l'usage des p...

Coupe des niches de la Citerne.

Plan de la Citerne

pompe

niches

pompe

Echelle du Plan de la Citerne.

Echelle de l'Elévation et de la Coupe qui lui repond

Echelle des profils Coupé sur la longueur et la largeur de la Citerne

assemble. In time of siege the stray shot and bombs might well cause such havoc in the barrack buildings that the troops would have to be removed to houses and cellars inside the town. Still, most engineers agreed that this one inconvenience was more than counterbalanced by all the good effects attendant upon the institution.

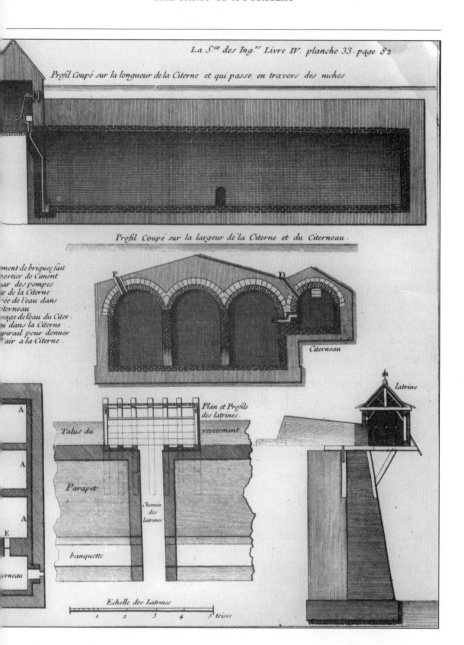

Barracks are built nowadays in all fortified places to keep up the discipline and good order in the garrison. They have been found so useful, that no place is built without them; and experience shows, that those garrisons which have them, are much more quiet, on account of the convenience which non-commissioned officers have to visit the quarters every evening, and to see that soldiers are shut up in their quarters, which cannot be done when they are lodged amongst the inhabitants, where they have the liberty of going out and in whenever they please. Besides, when the governor has a mind to make a detachment, or send out a party, he cannot do it without the knowledge of the whole town. If any alarm happens, the garrison cannot be assembled without great trouble and loss of time; whereas, when there are barracks, everything necessary for the good of the service may be done with ease.[13]

The barrack building of Vauban's time was a grim, rectangular construction of three storeys. The officers occupied relatively spacious quarters in their 'pavilions' at either end, while the men were packed twelve at a time in chambers which measured twenty-two feet long by eighteen broad. Three men were assigned to each of the four beds, on the assumption that at any given time two of the trio would be on duty. In the nineteenth century General Prévost de Vernois looked back with nostalgia on the days when barracks were arranged on cosy 'family' lines such as these, and he claimed that the system was to be preferred to the one prevailing in the vast dormitories in the modern barracks, where the soldiers were supervised like a flock of sheep.[14]

THE FORTIFIED BOG-HOUSE

In some fortresses the latrines were accommodated in special chambers which were hollowed out of the bastions, directly above the town drains. Elsewhere the latrine took the form of a masonry or wooden shed, which projected from the rampart on beams or corbels, so that the droppings fell into the ditch clear of the revetment. In time of siege the soldier who patronised such an establishment must have been exposed to a danger that is too horrible to contemplate.

Chapter 5
The Service of a Fortress

THE COMPOSITION AND SIZE OF THE GARRISON

We encounter two distinct methods of garrisoning a fortress. In the Prussian and English services the places were held by special garrison formations, which went by the respective names of 'land regiments', 'free companies' and 'independent companies'. These units (and the corresponding garrison artillery) comprised a high proportion of men who were elderly, sick and crippled from the outset, or who (like the English independent companies and detached regiments) were allowed to become so with the passage of time. The old German term *Mauerscheisser is* an accurate indication of the esteem in which the fortress troops were held by the field arms.

Friedrich Baron v. Trenck (cousin of the famous 'Pandour' Trenck) was something of an expert on the insides of Prussian fortresses, having spent most of his life in prison at royal command, without ever being able to discover precisely why. He recalls that during his incarceration at Glatz in 1744 and 1745 he discovered that most of the Prussian lieutenants were every bit as willing to desert as he was to escape:

> The greater part of them are poor devils who are loaded down with debts, or are under a cloud for still worse offences . . . Young officers are hardly ever sent to the garrison regiments unless they have given some cause for dissatisfaction. They are chagrined at their wretched state, paid in the most miserly fashion and despised by the rest of the army. They all, or nearly all, seize on the slightest chance which promises anything to their advantage.[1]

The French garrisoned their strongholds on the alternative system – that of tours of duty by the field regiments. This arrangement had inconveniences of its own, and in 1765 some unappreciative soldiers banded together to complain to the king about their seemingly endless tramping from one fortress to another.

> Your Majesty would render a most useful service if you would be so good as to leave us in our garrisons for two or three years at a time, instead of marching us from one end of the kingdom to the other, which has just happened to the regiment of Médoc, which came to Valenciennes from Briançon. Our comrades have worn out two or three pairs of shoes on the march, and ruined their gaiters, stockings, shirts and other items of clothing.[2]

Whatever the system prevailing in peacetime, a fortress which was under threat of siege would almost certainly be reinforced by troops who were detached from the field forces. Occasionally, after some catastrophic defeat in battle, the fortress might be jammed with the remnants of an entire army, and the commander-in-chief would take over from the governor.

The size of the garrison was calculated in the textbooks on the basis of so many troops for each bastion of the fortress. Five or six hundred men per bastion was considered a reasanable allowance for a fortress in a theatre of war, which yielded between 3,000 and 3,600 infantry for a fortress of six bastions. A force of five or six hundred horse, preferably dragoons, was added to this number to help the infantry to escort the convoys, and to carry out reconnaissances and sorties.

PROVISIONS

Most reputable soldiers agreed that a satisfactory daily siege ration for one man comprised two pounds of bread, one pound of fresh or salt beef, and about eight pints of water for drinking, the preparation of soup, washing and laundry. There were some special allowances for the officers and the sick and wounded. Carnot protested against the 'rational' calculations of French eighteenth-century officialdom which used to hold a man to one night's sleep in three, and a daily sustenance of twenty-four ounces of bread or eighteen of biscuit, five ounces of beef and one-sixth of a bottle of wine. 'We may scarcely doubt,' he commented, 'that the feeble defence of fortresses may be attributed to the pernicious practice of cutting down the subsistence of the troops. Two undernourished soldiers are worth less than a single man who is well fed – you cannot defend ramparts with skeletons.'[3]

Vauban went into almost obsessive detail on the matter of provisions. He reckoned that one pound of that morale-raising substance, tobacco, could be divided into 112 pipefuls, and would permit twenty-eight soldiers to enjoy four smokes each for one day.

> Tobacco is essential for keeping the soldiers happy. Indeed they have become totally dependent on it, as we may observe from several sieges where the only complaint uttered by the troops was that they had nothing more to smoke. This addiction reaches such an extreme that I have seen men smoke oak or walnut leaves in the absence of tobacco.[4]

A horse required a daily ration of ten pounds of hay, and six pounds of oats and four of wheat or barley, as well as three bundles of straw a week. The fodder could be stretched by putting the horses to graze in the ditch or even on the glacis of the 'safe' fronts, and in any event the hungry garrison would regard the equine rations as a worth-while investment in horsemeat.

The consumption of provisions was a function of the size of the garrison and the length of the siege. The daily requirement of the defenders could be calculated easily enough, but not even a Vauban, for all his efforts, could make a realistic estimation of how long a given fortress would hold out under attack.

ARMAMENT AND AMMUNITION

The 16- or 18-pounder 'culverin' was the mainstay of the artillery defence. This piece consumed far less powder than the 24-pounder battering piece, yet its shot carried nearly as far and it had the power to wreck the parapets of the enemy siegeworks, which were so much thinner and less well consolidated than the breastworks of the fortress. The lighter pieces – 12-pounders, 8-pounders and 6-pounders – served very well on the ravelins and other detached works, while 3- or 4-pounders could be mounted on the places of arms of the covered way, and could accompany the sorties into the country beyond. Mortars and pierriers (special stone-throwing mortars) were capable of being planted almost anywhere within the fortress, thanks to the high trajectory of their fire.

Much good work could be done by the wall-piece, a massive musket or punt-gun, which rested on a pivot or fork.

> These little guns inflict more casualties than the heavier ones – they have a faster rate of fire and they burn up less ammunition, but they still have a long range and the capacity to penetrate the thickest armour. It is worth while firing a wall-piece when you see just two or three enemy soldiers in a group, whereas if you shoot off a cannon you waste a considerable weight of ammunition when you miss.[5]

Vauban's garrison carriage (Saint-Rémy 1702). The specimen shown here was the design for a 16-pounder in 1689. The cheeks of the carriage were of compound construction, to permit the use of smaller and therefore cheaper pieces of timber.

Vauban was responsible for the general introduction of the 'garrison carriage', which was made up of two timber brackets and two or four small iron-shod wheels. Almost identical with the contemporary naval carriage, Vauban's invention occupied far less space than the two-wheeled field and siege-gun carriages, with their large wheels and their wide spans and long trails. Hardly less influential was the 'Gribeauval' carriage of the 1770s, a high-cheeked mount which enabled the barrel to be pointed *en barbette* over the parapet, without embrasures.

Gun-carriages were much less robust than the cannon barrels which they supported, and it was wise to set aside a large number of spare carriages to allow for breakage. On the continent of Europe it was also the custom to dismount the gun barrels in time of peace and keep the carriages in store. In 1740 the English *General Instructions for Engineers* commented on this matter:

> As it is observable that we have more guns in our places than our most powerful neighbours, although they are joined upon the same Continent and we on an island, so we

expose all our guns mounted on outworks to the injuries of the weather, both carriages and platforms, and even subject to surprise in the outworks, whereas theirs are secured both from weather and surprise under proper sheds except some few for alarms and salutes.

A six-bastioned fortress was considered to be reasonably well armed if it possessed between fifty and sixty cannon, and about twenty or thirty mortars and pierriers. In calculating the consumption of ammunition, the governor reckoned that each cannon round would burn a weight of powder equivalent to one-third of that of the shot, in other words an average of four or five pounds. A charge of one-and-a-half pounds might be enough to launch a mortar bomb on its course, though this economy was more than offset by the sixteen pounds or so of gunpowder which were stuffed into the missile. All the time the chemically

Twelve-pounder on a Gribeauval garrison carriage.

treated cord in the gunners' linstocks would be burning away at a rate of more than one foot every three hours.

One pound of powder would yield roughly eight charges for a wall-piece, or fill between thirty and forty musket cartridges – which would be rather less than half the quantity an infantryman would fire away on a single turn of normal duty on the ramparts. The musket balls were cast from bars of lead, of which one pound produced twelve or more rounds. One day's firing by a single musketeer would therefore deplete the munition stocks by more than two pounds of gunpowder and over five of lead.

Mines and fougasses were always expensive in powder, and they became still more ravenous after the supercharged mine was invented in the middle of the eighteenth century.

As a specific example of the requirements of a first-class fortress we may take Louis Roland Hué de Caligny's estimate in 1723 for an adequate defence of the elaborate eight-bastioned stronghold of Landau, assuming a garrison of 8,800 officers and men and a period of 160 days of investment and siege. This worked out at 9,338 two-hundred-pound sacks of flour, 205,700 rations of fodder, 128 cannon and 44 pierriers and mortars (an unusually powerful armament), 1,210,000 pounds of gunpowder, 102,400 roundshot, 11,000 bombs, 6,000 pierrier loads, and 1,430,965 pounds of lead.[6]

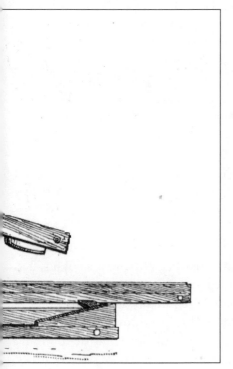

SECURITY

Even in time of peace, or when the fortress was not under immediate threat of siege, the most important duties of a garrison were those which were directly connected with the security of the fortifications and the gates. At no time could the governor be absolutely sure that some enemy might not seek to take over the fortress by surprise or stratagem. Austrian generals were told in 1769 that

> there are a number of circumstances which will require you to shut the outer entrances, gates and barricades. These are whenever a large crowd gathers in the town for functions, processions or executions, whenever suspicious or disorderly folk pay a visit, whenever services are held in the principal churches on Sundays and feast days, and whenever your visibility is limited by thick fog, heavy rain, storms or dust clouds.[3]

A narrow watch was kept on the daily traffic through the gates, and the guards usually required a stranger to furnish his signature and the name of the inn where he intended to lodge. In some places, as an additional check, the inn-keepers were ordered to bring a list of their guests to the governor every evening. In Austria the post officials were obliged to

> provide the commandant with detailed notification of the arrival and departure of passengers, posts, couriers and messengers, as well as to submit the passes of these people for his signature. Likewise in time of war, when the enemy are about, all the incoming postal packets are to be opened in the presence of the commandant.[8]

The guard was usually changed about one hour before sunset, and as the sun went down the gates were shut and locked and the keys carried to the governor by the sergeant-major. People who announced themselves at the gates at night-time were admitted through the wicket-doors only for a very good reason, or if they responded with the appropriate password. In tightly run fortresses the password was changed after every time that the gate had been opened, a soldier had deserted or an alarm had been sounded.

To give good warning of the approach of any suspicious body of men, the governor posted intelligent and keen-sighted soldiers in the highest church towers, and sent cavalry patrols into the surrounding countryside. Within the fortress the watch was kept by street patrols, regular rounds of the ramparts, and standing guards at the gates, guérites, aqueducts, sluices and magazines.

> To prevent the sentries from sleeping, or at least to detect such sentries as have fallen asleep, we furnish all the guérites with little bells. Every time one of the watches sounds a bell, all the other sentries must strike on theirs, beginning with the nearest guérite, and so on around the whole perimeter of the fortress.[9]

The sentinels gave the first notice of threatening danger by firing their muskets. If a large-scale assault seemed likely, the alarm would be relayed to the whole town by the sounding of the 'storm-bells' from the churches.

COMMAND AND ADMINISTRATION

The fortunes of the stronghold were entrusted by the sovereign to the official variously named the 'governor' or the 'commandant'. A well-tried officer, he disciplined and trained the garrison, saw to the upkeep of the fortifications, maintained an intelligence service, and commanded the defence in time of siege. His life and duties were summed up in a most vivid fashion by Vauban, when he congratulated his nephew on being appointed governor of Béthune.

> Live on good terms with the officers of your staff. Consider them as your brothers, and do not curtail any of the privileges which your upright predecessors allowed them – in fact, you should be prepared to spend out of your own pocket for their benefit...
> You should make frequent tours of the fortress in both the daylight hours and darkness. At night-time you must make sure that the guards are doing their duty, and that the sentries are alert and well-posted; in daytime you have to check up on the same items, but in addition you must make sure that all the gates and barricades shut tightly, and that there are no breaches, sewers or aqueducts which may

facilitate a surprise attack. You should frequently watch the guard being changed, and you must learn everything that has to do with the routine of the fortress – no guard or sentinel should be placed in position without your knowing the reason why.

Make tours of your magazines, and order the officials to draw up lists of what they contain. Verify what they tell you by making a personal inspection.

Get to know the ins and outs of your fortress, and meditate every day of your life on how you would defend the place if it came under attack...

Install yourself in the castle. Furnish your rooms plainly and without frippery. When exercising your command you should bring your officers in to dine regularly, and feed them once daily with good plain food.

Be a good friend to your citizens. Govern them gently, and avoid any suspicion of rudeness or oppression. Not only the bourgeoisie but the common people deserve to be treated with every consideration by you and by all the men under your command.[10]

There existed a clear distinction between the terms 'governor' and 'commandant' only when the king dispatched a special 'commandant' direct to an imperilled fortress to assume the control, or when a senior officer brought his field forces into the fortress and took command over the head of the permanent governor. In either event the governor was not likely to take kindly to being set aside in such a cavalier fashion. At Tournai in 1709 the Marquis de Surville was set up as commandant over the veteran governor the Comte de Mesgrigny, who had actually built the citadel and was far from inclined to put himself at the service of the newcomer; Saint-Hilaire remarked that this episode 'ought to persuade ministers how dangerous it is to make over the defence of a fortress to a strange commandant, especially when he enjoys less seniority than the governor'.[11]

The governor was assisted by a number of aides-de-camp, and by a private secretary who conducted delicate negotiations and supervised the network of spies inside and outside the fortress. Under the authority of the governor the second-in-command, or *lieutenant du roi* as he was called in France, directed the activity of the senior staff officers – the fortress major (who commanded the garrison troops), the chief gunner, and the chief engineer. The miners stood under the command of the artillery or the engineers, according to which one of these two arms had won control over the mining branch.

The muster-master, the paymaster, the commissary, the director of medical services and the chief of police fulfilled a number of vital tasks, but they were not always summoned to the governor's council. In the French service there existed a special *commissaire ordinaire de l'artillerie*, who saw to the service of the powder magazines and the arsenal, and the transport of ammunition and guns.

In time of siege the governor's council met daily in the guise of a 'council of defence', and the membership was usually widened to embrace all the heads of the military departments and some representatives of the municipality. 'It was there that all the deliberations were conducted concerning the security of the fortress, the most important enterprises, the intelligence messages, the supplies and regulations and other matters of the same kind.[12] These 'regulations' extended to the policing of the fortress, the fire service, the fixing of food prices, and the drawing-up of a sanitary code such as the one issued by the Lorrainers at La Mothe in 1634, which stipulated that

> the doctors, apothecaries and surgeons are to take measures to prevent the causes of contagious diseases in the town; to this end they will visit the wells and cisterns, and in the event of their discovering any infection they will arrange to have these reservoirs emptied and scoured as thoroughly as possible; they will prevent garbage, excrement and other filth from rotting too long in the streets and infecting the air; they will see that the butchers sell only untainted meat.[13]

If the paymaster ran out of cash it was important to mint an authorised 'siege currency', for 'the soldier is like a statue which comes to life only when he is lit up by the rays of this golden sun'.[14]

This hierarchy of command was more complicated and weighty in appearance than it was in effect. If the governor happened to be a grizzled veteran who was living out his days in semi-retirement, the real direction of the defence devolved upon a strong-minded individual who seemed to know what he was about – the second-in-command, perhaps, or more likely the chief engineer, who by the later eighteenth century was probably the only offficer in the garrison who had a clear understanding of fortress warfare. The Prussian engineering regulations of 1790 recognised this state of affairs by putting the *Platz-Ingenieur* in the first place next to the governor.

Citadels were usually placed under a governor and a staff of their own, an arrangement which was supposed to preserve them from any contagion of treason or cowardice that might emanate from the main fortress.

During a siege the bulk of the infantry served three watches: one spent in service on the ramparts, one in readiness nearby or on fatigues, and one at rest. The troops actually engaged in firing from the banquette were relieved every one or two hours. The rest of the men were assigned to help in the service of the guns, to bring up the ammunition or tend the sick and wounded.

We have decided why we want to build our stronghold. We have sited our fortifications, raised them, armed and provisioned them and furnished them with a garrison of sorts. It now remains to subject the place to the horrors of a siege.

Chapter 6
The March of the Siege

PLANS AND PREPARATIONS

The decision to besiege a fortress could be inspired by any motive ranging from naked aggrandisement to the morally impeccable desire to divert the enemy from attacking your own territory. Whether you could ever put the project into effect would depend on such factors as the state of your army, whether you had enough siege guns and materials nearby in friendly fortresses, and whether there was any risk of the enemy army intruding on the proceedings. As for the timing of the operation, the Austrian field-marshal Lacy stipulated in 1769:

> Without the most powerful motives you must never undertake a siege in an advanced season, let alone in the winter. This is because sickness will carry off too many of your troops, and because the countryside can furnish no fodder. Even the early spring is somewhat inconvenient, owing to the continuing absence of green forage, though you can make up the deficiency by establishing large magazines in the vicinity.
>
> The best time is undoubtedly the summer. By the same token, however, this is when it is easiest for the enemy to frustrate your enterprise.[1]

THE SIZE OF THE SIEGE ARMY

The prudent commander liked to be certain that the attacking army would outnumber the garrison by a ratio of anything between five and ten to one. It is easy to appreciate why the besiegers had to possess such an overwhelming superiority of force. At any given time the siegeworks would have to be held by a corps equivalent to three-quarters of the size of the garrison, while the rest of the army was busy digging and improving the trenches, transporting and serving the guns, bringing up the ammunition, looking after the sick and wounded, preparing siege materials, and warding off attempts at relief.

THE SIEGE TRAIN AND ITS TRANSPORT

In the eighteenth century the siege army was commonly accompanied by an artillery train of between thirty and sixty heavy pieces, of which rather under a third were mortars and howitzers. For their Netherlands campaign of 1744 the French astounded Europe by bringing out a train of no less than ninety heavy cannon and seventy mortars.

Perhaps the neatest definition of the function of the various calibres of guns was given in 1683 by the Imperial artilleryman Miethen:

> The demi-cannon [24-pounders] are the most generally useful pieces in the attack on a fortress: they breach and shatter the walls, and the fragments are then broken up by the quarter-cannon [16- and 12-pounders]. The falconets and regimental pieces strike at the enemy embrasures, and take up the duel with the batteries on the towers... they are also the most suitable pieces for shooting red-hot shot.[2]

The falconets and regimental cannon were light pieces, borrowed from the artillery complement of the field army. Of the siege train proper, four-fifths of the cannon were comprised of the 24-pounders.

Most authorities recommended that between 1,000 and 1,200 shot should be allowed for each battering piece, and between 500 and 1,000 bombs for every mortar and howitzer. A demi-cannon firing only 40 rounds a day would gobble up over half a ton of powder and shot at a time. Not surprisingly, a minimum allowance of powder for a serious siege was considered to be about 700,000 pounds.

The effort required to transport and administer this mass of material was nothing short of colossal. Seventeen drivers and 33 horses were needed to convey the dismounted barrel of the 96-pounder double cannon of the Emperor Charles V's time, leaving 3 further drivers and 6 horses to draw the empty gun-carriage; 7–8 drivers and 156 horses were assigned to cart the powder and shot for eight days' firing (at 30 rounds per day); additional transport was required for the conveying of tools and baggage, which gave a grand total of 32 vehicles, 213 horses, 107 drivers, 2 gunners and 10 assistants, while the service and movement of the whole park of 128 pieces engaged 2,675 horses, 890 drivers, 5 transport overseers, 124 gunners and 630 assistants.

In 1697, by when the artillery was much lighter than it had been in the early sixteenth century, the Austrian general Börner made some calculations for a projected siege of Temesvár, and decided that he would need 1,849 pair of oxen and 753 vehicles to transport a small train of ten 24-pounders and ten mortars and the downright inadequate stock of 3,000 roundshot and 2,000 bombs.

Small wonder that the more backward governments and armies were not always up to the task of bringing a powerful siege train against a selected fortress. John Muller writes in admiration:

> To determine the quantity of guns, ammunition, stores and everything else necessary in the field or a siege, so as to have enough, and no more, requires more knowledge and experience than can be found in one man. The French have a set of officers [the *commissaires*] whose business it is to master these things, and who are gradually initiated in it step by step. It is from their works that most nations of Europe copy the quantities of stores wanted upon different occasions.[3]

The French military effort was seconded by all the resources of the dedicated and efficient civil administration which had been set up by Louis XIV. Carts and teams were hired or requisitioned by their hundreds at a time, while peasant pioneers toiled in their thousands (20,000 in Flanders in 1744) to repair and widen the roads and fit out the siege parks.

In contrast, Muller's own masters, the English, had the reprehensible custom of signing on their commissaries of stores in time of emergency, and discharging them as soon as the war was over.

The eighteenth-century road appeared in one or other of three guises – the bottomless quagmire, the stony *via dolorosa,* or the exceedingly rare metalled carriageway of the type of the Austrian *Kaiserstrassen* or the Dunkirk–Ypres–Lille highway. There was a good deal to be said for piling as much equipment as possible on barges or boats, and proceeding to attack only such fortresses as stood within easy reach of canals or navigable rivers.

DEFENSIVE PREPARATIONS

The governor could not afford to wait the coming storm in idleness. He had to review and sort out the stocks of ammunition, round up the cattle from the countryside, grind as much grain into flour as possible (for the mills were very vulnerable structures) and make a list of the townspeople and their resources of food. Above all he had to reverse the process of decay which would almost certainly have set in among the works of the fortress: the glacis had to be cleared of houses, trees and other accretions; the casemates demanded to be cleaned out and fitted up to accommodate magazines and the sick and wounded; there were the palisades to be cut and planted, and the subsided parapets of the rampart and the covered way to be restored to their original slope by the process of *recoupe,* or cutting-back. Additional embrasures were cut through the thickness of the parapet, and, for the protection of the musketeers, the crest between the embrasures was crowned with an additional loopholed parapet of sandbags, small gabions or sods.

At the staff level the garrison records were ransacked for whatever plans or memoranda related to the fortifications and mines, and troops were earmarked to assist the professional gunners and miners. For the latter, dangerous work the governor was on the lookout for 'miners, bricklayers, carpenters, stone-breakers, stone-masons, ditch-diggers and men of the same kind'.[4]

INVESTMENT

The besiegers made their first appearance in the shape of a number of highly mobile columns which converged on the fortress from several directions at once. The leading squadrons spurred forward as boldly and rapidly as they could, in the hope of rounding up a good number of stragglers and cattle before they were brought up short by the fire from the ramparts. The main army arrived on the scene about three or four days after the advance guard had thus clamped down the preliminary investment.

The siege commander lost no time in determining the course of the line of countervallation, the entrenched position which covered the army against the sorties of the garrison. Since the tactical purpose of the countervallation was purely defensive, the general was careful to site the

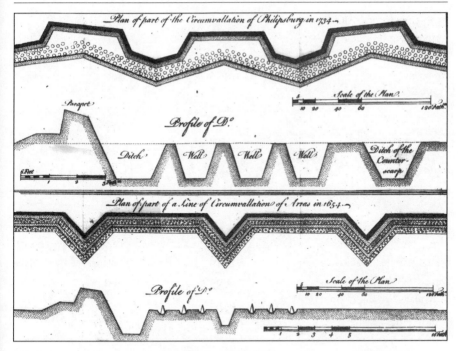

The circumvallations at Philippsburg (1734) and Arras (1654).

line out of effective cannon shot from the fortress. In form the position was a continuous semi-circle of redans and curtains, preceded by a ditch which was about five feet deep and eight feet wide across the top.

Our period witnessed an important change of view as to the best means of securing the siege against interruption by any army of relief. Until the second quarter of the eighteenth century most commanders held to the ancient example of Prospero Colonna at the siege of the castle of Milan in 1522, and surrounded their camps on the country side by lines of circumvallation. These entrenchments were designed to withstand a full army, and they were consequently more powerfully built than the countervallation.

The redans of the circumvallation were sited at intervals of about three hundred yards between salients, and they possessed faces between thirty-five and fifty yards long; the ditches were dug six feet or more deep, and extended up to eighteen feet wide across the top. If enough peasants could be conscripted to help in the work, both sets of lines could be completed in about ten days.

113

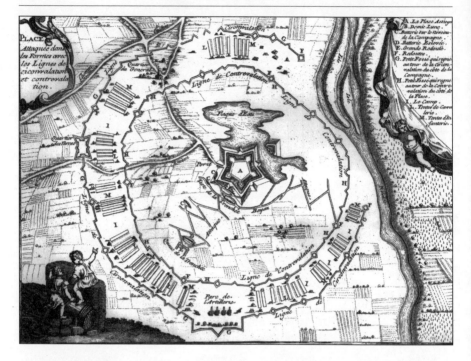

Formal siege à la Vauban, showing the trench and lines of circumvallation and countervallation.

Most people's faith in the efficacy of lines of circumvallation remained firm, even after the Spanish suffered spectacular defeats when they were holding positions of this kind before Arras in 1654 and Valenciennes in 1656. Thus in 1691 the Duke of Luxembourg could still argue that the French ought to stay in their lines in front of Mons, instead of coming out to fight the Prince of Orange and the army of relief. He reasoned that 'when there are troops enough to encamp in two lines, investing the whole circuit of the place besieged, it is best to avail oneself of the advantage derived from a good entrenchment, especially as by that means the siege is neither interrupted nor slackened'.5 King Louis deferred to Luxembourg's opinion.

Vauban, who was ahead of his time, maintained on the other hand that circumvallations were inherently defective, for they were always too extensive for the number of troops available to hold them.[6] He said that it was much better to hold the enemy field forces at a distance by a separate army of observation. The validity of Vauban's argument was borne out when the Swedes broke through the Russian lines at Narva in 1700, and the Austrians and Piedmontese smashed the French at Turin in 1706. The old ways were finally discredited in the Netherlands campaigns of the 1740s, when the Marshal de Saxe employed armies of observation with brilliant success.

Whatever the means adopted, the investment, or isolation of the fortress from the outside world remained the first and one of the most vital of all siege operations. The defences of Ostend 1601–4, Candia 1667–9 and Verrua 1704–5 proved that the fortifications of a place could exercise something like their full geometric strength, as long as manpower and materials were being replenished from the outside.

The process of investment afforded the defenders their last opportunity for preparation before they came under serious attack. The governor spent this time looking for any clue which might show him where the enemy intended to open the siege. The soldiers on the ramparts, the lookouts in the church towers, the pickets in the open country – all were on the watch for tell-tale signs like the planting of the siege park and the assembling of the heavy artillery. It was a good idea to keep up a half-hearted fire from a few undercharged guns, so as to tempt the enemy to plant his camp and parks within easy range of the fortress. You could then expect spectacular results when you opened a furious fire with every piece you could bring to bear, 'a hackneyed but often very successful stratagem'.[7]

Several means of action were open to the commander of an army of relief which was separated from the fortress by a hostile host. If he was a bold and resolute kind of person, he could form his troops into several columns and try to pierce the line of circumvallation at its weakest points. Failing that, he could besiege an enemy fortress by way of diversion, or attempt to send in a picked force of cavalrymen bearing gunpowder or some other vital commodity on their saddles. Six tons of gunpowder reached Turin in this way on the night of 30/31 July 1706, two-and-a-half months after the French had first appeared before the place.

The garrison might second the operations of their friends by means of sorties, if some means of communication could be arranged across the enemy lines: simple messages could be conveyed by flags, rockets or some other pre-arranged system of signals; more elaborate communications could fly over the heads of the besiegers by pigeon post (Haarlem 1573) or in empty mortar bombs (Turin 1640, Poltava 1709). Santa Cruz seriously suggests that the army of relief should get hold of a dog who lived in the fortress, and treat the animal so badly that he could think of nothing but getting home again; a message should then be attached to his collar, and after a final beating the poor creature would streak away across the siege lines and into the town.

> I have heard from several officers, who were at the last siege of Milan, that there was a dog whose master was shut up in the citadel, and whose mistress was in the town. The animal came and went with various letters, until the Imperialists found out what was going on and killed him.[8]

MEANS OF REDUCING A FORTRESS SHORT OF FORMAL SIEGE

Rather than face the prospect of long-drawn-out siege operations, many commanders were inclined to stake their reputation on the success of some enterprise in which the prospect of immediate gain was balanced by the likelihood of heavy and useless expenditure of ammunition in the event of failure. For every ten generals who could conduct a passable siege, there was only one who had the nerve and judgement to carry off one of these risky enterprises with panache and success. Vauban, Coehoorn and the mid-eighteenth-century Austrian general Loudon are among the few who deserve to be numbered among this select band.

SURPRISE

The most ingenious and entertaining kinds of surprise were those where the enemy tried to gain entrance to the fortress at some particularly vulnerable or unregarded point. Thus a Dutch storming party hid itself in a peat boat so as to gain access to Breda in 1590, while the Austrians wormed their way by an aqueduct into the heart of Cremona in 1702.

The gateway could be forced in one of two ways. The first, and the more cunning method was to jam the doors and the portcullis in

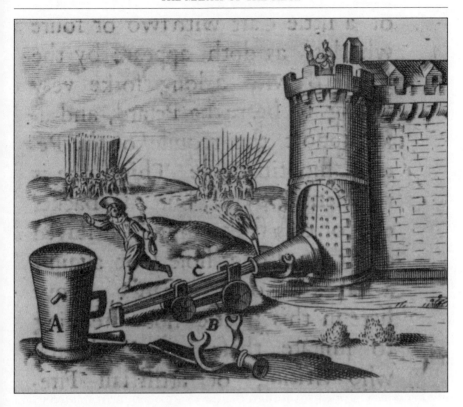

The petard (Malthus 1629).

the open position by means of a 'broken-down' waggon, and then bring a force of disguised soldiers so close to the gateway that they could rush the entrance while the enemy were still trying to sort out the tangle. The Spanish brought off the feat with conspicuous success at Amiens in 1597, as did the Dutch at Ypres in the following year. More than a century later, at Breisach in 1704, the Austrians made an attempt which was attended with very much less success. Four thousand of their élite troops stole down on the place early on 10 November. The way was supposed to have been prepared by thirty hay carts which were crammed with men and weapons and accompanied by a group of officers in peasant disguise. These people had the misfortune to attract the attention of a French foreman, who had the job of checking the labourers as they arrived early each morning at the Porte Neuve to report to work.

He became slightly suspicious of their identity, on account of their gentlemanly bearing. He began to question one of them, and since the 'peasant' seemed to be struck dumb, he belaboured him with his stick. The 'peasant' in question was the lieutenant-colonel of the regiment of Bayreuth, who did not have the patience to put up with this kind of treatment: he leapt to a nearby cart, pulled aside the bale of hay which blocked the rear, drew out a musket and fired.[9]

Thus the secret was betrayed, and the French hastened to raise the drawbridge before the main body of Imperial troops could intervene. A noisier and more straightforward means of breaking in at the gate was offered by the petard. A hollow, bell-shaped metal container was filled with well-rammed layers of fine powder, and screwed or chained down to a stout iron-bound beam. The device was then wheeled up to the gate on a wheelbarrow or similar vehicle under cover of darkness, and was screwed, nailed, hung or propped against the door, beam first. The bold petardier ignited a fuze at the base of the bell, and retired as fast as he could. The charge went off with a thunderous fart (to use the ety-mologically correct term), the bell shot backwards, and the beam was simultaneously propelled through the door, smashing it to splinters.

The petard was first used with notable success in 1580, when the young Henry of Navarre (later Henry IV of France) descended upon Cahors. At midnight on 5/6 May Henry's petardiers blew small holes in three of the gates, then stood aside while the axemen widened the gaps sufficiently to allow soldiers to crawl in on all fours. Inside the town the troops encountered a scratch force of forty pikemen and two hundred arquebusiers, and

> in the flash of the arquebus volleys you could see that most of the defenders were bare-legged, not having had time to put on their stockings and breeches. The church bells made a wonderful clangour, sounding the alarm in every part of the town. The noise was swelled by cries of 'Charge! Charge! Kill! Kill!', and by the reports of arquebuses and the flashing of arms. All the time we were being showered from the roof-tops with tiles, stones, pieces of timber and flaming brands.[10]

Henry's troops had to stage a dozen battles of this kind before the enemy gave up the fight in the morning.

The success of the petard against Cahors, Dreux and other places created a European demand for French petardiers. The Emperor himself was at pains to hire French experts, and one of these mercenaries, Corporal La Marche, proved his worth by blowing in the gate of the Turkish fortress of Raab in 1598.

This spectacular weapon disappeared completely in the second half of the seventeenth century. The Chevalier de Guignard states that since 1689 he had neither seen nor heard of the petard being used to any effect. [11] His contemporary Saint-Remy offers the explanation:

> To be perfectly frank ... hardly any officers ever return from these uniquely hazardous expeditions; as soon as the garrison troops see what is going on, they open fire on the petardier from the gate and the flanking defences. They seldom miss.[12]

The failure of a petard was usually accounted a setback, rather than a disaster, involving as it did only a fairly small number of troops. The same was rarely true of escalade – an attempt to climb the rampart by ladders.

It was fortunate that artillery fortifications were massive and thick, and did not confront the escalading troops with a precipitous drop on the far side, as had been the case in medieval times, but this one small mercy was more than offset by the appalling danger of coming under enfilade fire from the adjacent bastions. A comparatively low wall, just thirty feet high, would require a ladder at least thirty-seven feet long, while higher ramparts might call for a monster that would have to be carried by twenty men and raised by forty.

Until about the middle of the seventeenth century many commanders were willing to throw away hundreds or even thousands of lives by attempting open escalades against a waiting enemy. In one of these desperate enterprises, against Nördlingen in 1634, Sydnam Poyntz lost an argument with another Imperialist soldier as to who was to be the first to mount a ladder.

> A proper young man he was and up he went and I followed him at heels; so soon as he came to the top of the walls, his

head was no sooner peeped above the walls, but it seems someone thrust at him with a halberd and thrust off his bever [helmet]; his bever was no sooner off but with a sword one struck off his head and fell to the ground the head being off the body falls upon me and there it lies very heavy upon me and blooded me wonderfully that I was almost smothered with blood.[13]

In later times escalade came to be regarded more as a particularly risky kind of 'surprise' than as a method of taking a town by open storm. The commentator Bonneville noted in the middle of the eighteenth century that 'we can hardly be surprised that escalades of fortresses are so rare, when we consider that this sort of enterprise must be planned with great care, and that all the arrangements must be so accurate and precise'.[14]

The very few successful escalades of the later period had a number of significant features in common: the attempt always took the defenders by surprise, whether in the timing or in the place of the attack; the troops came on in several columns, so that at least one of the detachments had a chance of breaking in at a weakly defended sector; and the troops, once they had reached the rampart walks, hastened off to right and left and opened the gates to the main forces waiting outside (Prague 1741; Badajoz 1812; Bergen-op-Zoom 1814, despite the later repulse; Delhi 1857).

We have a classic description of such an escalade from some of the French officers who accompanied the attack on the Austrian-garrisoned city of Prague on 26 November 1741. Maurice de Saxe was told off with some 2,600 troops to tackle the main town wall on the west side of the Moldau. He writes:

> The ladders having been distributed to the grenadiers, I ordered the first sergeant to climb up with eight men. I told him that on no account were his grenadiers to open fire, but that they were to stab the sentries, if they could take them by surprise, and to defend themselves with the bayonet if they encountered resistance. This sergeant was to be followed by Colonel de Chevert, at the head of the grenadiers, dragoons and fusiliers who were under the orders of the Comte de Broglie.

Chevert was meanwhile giving instructions to the leading grenadier under his own command:

> 'Do you see that sentry over there?'
> 'Yes, colonel.'
> 'He will shout out "Who goes there?" You will say nothing in reply, but just keep on going.'
> 'Yes, colonel.'
> 'He will fire at you and he will miss.'
> 'Yes, colonel.'
> 'You will then cut his throat. I shall be there to back you up.'

We return to Saxe:

> After the sergeant and the eight grenadiers had reached the summit of the rampart the sentries gave the alarm. I was sitting at the edge of the ditch, on the end of a platform of rubble, and opposite the bastion which Chevert was about to climb. I had concealed the dragoons thirty yards behind me, and now I rose and cried: '*A moi, dragons!*' They appeared at once. All the enemy on the bastion and the curtain could see us, and they began to shoot. I replied by a very heavy fire. Meanwhile Chevert and his grenadiers climbed the revetment. The enemy did not notice them until there was a company on the rampart. The Austrians then delivered a counter-attack, blazing away with their muskets and coming to hand-to-hand fighting with our grenadiers. The grenadiers stood firm without firing, and defended themselves by powerful bayonet thrusts. Chevert was soon followed by three other grenadier companies and by Broglie and his pickets. These troops were eager to scale the rampart, but many of the ladders gave way under the great press of men, which nearly wrecked the whole enterprise. I sent an officer hurrying off to put things right, and I hastened with my dragoons to the gate, leaving my remaining pickets to take our place and keep up a covering fire. At the very moment I arrived the drawbridge was cut down for me by

Chevert, who had approached from the interior of the city and overpowered the guards at the gate. [15]

A final dash through the streets brought Saxe to the Town Hall, where the governor made his surrender.

BOMBARDMENT

A bombardment may be defined as a general cannonade by which the besieger intended to open the fortress by striking directly at the morale of the garrison and townspeople, rather than destroying the works.

Every kind of artillery could join in a bombardment, though certain missiles and pieces were found to be particularly effective. The explosive mortar bomb was probably first employed in continental warfare for the purpose of terror bombardment in 1588, when the Spaniards were attacking Wachtendonck. Mortars were commonly used in this way throughout the rest of our period. One of the defenders of La Mothe in 1634 remembered how the 200- or 300-pounder bombs

> left the muzzles of the mortars with a muffled report, climbed slowly to a height of several hundred feet above the town, then descended with increasing force, advertising their fall by revolving in the air and giving off sparks from their fuzes. They landed in the town with such an impact that their weight sent them crashing through the most stoutly-built roofs and the floors below. When their filling exploded, the splinters and the blast instantaneously stripped the roofs from the houses, smashing the timbers and carrying away the gable-ends and the guttering. A single bomb was capable of wrecking several large dwellings at a time. [16]

In 1672 an engineer of the Bishop of Munster set a vogue for the acorn-shaped incendiary missile called the 'carcass'. The iron cup *(culot)* at the broader end of the missile supported a body framework of iron hoops or bands. The interior was filled with a composition of melted pitch, gunpowder, saltpetre, and sulphur, in which were embedded small grenades and loaded pistol barrels for the entertainment of the municipal firemen. The carcass was discharged from a mortar, and described a

Scene in a mortar battery (Rigaud, in Belidor, 1731).

wobbly flight until it either blossomed as a harmless fireball in the air, or descended all the way to its target. By the middle of the eighteenth century, if not before, the carcass was recognised to be expensive and inaccurate, and not much superior in incendiary effect to the ordinary black-powder mortar bomb.

The red-hot shot remained one of the most potent instruments of bombardment until the advent of rifled artillery in the nineteenth century. The besiegers began their infernal work by digging a pit, filling it with coal or charcoal, and laying an iron grill over the top. When the fire was at full force, only a short time was required to raise any shot placed on the grill to incandescent heat. In 1781 the Hanoverian soldier Schwependik was said to have invented a portable red-hot-shot oven, and persuaded the grateful English government to give him enough alcohol to drink himself to death. He accomplished his desire within a year. [17] The Austrian major Smola improved the oven in 1808, and about the same time the French general Meunier devised a brick-walled reverberating furnace, which held large numbers of shot in sloping racks.

The glowing shot was retrieved from the flames and carried to the waiting gun (a long 8- or 9-pounder was best) in a spoon, an iron scuttle or a pair of long-handled pincers. The cannon was already loaded with powder and a wadding of clay, turf, or partially-dampened hay, and the shot was dropped down the highly elevated barrel and allowed to roll to the bottom. The gunner at once touched off the charge, for it was undesirable to let the shot burn through the wad and ignite the powder from the front.

Miethen observed that 'it is almost impossible for one or two out of every twenty red-hot shot not to land on some inflammable material'.[18] The shot were most dangerous of all when they embedded themselves deep in the timber of a building and smouldered away undisturbed.

The French armies were profoundly influenced by the views of Vauban, who held that bombardment was a barbaric and not very effective means of reducing a fortress: 'It is hardly ever employed except against rebel towns, or when we have been insulted by the inhabitants of the besieged fortress.'[19] The bombardment of Brussels in 1695 was the last of its kind. The commander of the French artillery wrote on that occasion:

We can see that most of the houses of Brussels are on fire. The neighbouring hills are crowded with troops, both French and of the enemy, who are watching this wonderful spectacle. I have been on several military expeditions, but I have never seen such a blaze or such destruction. I trust that the intentions of the king have been carried out, and that he will be pleased with my labours and our speed.[20]

The German states and the English had less choice in the matter, for their engineer establishments were not always up to the skilled work of formal siege.

Bombardments achieved their greatest successes when the siege commander took the trouble to lay in a large stock of ammunition beforehand, and then, once he had opened fire, he kept up a continuous and furious bombardment with everything that would shoot. The Austrian field-marshal Loudon took Belgrade by this means in 1789. Ten years later his compatriot Colonel Reisner brought 138 pieces against Turin, and reduced the place in twenty-four hours (3–4 December 1799) by firing about 200 rounds from each of his cannon and 150 from every howitzer and mortar. These performances were particularly impressive when we compare them with the long-drawn-out sieges of Belgrade and Turin earlier in the century.

STARVATION

The long, passive blockades of earlier times went out of fashion almost completely in the second half of the seventeenth century. The French, for example, never again staged anything which compared with their blockade of Perpignan in 1642. This was partly because commanders now had more positive siege techniques at hand, and partly because so many small and inaccessible places were being demolished – the sort of stronghold which had been so often blockaded in the past.

If the 'pure' blockade became something of a rarity, the starving-out of the garrison and population could still hasten the end of an active siege. The wise governor therefore compelled the well-off townspeople to lay in stocks of provisions, and he expelled the rest as 'useless mouths' before the investment was complete.

Generally speaking, a besieged town in the civilised eighteenth century would capitulate long before clinical starvation set in. But even then there were determined folk who were prepared to hold out longer than could have been expected of brave, or even decent men. Thus when the Piedmontese relieved Alessandria on 11 March 1746 they discovered that the garrison, having consumed the horses, the cats and the dogs, was left with three days' supply of bread, of which even the officers received only a ration of five ounces. The wretched soldiers were seen to eat the flesh of their dead comrades. They were in a terrible state, but nobody talked of surrender.[21]

FORMAL SIEGE

THE CHOICE OF THE FRONT OF ATTACK

Every later operation of the siege had to wait until the commander and his engineers had determined which of the sides of the fortress they were going to attack. It was very rarely that the besiegers did not have a reasonably complete knowledge of the fortress before they arrived on the spot. It was generally accepted

> that if in time of peace a considerable project of mines be executed, the position of the principal galleries may soon be known to anyone who wishes to be informed of them. Indeed the plans of mines of any consequence, ancient as well as modern, and even those of the projected systems, are in the hands of everybody, and it will be the same with regard to every new work; because it is always necessary to entrust the design to so many persons that the fidelity of all cannot be relied upon.[22]

The same was true of the surface works. Plans of varying accuracy could be purchased from print-stalls in the open street, and any remaining doubts could be cleared up by sending agents or officers to pay a visit to the fortress in time of peace. Vauban and Frederick the Great were among the very few commanders who were at all concerned to keep their fortifications secret. Most people did not bother. In 1754 a young English amateur of engineering, Sub-Lieutenant

126

Robert Clerk, called on the governor of Rochefort in full uniform.

> I told him that I was upon my way to England from Gibraltar, and that I came on purpose to see the place, the dock, and the men of war. He was very polite; I was shown everything; went about the ships of the line new built, and an engineer attended me in going round the place.[23]

There still remained the difficult task of relating the designs on the map to the actual ground as it presented itself to the eyes of the besiegers. From a distance most fortresses looked like collections of grassy mounds, among which it was not at all easy to distinguish the ravelins from the bastions – though a few clues might be provided by the positions of the gates and guérites, or by the shadows that were thrown on the works when the sun was low. Telescopes were on general sale by 1609,[24] but when you looked through the tube you were rewarded with a small, dancing image with yellowish edges. There was really no alternative but for some high-ranking officers to go forward in person and investigate the works at close range. It certainly repaid the defenders to fire their light cannon at any enemy officers who seemed to be displaying an unhealthy curiosity in the fortifications. 'For that purpose it is wise to employ your best gunners, for among these curious folk are probably all the most highly-qualified officers in the enemy army.'[25]

An engineer officer, provided he was impudent enough, might be able to satisfy his curiosity without having so much as a single shot discharged in his direction. When the Swedes marched to attack Copenhagen in 1658 Erik Dahlberg hastened ahead and had himself invited inside the fortress by a number of Danish officers of his acquaintance. Over several days

> I was exceedingly well and courteously received by these people and many others ... However I inspected the city in the early mornings, before anyone was up, and I fulfilled my errand so well that in four days' time I had a tolerably good representation and plan of Copenhagen, which afterwards stood us in very good stead. This was not done without great danger.[26]

Likewise in 1691 Vauban and some of his colleagues approached to within musket shot of the ramparts of Namur. The party then

> made a confident and open circuit of the walls, walking, like townspeople do, with our hands behind our backs, so that I am quite certain that everyone we met, including the sentries, took us for citizens out for a stroll. Sometimes we staged a little horseplay, and ran after each other. Sometimes we lay down as if we were tired – that was when we drew up our plans, making sure that the maps were concealed by stretching ourselves out with our stomachs to the ground and our backs towards the fortress.[27]

Usually the defenders were very much more on the alert. The Saxon officer Tielcke reports how he and the Russian engineers tried to sound out the works of Kolberg in 1758:

> We used to approach within grapeshot range of the fortifications; two generally went together, one of whom kept his eyes fixed on the enemy's batteries, and when they prepared to fire, both threw themselves flat on the ground, and let the balls go over their heads. On moonlit nights we used to steal up to the palisades of the covered way, and endeavour to form some idea of the works by the shade. It was very astonishing that with so few experienced artillerymen, they fired so well and so quick from the fortress, as to make it dangerous to reconnoitre on horseback.[28]

Not surprisingly, the Russians made the mistake of attacking the northern side, which turned out to be the strongest of all.

As a general rule the attack was directed against a 'front' of two bastions and an intermediate ravelin, on whichever side of the fortress the siege commander judged to be the weakest. Yet Vauban himself did not hesitate to break with custom when he took on the strong Porte d'Anzin at Valenciennes in 1677, for he had noticed that this side of the fortress was well served with roads from the French-held strongholds, and that there were woods nearby that would yield plenty of material for the gabions and fascines.

Above: The great-grandfather of all ravelins. This massive, prow-like work was built at Sarzanello Castle (Italy) in 1497. Embrasures have been cut into the older drum towers behind, so as to bring a flanking fire to bear on the ditch in front of the ravelin.

Below: Bastion La Libertà at Lucca (Italy). Part of the very well-preserved town fortifications begun by Pacciotto of Urbino in 1561.

Above: The town within the ramparts. The compact perimeter of Berwick-upon-Tweed. To the right we see the rearward slopes of the Elizabethan fortifications.
Below: The Marienberg, citadel of the Prince-Bishop of Würzburg.

Above: The fortress on the rock. The Castello at Porto Venere (Italy).
Below: Covered way at Fort George, Inverness. The wall spanning the ditch to the left is a batardeau, a dam designed to retain water in one sector of the ditch; the little tower on the batardeau (in line with the guérite behind) was an obstruction intended to prevent besiegers from using the batardeau as a path across the ditch.

Above: *Brick-lined embrasure (Lucca).*
Left: *Guérite overlooking the Queyras gorge, Mont-Dauphin.*

Front and rearward views of parts of the massive 'Carnot' scarp at Verona, the chief fortress of the Austrian 'Quadrilateral' in northern Italy. In the 1830s the Austrians reshaped the sixteenth-century fortifications into grassy banks, and built their new walls around the foot.

Above: *Chemin des rondes with garde-fou (Excavation at the Brass Bastion, Berwick-upon-Tweed).*
Below: *View from the upper battery of a double casemated bastion flank, showing the lobe of the protecting orillon on the right (Lucca).*

Above: Bastion flank, with curved orillon and double retired flank (Bastion San Colombano, Lucca).

Below: Close-up of the Bastion San Colombano, Lucca. The upper storey has three open embrasures. There are two casemated embrasures in the lower storey, each with a slot-like chimney to permit the smoke to escape.

Above: Counterscarp at Mont-Dauphin, with pas de souris ('mouse steps') giving access from the ditch to the covered way.

Opposite page, top: Mont-Dauphin, an example of Vauban's First System, with (from left to right) bastion with rounded orillon, ravelin, and counterscarp with pas de souris, and covered way.

Opposite page, bottom: View of ravelin with redoubt (Almeida). Possibly the most formidable ravelin still in existence.

Below: Tips of stakes in the covered way, as seen from the crest of the glacis.

Right: View from the left-hand shoulder angle of a bastion (Almeida): ravelin in right middle ground; guérite in right foreground; flank and face of adjacent bastion in centre-left background; curtain in left middle ground.

Below: The mortar of Belgrade, a 10-pounder cast by Leopold Halil in Vienna in 1714. In memory of its rôle in the siege of Belgrade in 1717 it was inscribed as follows: On 14 August 1717 I was planted before the fortress of Belgrade, causing great consternation. And my little bomb must have sped many folk to their deaths. It landed on the powder magazine, and left nothing in the place Save lamentation, death, horror and the most frightful ruin. *(By courtesy of the Heeresgeschichtliches Museum, Vienna)*

Below: Characteristic nineteenth-century casemated coastal battery (Waxholm Fort, Stockholm Archipelago, 1833–63). Works of this kind became very vulnerable after rifled artillery was perfected. People said that the stony-faced Prussian chief of staff, Moltke the Elder, smiled only twice in his career – once when he heard that his mother-in-law had died, and again when he saw Waxholm Fort.

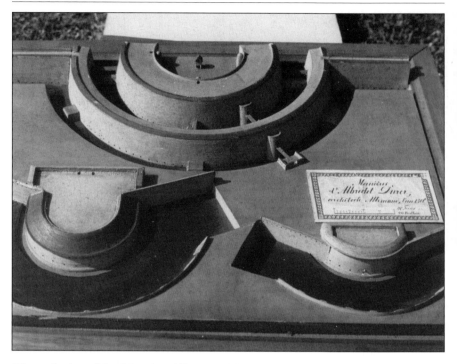

The evolution of fortification, illustrated by a series of demonstration models made for the RMC Woolwich at the turn of the eighteenth and nineteenth centuries. (By courtesy of the Librarian, RMA Sandhurst.)

Above: *Transitional fortification, represented by three designs of the German artist and architect Albrecht Dürer (1471–1528). These were characterised by squat casemated towers called 'roundels', which offered good long-range defence, since the masonry was mostly screened from the open country. Unfortunately the medieval ground plan remained fundamentally unchanged, and every roundel had a patch of ground in front of the salient which could not be commanded by the fire of the adjacent towers. The individual roundels therefore saw to their own close-range defence, and were provided with a tier of casemates around the base which weakened the works and added considerably to their cost. Dürer's influence is shown in the Munot Tower at Schaffhausen, and in the coastal forts (notably at Deal, Walmer and St Mawes) built by Henry VIII of England in the 1540s.*

Opposite page top: *Early Italian bastioned fortification. The works have now been angled into geometrically interrelated planes, making sure that every yard of the ditch was swept by fire. The two examples illustrated here show the characteristic Italian hammer-headed bastion with casemated flanks. The upper 'front' is protected by a simple ravelin, and the bastion on the top right owns a 'cavalier', or raised interior battery.*

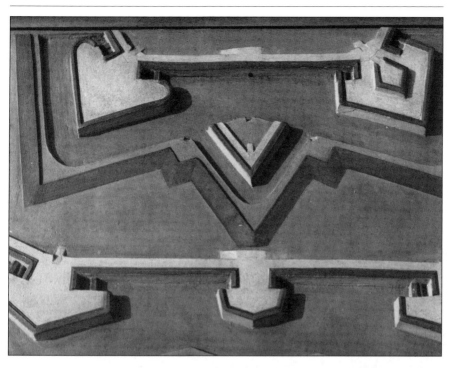

Above: *Netherlandish fortification (Adam Freitag 1630). Low-lying earthen fortifications, with wet ditches, and acute-angled demi-lunes in front of the bastions. The main enceinte is a double one, sporting an outer fausse-braye.*

Right: Coehoorn's 'first system' (1685). Elaborate bastions and ravelins, each consisting of an inner core in demi-revetment, and a powerful fausse-braye of earth: these two components are connected by casemated caponnières which run along the capital lines of the works. The ditches are wet, and in the dark-shaded areas between the cores and the fausse-brayes the earth has been cut down to within a few inches of the water table. Square redoubts have been planted in the spacious places of arms of the covered way – works of

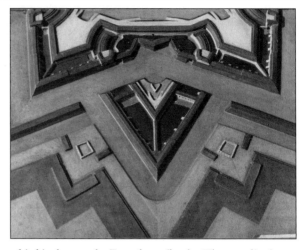

this kind gave the French a great deal of trouble in the siege of Bergen-op-Zoom in 1747.

Below: Vauban's 'first system'. An example showing bastions with orillons and concave

flanks. The ravelin is preceded by an unusually elaborate set of outworks – a bonnet in front, and tenaillons to either side.

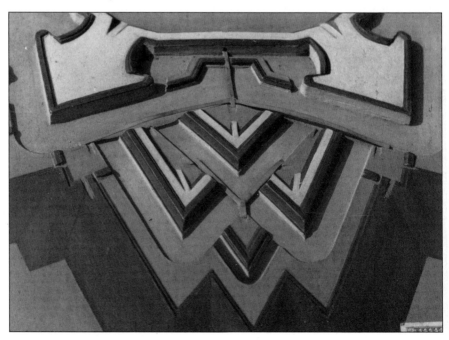

Right: Vauban's 'third system', as built at Neuf-Brisach in 1698. The bastion consists of a case-mated 'bastion tower' and a massive covering counterguard. The rav-elin has a redoubt, and the covered way is inter-cepted by a number of powerful traverses. The ensemble represents prob-ably the furthest realistic development of the bas-tion system.

Below: The Cormont-aigne–Fourcroy trace, as taught in the French engineering school at Mézières in the later eighteenth century. Vauban's 'bastion tower' has been replaced by a large casemated redoubt. The ravelin is notably long, and the fortific-ation is carried deep into the country by means of lunettes, one of which is seen in the bot-tom left-hand corner. The scheme was impos-sibly elaborate, but as a theoretical exercise it influenced French mili-tary engineering until the 1860s.

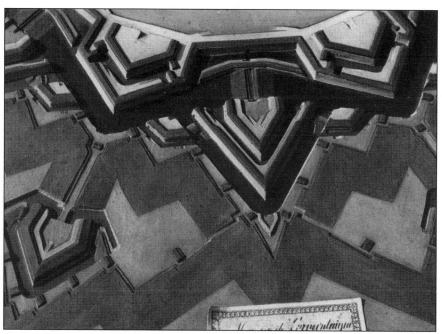

Three stages of a siege wargame, played by the Kriegsspiel Society of the RMA Sandhurst.
Top: *Fire is opened from two batteries in front of the second parallel. The battery to the right of the view is well sited to enfilade the left-hand branch of the covered way of the ravelin. The battery on the left has not been so advantageously placed.*
Centre: *A third parallel has been completed around the foot of the glacis. The defenders have just launched a sortie.*
Bottom: *The sortie has been decisively repulsed, and bitter fighting is in progress as the besieging troops push their way after the fugitives into the ravelin. In the next two 'moves' the defenders lost the ravelin altogether, and the fortress governor sought (and was granted) a capitulation upon lenient terms.*

Sheer vanity might also dictate a departure from the normal proceedings – that seemed to Santa Cruz to be the only explanation for the different methods of attack which were employed at the four sieges of Barcelona in the 1690s and 1700s.[29]

People could not agree as to the best course of action when the fortress happened to be equipped with a citadel as well as a town enceinte. On the one hand you could attack the citadel first, and thus engage yourself in a single, difficult siege which, if successful, would certainly bring about the fall of the town. Alternatively you could begin with the town, and then go on to mount a second operation against the citadel, in the hope that the enemy would have run through his resources in the first siege: this was the sequence which Vauban preferred.

Circumstances might well force you to split the siege army into more than one attack. At the turn of the seventeenth and eighteenth centuries, in the sieges which were undertaken by the anti-French and anti-Swedish coalitions, it was the practice to subdivide the siegeworks among the various national contingents – one for the Dutch, one for the English, one for the Prussians and so on.

The French usually preferred to stage a single, broad attack, but in their Netherlands sieges in the 1740s they frequently came at the fortresses from two directions at once, with the object of compelling the small garrisons to divide their forces (Menin, Furnes, Mons, Charleroi).

There were some pundits who maintained that from now onwards the length of the siege was simply a matter of arithmetic. They could point to calculations like the ones that Vauban made concerning the expected resistance of his new citadel at Lille. He estimated that the work should be provided against a siege of forty days.

> After the town has surrendered and the enemy have entered, we may suppose that they will spend two days in establishing their lodgments, throwing up protective breastworks against the fire from the citadel, draining the water from the inundation, etc...
>
> Two days
>
> NB We do not count the several days' truce to allow the garrison to retreat to the citadel.

From the opening of the trench on the esplanade to the time when the enemy are within reach of the outer covered way...

Five days

Passage of the outer ditch...

Three days

Attack and lodgments on the salients of the covered way...

Five days

Complete occupation of the said covered way...

Two days

Passage and descent of the ditch of the ravelin...

Three days

The attaching of the miner to the ravelin, the blowing of the mine, the lodgment on the salient of the ravelin and the overcoming of its inner defences...

Five days

Descent and passage of the main ditch, undertaken before the-capture of the ravelin...

Four days

The attaching of the miner to the rampart and the blowing of the first mines...

Three days

Progress of the attack until the second mines are blown and the lodgments are made on the summits of the bastions...

Three days

Allowance for malfunctions and other delays...

Five days

Total time for the attack on the citadel by way of the esplanade...

Forty days.[30]

Our experts forgot that Vauban was not laying down an exact timetable for a siege. He was stocking the place with supplies, and he needed to have a rough idea of how long it might be expected to hold out.

In the real world all mathematics were liable to be thrown out by a mass of imponderables. Thus in 1744 a powerful French and Spanish army failed dismally against the Piedmontese fortress of Cuneo, which happened to be commanded by an obstinate old governor, and the besiegers were compelled to march back over the Alps, having fired away 43,000 rounds of shot and bombs, and having lost 15,000 men through enemy action, sickness and desertion. Marc-René Montalembert was there as a young officer, and he was 'forced to recognise, with great regret, how utterly uncertain is the course of a siege attack, and how many circumstances may combine to retard it'.[31]

SIEGE PARKS

Once the point of attack had been chosen, the gunners and engineers could determine the ground where they were going to lay out or prepare the guns, platforms, magazines, gabions, fascines and other requisites for the siege.

The artillery and engineering parks, whether combined or separate, were planted up to 2,000 yards from the fortress in concealed spots which were readily accessible from the roads. The cannon and mortar barrels, as the heaviest materials, were arranged in rows on the side nearest the siegeworks (it was usually only after the barrels reached the park that they were hoisted on to their wooden carriages or beds). All the forges, saw-pits, carpenters' workshops, and stores of inert materials like tools, gabions, shot and unfilled bombs could be arrayed in the middle of the park. The powder, on the other hand, had to be stored behind breastworks somewhere outside the perimeter. Close by these magazines were the plank- and earth-covered 'laboratories', where the artificers were left in peace and isolation to fill the bombs and grenades with gunpowder, and make up the cartridges.

It was advisable to let the engineers and gunners take their time about things, 'for it is better to delay the opening of the trenches, which merely loses time, than to run short of some indispensable commodity during the course of the siege, which will cost blood as well.'[32]

The materials from the parks and magazines were transported a little at a time to small depots which were positioned at the 'tail' (entrance) of the trenches, from where they were carried to the siegeworks as the need arose. Commanders liked to keep all of this activity as secret as possible from the garrison, and Lefebvre recalled with a shudder that 'at the siege of Menin [1744] I saw the soldiers who were carrying the fascines make a short cut to the depôt over the glacis of the fortress. You will hardly believe it, but they stopped to chat and smoke with the enemy soldiers in the covered way.'[33]

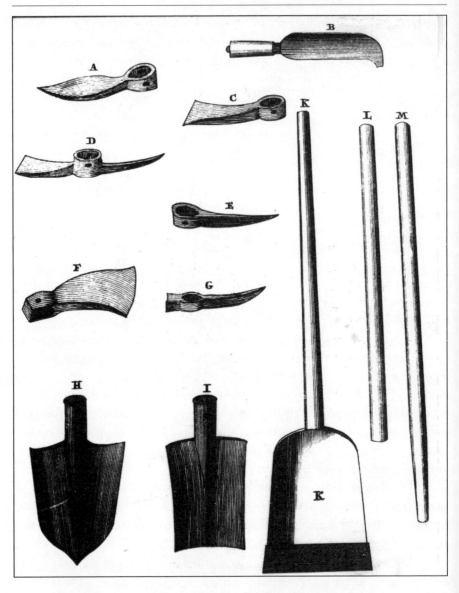

Near the small depots was established a first-aid post, complete with tents, surgeons and stretchers. The more serious casualties were sent back to the main field hospital *(hôpital ambulant)*.

In the French service all the medical facilities were placed under the authority of the intendant who directed the administration of the siege army. His duties were summed up in a memorandum dating from the middle of the eighteenth century.

Opposite page: Kinds of tools used in siegework (Saint-Rémy 1702): A, D, E, G – picks; C – mattock; B – billhook; F – axe; H, I – spades; K – wooden shovel with iron-reinforced blade.

The intendant is usually warned when we are about to attack any work or covered way. He must then calculate the likely quantity of wounded from the size of the assault, and make provision:

Firstly, for the appropriate number of stretchers to be assembled in the trenches.

Secondly, for the necessary surgeons and orderlies to be at the depôt.

Thirdly, for the requisite quantities of brandy, slings and dressings.

Fourthly, for the waggons to be standing by covered with straw and ready to convey the wounded, once they have been given first-aid, to the main field hospital, where everything must be prepared to receive them.[34]

All this time the cavalrymen were hard at work stripping the nearby woodlands of supple branches to provide the materials for the parapets of the siegeworks. The parapets of the trenches and many of the batteries were built up of earth-filled cylindrical baskets called gabions. The ordinary gabion stood between two-and-a-half and three feet high, and had a diameter of two feet (a few inches more back in Vauban's time), though the sap roller, or gabion farci, which was rolled in front of the sappers as they worked, was a massive cylinder six feet long and four feet wide at the open ends.

The manufacture of gabions was a skilled work which was taken on by the miners and sappers, and troops like the Swiss who were good with their hands. The men worked two or three at a time, and began by tracing on the ground a circle with a diameter of two feet or slightly less, and driving a dozen or so pointed pickets into the earth at equal intervals round the circumference. They wove slim and supple branches round the pickets, starting at the bottom, and consolidated each layer as they went by hammering it down on the one below. When the wickerwork approached within a few inches of the top of the pickets, the upper layers were firmly bound with withies, and the completed gabion was uprooted from the ground. Thousands of gabions were consumed in the course of the siege, and each of them represented up to three hours' work by two or more skilful and well-paid men.

'Fascines' were bundles of branches which were used for crowning rows of gabions, for revetting batteries and for filling up ditches and marshy ground. They were clumsy affairs, about nine inches in diameter and up to eighteen feet long, and they required little skill in the making, apart from the process of 'choking' (compressing) the bundle into a cylinder by chains or ropes, and binding it together by withies. Cavalrymen and other unintelligent forms of life were usually up to this undemanding work.

Sandbags offered a speedy and economical alternative to the building-up of the parapets by gabions and fascines. They were forwarded to the siege by scores of thousands at a time, as ready-made sacks about two feet long by seven or eight inches wide. The labour required to fill and plant them was as nothing compared with the maddeningly tedious business of putting together the gabions. Sandbags were used extensively by both sides in the Eighty Years War, by the French in their sieges in the Netherlands in the 1740s, by the English in the Peninsular War and by both French and English at the siege of Sevastopol. The wonder is that the preference was so often given to the gabion.

THE COMMAND AND DIRECTION OF THE SIEGE

The tensions of a siege were liable to strain beyond breaking-point the delicate relations which existed between the commander-in-chief, the engineers and the gunners.

The commander of the army was in an awkward position, for he was the fountainhead of authority, yet he depended upon the advice of the engineers and gunners in technical matters. As La Mina pointed out in the eighteenth century, a really able general might be able to obviate some of the difficulties if he took the trouble to equip himself to make the final decisions.

> He must give separate and joint interviews to the most able
> and prestigious engineers. He must get hold of old plans,
> and he will find it an illuminating experience to obtain a

diary of an earlier siege. With these preparations, and helped by information from the local people, the commander ought to be able to follow the right course – neither disagreeing too petulantly with the opinions of his engineers, nor following their proposals too slavishly.[35]

The commander's immediate deputy was the *tranchée major*, who supervised all the operational detail of the siege. 'For this work must be chosen a zealous, alert and tireless kind of man. He must be a lover of order. He must understand detail, and he must have an adequate knowledge of all matters pertaining to a siege. His duty lasts without a break from the beginning of the siege right through until the end.'[36] Further *tranchée majors* were appointed to command in any additional 'attacks'.

The tactical direction of the troops was entrusted to a temporary *tranchée général* (sometimes also known, according to his rank, as 'lieutenant general of the day' or 'major general of the day'), who was the divisional commander of the regiments which happened to be manning the trenches.

The divisions served in the trenches by rota for twenty-four hours at a stretch. As the division entered the siegeworks the divisional inspector or equivalent officer took on the responsibility of assigning the individual regiments to their posts. The Duke of Luxembourg explained to the war minister Louvois

> that the regiment which garrisons a stretch of the trench is also entrusted with pushing on the work. This has one good effect: namely, that each regiment strives to outdo the others in advancing the trench during its night of duty. However there are sectors where a regiment will suffer hardly any casualties at all, and other places where there will be a veritable massacre, which is a hard blow to an individual battalion.[37]

The troops were awarded extra pay for siege labour, an arrangement which seemed undesirable to pure-hearted warriors like Santa Cruz, 'for the soldier ought to be under just as strong an obligation to serve his Prince with pick and shovel as with sword and musket'.[38] At the end of the twenty-four hours' duty the regiments left the trenches and the *tranchée général* relinquished his command to a successor.

The chief engineer made regular reports to the commander on the progress of the siege, and he notified the adjutant-general in good time of how many infantrymen would be required to help in each day's or night's work. A couple of 'directors of approaches' stood next in line in the engineering hierarchy. It was their job to supervise the 'brigades' of engineer officers, who served in the trenches for watches of about eight hours at a time. The chief gunner organised his own officers on similar lines.

Throughout our period the engineers and the gunners were engaged in furious disputes as to the extent of their responsibilities in a siege. They did not hesitate to spirit away the soldier-labourers in secret at night-time, and, according to which arm was in the ascendancy, either the engineers found that their parallels were badly aligned by the artillerymen, or the gunners discovered that their batteries had been badly sited by the sappers. De Ligne says that in eighteenth-century Austria the infantry officers used to take a hand as well:

> The commanders ask the infantry colonels whether they have any officer who knows how to draw and have a little acquaintance with geometry. The colonels take the opportunity to produce such officers as they want to get rid of, or those that they wish to favour; in either event they boldly assert that the gentlemen in question are well qualified. These officers are thrown into confusion as soon as the first pistol shot rings out. Up rides the artillery commander at a gallop, asking to have a battery laid out, and up strides the engineer, who wants to dig a retrenchment. Now we have a quarrel on our hands. Everything is delayed until a general comes on the scene and loses further time in hearing the three parties out – often without having the foggiest notion what they are talking about. He is frequently guided by the most stupidly persistent of the trio (for he is looking for somebody to tell him what to do), and he ends up by following the worst of all the possible courses of action.[39]

From 1755 until 1758 the French government made an unhappy experiment in combining the engineers and gunners in a single corps. Maigret, for one, had been firmly against any union of the sort, for 'by uniting both into one corps, the knowledge of each man's duty would become so diffused that you could expect only men of moderate abilities in either profession; for the more the object of our researches is limited and confined, the easier it is fathomed by those who apply themselves; whereas vast objects require vast geniuses to comprehend them, and such spirits are rare'.[40] In 1783 Louis Duportail took the contrary view, and told his American employers that the only way to avert the 'frequent disputes and dissensions' among the gunners and engineers was to join them together. He explained that the French essay in a combined corps had failed because the time was not proper [in the midst of a war], and the operation was formed upon a bad scheme. Besides the private interests of many individuals principally of the first officers were much hurt by it. Add to this that as those corps existed in France a long while ago, each of them had acquired a particular *esprit* which makes it very adverse to such a union.[41]

Over the centuries, however, the advantages of separate corps have proved to be the stronger. General Lamare concluded from what he saw of the Peninsular War that the engineers and gunners would always manage to get along well, provided they were commanded by an intelligent and energetic general.[42]

THE FIRST PARALLEL

From Vauban's time onwards the regular siege proceeded by two kinds of trenches – the parallels (transverse support trenches) and the zigzags (approach trenches).

The parallel was a wide and deep trench that was traced in an arc round the fortress, so that it lay equidistant from the works along its whole length. It acted as a covered road between one side of the siege-works and the other, and as a strong position from which the infantry could repel sorties and otherwise support the zigzags in front.

The first of these parallels therefore formed the foundation for all the later work of the siege. The 'opening' was attended with due precaution and solemnity. Covering parties of infantry issued from the countervallation on the chosen night, and crept forward to within four or five hundred yards of the covered way of the fortress. The soldier-labourers (up to 3,000 at a time) now took up their entrenching tools and short 'tracing fascines' and advanced in several columns until, at about 600 yards from the covered way, they wheeled to left or right and deployed along the intended course of the parallel. There were engineers at hand to supervise the operation, and they arranged the tracing fascines in a line to show the men exactly where they were supposed to dig.

The men disposed themselves behind the fascines at intervals of four or six feet, and set to work in the remaining hours of darkness to dig a trench about three feet deep and three feet six inches wide. A space of a couple of feet was left between the line of fascines and the lip of the trench to serve as a banquette (firing-step), and the excavated earth was thrown beyond the fascines in order to pile up the parapet. Special parties were told off to build a redoubt at each end of the parallel, and to dig a number of 'boyaux' (communication trenches) in the direction of the countervallation behind.

If all went well, the garrison would know nothing of the 'opening of the trenches' until daylight revealed a scar of raw earth stretching for several hundred yards round the threatened side of the fortress. On the other hand the sun could easily rise on a scene of utter confusion. At Tournai, on 30 April/1 May 1745 the French discovered too late that they had built their parallel in two disconnected halves, one 240 yards from the covered way, and the other a good seventy yards further to the rear. A couple of generations later Ensign William Grattan witnessed his first siege, at the abortive British attack on Badajoz in 1811, and he writes that 'nothing astonished me so much as the noise made by the engineers; I expected that their loud talking would bring the enemy's attention towards the sound of our pick-axes, and that all the cannon in the town would be turned against us... I scarcely ventured to breathe until we had completed a respectable first parallel.' The French opened fire as soon as they had an inkling of what was going on, and 'by ten in the morning our line of batteries presented a very disorganised appearance: sandbags, gabions and fascines knocked here and there; guns flung off their carriages, and carriages beaten down under their guns. The boarded platforms of the batteries, damp with the blood of our artillerymen, or the headless trunks of our devoted engineers, bore testimony to the murderous fire opposed to us.'[43]

Assuming that the first night passed without mishap, the trench was strengthened over the following week until it became a true parallel, about four feet deep below ground, and between six and ten feet wide at the bottom. The parados (rearward side) of the parallel was usually cut into a gentle slope, so that the width across the top could amount to as much as fifteen feet. The Austrians were fond of digging vertical-sided parallels up to nine feet deep, which left the men with no means of extricating themselves in the event of a sortie.

The duration of the siege was reckoned in the diaries from the date, usually the day following the opening of the trenches, when the first division of regiments manned the parallel. The troops came from the camp and through the countervallation with drums beating, colours flying and their muskets at the carry. On entering the trench they shifted the muskets to the support, and marched to their assigned posts, where they planted their colours on the parapet.

THE FIRST ZIGZAGS

On the first or second night after the opening of trenches, the besiegers breached the parapet at two or three points and struck out towards the fortress by the first series of their approach trenches. It was in watching this interesting operation that Charles XII of Sweden was struck dead at the siege of Fredriksten in 1718.

The trenches wound forward in a series of zigzags, each arm of which extended for about thirty or forty yards (successively less as the approaches neared the fortress) and terminated in a rounded-off 'crochet', or miniature parallel. The zigzag conformation reconciled two equally vital needs – that of winning ground towards the fortress, and that of preventing the trench from being enfiladed from the works. The arms were therefore aligned in such a way that their imaginary prolongations fell just clear of the covered ways, which accounts for the increasing acuteness of the angles as the zigzags snaked closer to the fortress. The Huguenot officer Goulon observed that 'the most skilful engineers are the ones who align the trench as near to the salient of the covered way as is consonant with avoiding enfilade. By this they hasten the march of the siegeworks, which would be considerably delayed if they made frequent changes of direction.'[44]

The first zigzags were traced and dug in much the same way as the first parallel. The final dimensions, however, were more modest, since the zigzags were intended to serve as approach trenches rather than fighting positions.

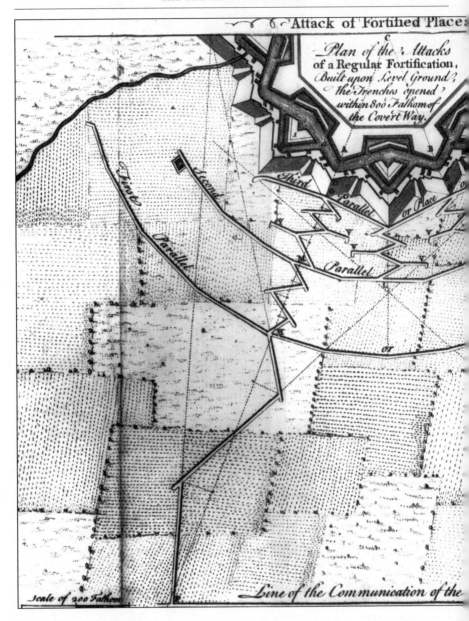

THE ARTILLERY ATTACK

Saint-Rémy remarks that 'as soon as the siege begins, the troops usually show their impatience to hear the cannon of the batteries open fire'.[45] Their wish could seldom be gratified before the fifth day of 'open trenches', but then there was a mighty roar as a simultaneous volley was

Plate 6.

Left: Formal siege, with parallels and zig-zags (Müller 1746).

delivered from the pieces that were installed in batteries a short distance in front of the first parallel.

There were about three batteries of mortars, lobbing their bombs into the interior of the fortifications, and eight or so batteries of cannon, which had the task of clearing the infantry and guns from the ramparts and covered ways.

Later in the siege, further mortar batteries and about a dozen batteries of cannon were emplaced in or near the second parallel. The final advance to the lip of the covered way was supported by six or so cannon batteries and several batteries of pierriers and light mortars, which were disposed in front of the third parallel.

When these pieces had done their work, the defending artillery on the ravelin and the faces of the bastions had been dismounted, and the parapets presented a decidedly ragged appearance. The final batteries were then arranged along the crest of the covered way: the counterbatteries knocked out the cannon still skulking in the bastion flanks, while the breaching batteries broke open the revetments of the ravelin and the bastion faces. Leaving aside the work of the high-trajectory pieces and the counterbatteries, we may sum up the process of the artillery attack as firstly, a period of long-range fire which silenced

Above: The opening of the trenches (J. Rigaud 1732). Part of a series of engravings which are remarkable for their reality and sense of space, and which lead us through the most important stages of siegework. In this engraving the first parallel stretches across the centre of the view; the labourers are carrying up fascines or wielding mattocks, while bodies of infantry and cavalry are stationed in close support. The setting is the city of Barcelona, as seen from the northern side. The hill of Montjuich may be dimly made out in the right background.

most of the enemy cannon, and secondly a phase of short-range fire which opened up the ramparts.

For dismounting work 16-, 12- or even 8-pounders served well enough, but nothing less than a 24-pounder would do for breaching fire.

For long-range fire the cannon were grouped in batteries of about half-a-dozen pieces at a time. Each battery comprised a solid parapet, which kept out the enemy shot, and a number of timber platforms which were disposed in the rear to support the gun-carriages. There were many instances of batteries that were made up of sandbags or woolsacks. Most commonly, however, the parapet was formed of large gabions or a solid earthen breastwork, the earth being obtained from a ditch about ten feet wide by six feet deep, which was dug in front of the site of the intended battery.

The battery parapet measured about 18 feet thick and 120 feet long, and it was pierced from about two-and-a-half feet above ground level with a number of embrasures, one for each cannon. The embrasures were arranged at intervals of between sixteen and twenty-three

143

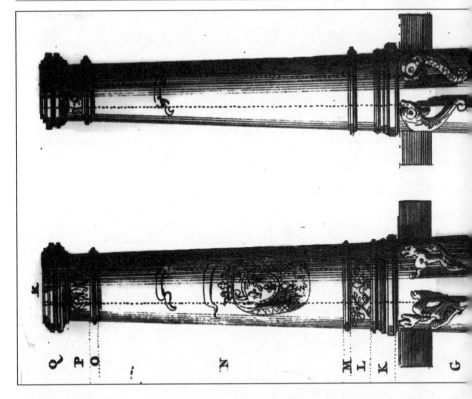

feet between centres, and they were designed with a pronounced splay, widening from two feet at the interior side to eight or nine on the outside. The merlons (the solid portions of the parapet between the embrasures) reached a height of about seven feet, and both they and the embrasures were roofed over with layers of fascines. In the case of an earthen parapet, fascines were used liberally to support the inner side of the breastwork and the cheeks of the embrasures.

Every cannon had to be provided with a wooden platform to save it from sinking into the ground under its own weight. The platform rested on a foundation of five or six eighteen- or nineteen-foot-long sleepers, which splayed out from a width of about nine feet at the front to eighteen along the rearward edge. The intervals were packed with earth, and the foundation was covered with a spiked-down layer of one-inch-thick planks, which were laid transversely across the sleepers.

The platform was supported in the rear by stout pickets, and at the front it was bordered by a transverse beam called the 'hurter', which prevented the wheels of the cannon from damaging the interior slope of

Left: French 33- and 24-pounder siege cannon (Saint-Remy 1702).

the parapet. A slight forward slope helped the crew to push the gun forward into the firing position after re-loading. The guns on the fortress ramparts were usually mounted on platforms of the same kind.

If the country around the fortress happened to be lightly wooded, the siege army would have to carry the timber for the platforms all the way from its base. This great mass of carpentry took up nearly half the transport space on the British expedition to Walcheren in 1809.

Each battery was provided with one or more expense magazines, lurking under cover of a breastwork that was cast up behind, or preferably to one side of the battery. The powder barrels were rolled along a boyau from the expense magazine to one of the still smaller magazines which were dug a dozen paces to the rear of every couple of guns. The powder was brought to the muzzle of the gun in leather sacks, open ladles, or cartridges of cloth or parchment. A quantity was inevitably spilled on the way, and by the end of a busy day's firing the ground round the battery might well be crisscrossed with a network of black trails, offering so many ready-laid powder trains which could be ignited by a stray spark or a dropped match. Thus at the single siege of Valenciennes, in 1793, there were seven major explosions in the siegeworks. However, the cannon balls, being solid iron, could be safely piled beside the platforms.

Commanders did not expect their armies to toil away at sieges from pure patriotism or a sense of duty. Every operation had its cash price, in the seventeenth and eighteenth centuries. In the French service it was the custom to award the chief gunner three hundred livres

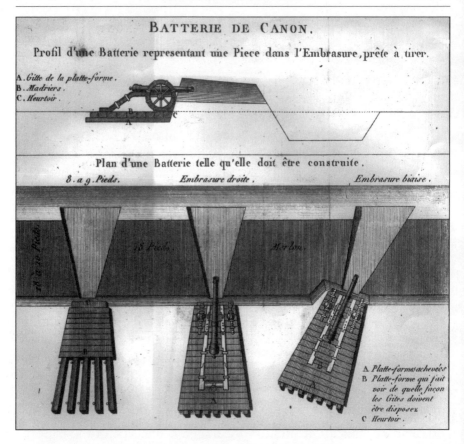

Profile and plan of siege battery (Vauban 1704).

for each piece placed in battery, and an extra thirty livres' 'subsistence' for every twenty-four hours that the gun remained in action. The chief gunners totted up the sum at the end of the siege, and distributed the money among themselves and the workmen and guncrews they had borrowed from the infantry. 'This work does not bring the same pecuniary profit to our majors as the other siegeworks,' commented Guignard. 'That is because they are too interested in the success of the operation to employ fifty men on the work instead of the nominal hundred, as usually happens in the other stages of the siege.'[46]

It could take eighty men up to forty-eight hours to build a battery and lay down the platforms. Their final task was to 'mask' the mouths of the embrasures with gabions or stout wooden boards, which were removed only when the order came to open fire.

That moment would almost certainly be delayed out of regard for some important tactical considerations: the cannon could be dragged up from the park and mounted in the batteries only at night-time, whereas the gunners needed daylight in order to see their targets; also, it was essential to wait until every battery was ready to open fire before you unmasked the embrasures, otherwise the fortress would be able to concentrate a superior fire on each battery in turn, and destroy the siege artillery piecemeal.

A cannon was loaded from the muzzle with a charge of gunpowder, a wad of hay, wood or some other substance, and a roundshot. A little fine powder was poured into the vent at the breech, and the

View of a cannon battery (Saint-Rémy 1702): A – the cannon is loaded; B – the cannon is pushed into the embrasure; C – the cannon is aimed; D – the cannon is fired; E – the powder is measured out in the expense magazine; F, G – powder kegs are brought to the expense magazine; H – the main magazine.

deposit was ignited by the application of a lighted match (treated cord) or portfire (tube of slow-burning powder). After every round the inside of the barrel was swabbed out with a wet mop, so as to extinguish any embers which might have set off the next charge as it was being loaded.

At least two gunners and half a dozen 'borrowed' soldiers were assigned to each piece. The gunners primed and aimed the cannon, brought up the powder from the nearest magazine and deposited the charge at the bottom of the barrel – either as a bagged charge or as loose powder in a ladle. Two gunners or two soldiers, one standing on either side of the muzzle, were responsible for introducing the wadding and shot, and wielding the rammer and mop. The remaining troops stationed themselves further to the rear, and used levers to elevate and traverse the piece according to the directions of the gunners, and to run it forward into the embrasure after reloading.

A rate of fire of twenty rounds per hour was considered a safe average for a cannon in a breaching battery. A well-trained crew could fire thirty rounds an hour, or up to 150 rounds a day with fair accuracy, but the brazen barrel would probably heat up so much in the process that the vent would become excessively enlarged, and the 'chase' (the unsupported stretch between the trunnions and the muzzle) begin to droop. At the siege of Verrua in 1704 the French guns were 'so worn that in order to be able to use them ... we had to saw off the muzzles. The resulting barrels were no more than half the original length, and they shot very badly.'[47]

Iron barrels were rarely used in land warfare before the nineteenth century: they were cheaper, lighter and harder than the bronze barrels, but they were much more liable to burst without warning.

The powder charge was the equivalent of roughly one-third of the weight of shot, though the quantity could be reduced a little after the barrel had heated up.

Saint-Rémy speaks in alarmingly casual terms concerning the fit of the cannon balls: 'a few fractions of an inch do not matter one way or another; it is actually better for a shot to be somewhat loose in the barrel than to fit so accurately as to be difficult to ram down'.[48] These were solid spheres of cast iron, a material that was cheaper and more tractable than the tougher wrought iron.

When the defenders ventured a sortie, the siege cannon could act as giant shotguns, discharging hails of canister (musket balls enclosed in a light metal cylinder) or the longer-ranged grape (shot of the size of billiard balls, which were packed round a solid base and an upright spike).

In ordinary siege-work, the best results were attained when all the guns in the battery concentrated their fire against one target at a time – a single embrasure, for instance, or a short stretch of parapet. Except when breaching a revetment, the guns were usually touched off in succession, beginning at the downwind end of the battery, so as not to obstruct the aim by smoke.

The thundering detonations of the low-trajectory fire were soon interspersed with a series of muffled thumps, as more and more of the gunners turned to ricochet fire and began to slaughter the garrison infantry along the ramparts and the covered ways. The technique was worked out by Vauban. In order to deliver this kind of fire the gun barrels were elevated by anything from three to fifteen degrees, and the powder charges were varied by an ounce at a time until the gunners arrived at a weight which caused the shot to graze over the top of the fortress parapets and bound along the length of the terrepleins behind. Even the slowest-moving ball exercised a great crushing effect. General Sir Howard Douglas recalled that at the siege of Burgos in 1812,

Siege battery in action (Le Blond 1746).

our shot having been all expended, soldiers were employed and paid for picking up shot fired by the enemy... Many of our soldiers were seriously hurt, some it was said killed, in attempting to stop 16- and 24-pounder shot which appeared to be rolling like cricket balls, and as if they might easily be stopped.[49]

From 1697, when Vauban first employed ricochet fire, at the siege of Ath, the parapets of a fortress ceased to offer any sure protection against siege artillery. The gunners, once they had overcome their first prejudices against the invention, were delighted to display their skill in a kind of fire which was so destructive and yet so economical in powder. Howitzers, too, came to be extensively employed for ricochet fire, in the second half of the eighteenth century, for they killed just as many men when the shell finally burst as they did when the missile was bouncing along beforehand.

At Valenciennes in 1793 one of the defenders saw that the enemy were lobbing howitzer shells towards him just as if

Attack on a horn work, with ricochet batteries firing from the left bank of the river.

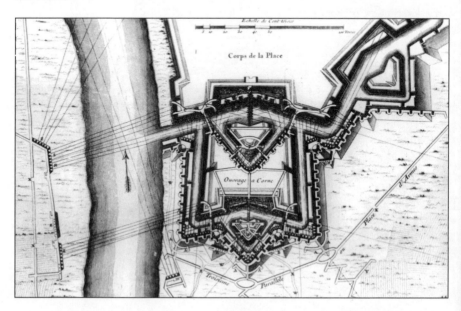

they were playing at bowls. If the shell was checked by a palisade the subsequent explosion used to shatter the stakes and send splinters flying into the sides and backs of the men who were sheltering behind. The effect was still more murderous when the shell stuck between two palisades. More often, however, the shell bounded over our heads and landed to the rear, placing us in little danger.[50]

By the middle of the nineteenth century the difficult art of ricochet had been almost completely supplanted by the firing of shrapnel shells. The first inspiration came from Captain John Mercer of the Thirty-Ninth Foot, who at the defence of Gibraltar (1779–83) fired 5½-inch mortar bombs from 24-pounder cannon, cutting the fuzes in such a way that the shells burst over the heads of the Spanish working parties. The young gunner Henry Shrapnel saw what Mercer had done, and in later years he perfected an air-burst shell of his own devising. The 'shrapnel shell' was packed with lead balls and just enough powder to burst open the cast-iron casing, causing the remains of the exploded shell to travel along the remaining line of the trajectory as a shower of lead balls and iron splinters. Shrapnel publicised his experiments in his *Gunner's Guide* of 1806, and the English went on to fire his shells from their long cannon in the last sieges of the Peninsular War. Wellington opposed the new invention, as we might have expected from his conservative habits of mind, but the notion of the shrapnel shell caught on throughout Europe in the post-Napoleonic period.

The mortars were sited in large pits called 'cauldrons', or behind earthen breastworks which were identical with the parapets of the cannon batteries, except for the lack of embrasures. Since the bombardiers had no direct view of the fortress, they sited an observer outside the battery and fixed a number of pegs along the crest of the parapet so as to record the correct traverse for each piece. The platforms in these batteries were somewhat squarer and stouter than was the case in the cannon batteries.

Mortars were essentially siege-pieces, and they came in a great variety of weights, from the tiny grenade-throwing coehorn to the monsters of 13-inch or greater calibre which were needed for the work of penetrating the cover of magazines or cisterns.

Opposite page: The firing of mortars (Mallet 1673). The mortar on the left has been stuffed with earth, in the French manner.

The spherical bomb was lifted by two cast-iron handles and lowered down the comparatively thin-walled barrel of the mortar until it came to rest above the powder chamber, which was a cylindrical, conical or semi-circular recess in the massive base. The two trunnions at the exterior of the base reposed upon a wheel-less carriage of timber, which gradually disintegrated under the tremendous shock of the discharges. The *mortiers à plaque* of the later eighteenth century had barrel and bed cast as a single piece of metal, which permitted the use of far heavier charges than in the conventional mortar. At the great siege of Gibraltar the Franco-Spanish *mortiers à plaque* were charged with up to thirty-two pounds of powder, and hurled their bombs nearly three miles.

The bombs were hollow spheres of cast iron. The thickness of metal was rather greater at the base than around the fuze-hole, so as to withstand the shock of the discharge and bring the bomb to rest fuze-uppermost when it reached its target. The artificers in the arsenal or the siege 'laboratory' poured the powder of the bursting-charge little by little into the bomb through the fuze-hole, and rammed each layer firmly down by a wooden rod. When the bomb was nearly full, a wooden fuze was inserted in the hole and the top hammered flush with the surface of the bomb.

The fuze had the shape of a gently tapering frustrum of a cone (in less pompous terms, like an elongated flower pot), and it was pierced from top to bottom with a hole of quarter-inch diameter, containing a composition of slow-burning powder. When a waterproof cap of parchment, pitch or wax was removed from the upper end, and a flame applied to the exposed powder, the composition took fire like the filling of a rocket, and the flame travelled to the bottom of the tube in a time which corresponded with the duration of the flight of the bomb when it was discharged at maximum elevation and with the largest propelling charge. The fuze could be adjusted to lesser ranges by cutting away slices from the bottom end which projected into the bomb. Except when he wished to penetrate cover, the bombardier liked to see his bomb explode at the moment when it touched the ground.

The process of loading and firing the mortar was strange and alarming. As Malthus sagely remarked, 'it is there that the hazards and dangers most great, do meet together'.[51] According to the practice which was followed by the French until at least 1747, the first step was to pour the propellant charge into the chamber and pack it down with a wad of hay and a quantity of earth; the bomb was then positioned fuze-uppermost in the centre of the bore, and the generous windage (space) between the bomb and the sides of the mortar was filled with earth. The fuze was uncapped, and at a given signal the bombardier took up a burning match in each hand, applying one to the bomb, and the other immediately afterwards to the powder-filled vent leading to the propellant charge. If the fuze took fire and the powder did not, there was nothing the bombardiers could do except run as fast as they could before the bomb burst in the barrel.

In the British service the bomb rested directly on the propellant charge, without a wad, and was centred in the bore by means of wedges that were driven into the windage. The fuze was uncapped, but not ignited, and at the instant of firing the flame of the charge licked round the bomb and touched off the fuze. The English technique of the 'single fire' was safer, speedier and more precise than the French, and caused less wear on the interior of the barrel. The only disadvantage, a slight one, was that the chamber had to be filled with a slightly heavier propelling charge, to make up for the absence of a wad.

Two means could be employed to adjust the distance at which the bomb fell. Some bombardiers had their mortar barrels at a fixed elevation of forty-five degrees, and varied the range by filling the chamber with greater or lesser quantities of powder. The alternative method was to elevate or depress the barrel by means of a wedge, and read off the angles from a gunner's quadrant which was inserted in the muzzle. In the Morea in 1686 the Venetian artillery commander Count San Felice caused consternation among the German contingent by employing this method against the Turkish strongholds. Any given target within range could be reached at two elevations, one above forty-five degrees and the other below. The lower trajectory was preferred when the object was a fortification filled with enemy troops, and the higher angle to break through overhead cover. In any event the relatively high trajectory of all mortar-fire carried the bombs over every obstacle between the battery and the target, hence mortars did not have to be sited in the same strictly geometrical relation to the fortifications as the long guns.

Marshall de Belle-Isle wrote glowingly of the effect of mortar-fire in sieges.

These bombs cause such devastation that the fortifications become well-nigh untenable. They smash the palisades, the tambours and the redoubts in the re-entrant places of arms, and they cause altogether greater disorder than ordinary cannon shot – not only are they larger and heavier than the roundshot, but, after they bounce a few times, they come to rest and burst.[52]

Mortar bombs produced their most spectacular effects of all when they managed to touch off a fortress magazine. Such a cataclysmic event was capable of curtailing a garrison's resistance at one blow, or even of ending it altogether (Nice 1691, Breslau November 1757, Schweidnitz 1762, Almeida 1809, and the many instances from the Turkish wars – Ofen 1686, the Parthenon 1687, Belgrade in 1690, 1717 and 1789, Azov and Ochakov 1737).

We know in fair detail what happened at Belgrade on the late afternoon of 14 August 1717, when a 10-pounder Christian bomb blew up the main Turkish magazine, sweeping away the minarets of the city mosques, and killing no less than 3,000 people. In 1775 Frederick the Great was lucky enough to uncover an eighty-year-old Hessian sergeant, Johannes Rau, who was able to give an account of how the deadly bomb had been fired. According to this testimony,

> there was a very young Pole present at the siege, who asked Prince Eugene [the Imperial commander] for permission to fire off three bombs, declaring that he was willing to answer with his head if one or other of his bombs did not blow up the magazine in the Wasserstadt. Prince Eugene was perfectly agreeable, but since thc gunners were too haughty to offer any help to our Pole, he had to betake himself to the Hessians. Soon enough he gathered some lads who were willing to lend a hand in return for a keg of Hungarian wine.
>
> The Polack then aimed the mortar and got me to set off the charge. Nothing happened with the first two bombs, and while I was applying the match for the third time he called out: 'If I don't land the bomb on the roof this time I shall have to make myself scarce!'

As it happened, the third bomb actually blew up the magazine. The whole town was reduced to ruins. Stones, timbers and Turks (both whole and in pieces) whirled through the air and were flung as far as the Imperial trenches.[53]

DEFENSIVE FIRE

The experts could not agree as to whether it was a good thing for the governor to order his outnumbered artillery to take up a serious duel with the siege guns. The defending artillery certainly had everything its own way in the precious few days which intervened between the opening of the first parallel and the first volley from the siege batteries. During this period the garrison gunners could bring their 3- and 6-pounders to the salients of the covered way and fire at the trenches with impunity, while the heavier guns rained shot on the uncompleted siege batteries. Any delay which was incurred in the finishing of a single siege battery would, as we have seen, cause all the batteries to postpone the opening of fire.

Early in the defence of Turin in 1706 the Piedmontese

> learnt from deserters that several enemy generals had arranged to dine in some farmhouses within artillery range of the citadel, so as to have a better view. We accordingly opened fire at noon with all the artillery of the citadel, aiming at all the farmhouses in the neighbourhood. This unpleasant surprise caused a horrid upset to the Frenchmen's lunch, and afforded great amusement to the people who were in the know.[54]

Things wore a different complexion after the siege artillery had come into action. Aggressive people like Frederick the Great advised the defending gunners to keep up the fight and attend religiously to the repair of damaged parapets and the remounting of barrels. In museums today we may still see the chipped, gouged and cracked pieces which bear witness to the ferocity of combats like these; we can only imagine what happened to the frail, expendable human beings who served the brazen barrels.

The eighteenth-century French authorities Cormontaigne and Vauban stand at the opposite extreme.

We believe that it is an excellent principle for the fortress artillery to refrain from duelling with the enemy guns before the final stage of the siege. Otherwise, as the experience of war tells us, the defending artillery will invariably be destroyed in a short time and rendered *hors de combat* for the whole of the rest of the siege. The reason is simple – the besieger cannonades the fortress with heavier pieces, and more of them, than the defender is able to pit against him.[55]

Cormontaigne even argued that the artillery should be withdrawn to the adjacent fronts immediately the first parallel had been opened, without making so much as an attempt to disturb the workmen who were labouring on the siege batteries. He intended thereby to conserve the whole artillery intact until the last stages of the defence, forgetting that the communications and the rampart walks would have been so ravaged by the end of the siege that it would have been very difficult to bring the guns back again. A reasonable compromise, and one that was often adopted in practice, was to employ a number of highly mobile *pièces ambulantes*. These guns would make an unexpected appearance, get off a few rounds, and vanish from view before the besiegers could reply.

THE SECOND PARALLEL

After the long-range fire had begun to take effect on the fortress, and the zigzags had approached to within about three hundred yards of the covered way, it was time for the besiegers to plant the second of their parallels. The second parallel was usually established by the technique of flying sap, which will be described later, but in almost every other respect it was identical in purpose and design with the first parallel.

THE SAPS

As the approaches neared the fortress, 'every cannon shot fired by the defenders is more deadly than five hundred discharged at the beginning of the siege'.[56] Moreover, the defending musketry and wall-pieces would begin to make themselves felt.

A special procedure was there adopted for the digging of the three or so zigzags which worked their way forward from the second parallel (one zigzag against the ravelin; one each against the bastions on either side).

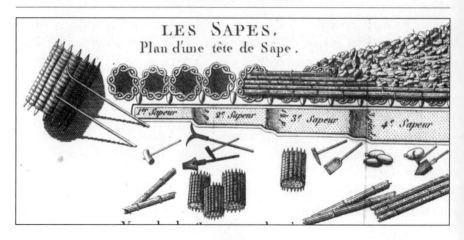

View of sap from above (Vauban 1704), showing how the trench was widened and deepened by successive sappers.

A number of muscular volunteers were designated 'sappers', and divided into four-man squads, each of which was made responsible for pushing forward one of the heads of sap. The leading sapper covered himself and the rest of his squad by cautiously pushing forward a sap roller, or a wheeled timber screen (mantlet). He took up a gabion, and gingerly positioned the basket beside the screen or just in front of it. He then advanced the screen a little more and dug a trench two feet long, and eighteen inches wide and deep, on the side away from the fortress, filling the gabion with the spoil. He left a berm of one foot between the gabion and the edge of his trench, and packed sandbags into the interstices between the new gabion and the one before. After that he pushed the screen forward and attended to the next gabion, while the second sapper crowned the newly planted gabion with fascines and widened and deepened the trench – this time the excavated earth was thrown over the top of the gabion to form a slope on the far side.

The third and fourth sappers continued the process until the sap was three feet wide and deep, and the spoil and the line of gabions and fascines constituted a parapet which could keep out all musket balls and many of the cannon shot. Over the following days and nights the less highly skilled workmen widened the sap to a breadth of ten or twelve feet, at which point it was designated a 'trench'. The ends of the arms of the zigzags were finished off with crochets, as before, though every now and then they might be prolonged into an 80- or 100-yard-long half-parallel, from which the infantry could direct an enfilading fire down the length of the covered ways.

After one hour the sapper team was relieved by another squad, in which time it would have planted and filled five or six gabions. In Vauban's time the head of the sap was said to proceed at a rate of 160 yards in 24 hours, an extraordinary speed, though in the nineteenth century the progress dropped to a more realistic 80 yards. Nobody could quite account for the difference between the rates, though the narrower gabion of later times, the replacement of the mantlet by the sap roller, and the fuss and commotion consequent upon more frequent reliefs of sappers all probably contributed to a general slowing-down of the pace. Perhaps also Vauban used to cheat a little and include a stretch of zigzag that was established by 'flying sap', in which the workmen planted and

Views of sap from sides and rear (Vauban 1704) .

filled a whole row of gabions simultaneously. This technique was adopted only when there was a marked slackening in the enemy fire.

Conversely, if the branch of the zigzag came under fire from two directions at once, then the full and flying saps were replaced by the wide 'double sap', which possessed gabion-and-earth parapets on both sides of the trench. In the event of progress on the surface becoming altogether impossible, even at night-time, the sappers could still burrow a few feet below the turf and proceed by means of 'covered sap'. Every now and again they had to break through to the open air with their picks, so as to ventilate the tunnel and see where they were going. It was odd to see the apparently disembodied heads appear in the grass, revolve once or twice, and vanish again no less mysteriously. In the War of the Spanish Succession the Allies employed saps of this kind in their sieges of Lille, Douai and Béthune.

At this stage of the siege, therefore, the progress depended very largely on the state of morale of the small bands of men who were working at the heads of the saps. Once they had offered themselves for this perilous work, the volunteers were exempted from all other duties and placed in tents apart. Sometimes they wore body armour, and massive and ugly morions with cheek-pieces which seem to have been inspired by the helmets of ancient Greece. Perhaps the sappers would even survive long enough to collect the cash reward for their valour and effort: in Vauban's time the going rates were fixed at forty sols for every two yards of sap between the first and third parallels, at two livres ten sols for the third parallel, and at no less than twenty livres for the same distance in the passage of the ditch. One can hardly blame the sappers for celebrating while they still had the opportunity. Vauban solemnly warns that 'there is one thing against which the officers ought to take every precaution, namely, the tendency of the sappers to get drunk while they are working at the head of the sap. They throw every precaution to the winds and have themselves killed off like brute beasts'.[57]

THE DEFENCE IN THE MIDDLE PERIOD OF THE SIEGE

The defenders rightly regarded the advance of the saps as 'the wave which was approaching to engulf them'.[58] The garrison gunners therefore scourged the siegeworks with mortar and howitzer bombs, and with grape and roundshot from whatever cannon were still intact – a lively fire of artillery would deter the enemy from attempting anything so perilous as flying sap, and might well deter them altogether from digging full saps in daytime.

Day and night, thousands of musket shots were discharged from the covered way. Most governors would certainly have agreed with the Prussian engineer Walrave that 'infantry fire is the most murderous of all weapons, and that we must therefore do everything possible to bring it to bear on the enemy'.[59] As we might have expected, Maurice de Saxe took a perverse delight in arguing that musketry was

> just so much empty noise. The soldiers are too lazy to load and ram in the proper way, which is tiring; instead they take a fistful of powder, empty it down the barrel, drop a ball on top and fire. Where do they shoot? Why, into the air! Their shoulders ache from so much firing, and since the officers cannot see them in the dark they are content to rest the muzzle on the palisade and blast away at random.[60]

As for sorties, de Ville sums up the view that prevailed in the era before Vauban invented the siege parallel.

> The defender will quickly lose his fortress if he allows the besieger to work at leisure in the country outside, for the siegeworks are like some poison which is deadly once it reaches a vital part. Men of every century have recognised that sorties are advantageous. History is full of examples of the severe losses in time and material which sorties have inflicted upon besiegers.[61]

In those days a governor did not hesitate to launch a sortie if he heard, for instance, that a stretch of trenches was held by a weak or bad regiment, or that the besiegers had failed to close off a length of sap with a redoubt. The Sieur de Puységur argued that the best hour for such an enterprise was at noon, 'the time when the trenches are most carelessly guarded: the infantrymen have been exhausted by their labours during the night, and most of them, having eaten, are now fast asleep; the cavalrymen too are vulnerable to surprise, for the majority have dismounted and unsaddled their horses'.[62] However, most authorities held that sorties were best undertaken at night.

Once the sortie-troops had entered the trenches they would tip up or burn the gabions, and render the cannon useless by knocking off the trunnions or jamming the vents with gravel or a spike: the best spiking nail was a thin, square-sectioned rod, the head of which could be snapped off flush with the surface of the cannon, and the point bent into a curl inside the barrel with the rammer; if no spiking nails were available, a cannon could be rendered unserviceable for some time simply by wrapping a roundshot in a hat and ramming it down to the bottom of the barrel.

Vauban did more than any other one man to make sorties unprofitable. By holding one of his parallels, the besiegers could deliver a couple of destructive volleys while the sortie was at a distance; if the garrison still came on, the procedure was for the troops to retire up the gentle rearward slope of the parallel and form up in battle array along the edge – in this case the parapet still offered a measure of protection, while the trench itself acted as a serviceable ditch. These considerations were more than enough to tip the balance of loss and gain against the garrison, for, as Vauban remarked, 'it is quite certain that the effect of one man lost to the defenders is the equivalent, or even worse, than of six or seven men lost to the besiegers'.[63]

THE THIRD PARALLEL

There was not much the garrison could do to prevent the enemy from establishing the third of their parallels. This work was usually effected by opening transverse saps to right and left, once the three zigzags had reached the 'tail' (foot) of the glacis – in other words about seventy or eighty yards from the crest of the covered way. The rearward batteries were supposed to keep up a heavy supporting fire all the time, though, as Bousmard says, 'I know from experience that when you have a battery shooting right over your head you feel an urgent desire to tell the gunners to desist. As a result, this kind of fire is possible in theory but almost always impossible in practice.'[64]

The third parallel was regarded as the main emplacement for the close-range anti-personnel weapons. Among these murderous devices the pierrier took pride of place. This was a special stone-throwing mortar that was invented, or re-invented, by Vauban. On 13 November 1672 he reported to Louvois that he had loaded stones of about the size of a fist into 12- and 13-inch mortars. They carried nearly four hundred

The last stages of the siege (Vauban 1704), showing third parallel, crowning of the covered way, positions of breaching batteries, passages of the ditch, and lodgements on the breaches of the ravelin and bastions.

paces, and fell with such force that even the smallest of them buried itself to a depth of six inches. Sixteen- or 18-inch mortars produced more gratifying results still: 'A mortar of this calibre can discharge the equivalent of up to two wheelbarrows' load of stones at a time. The stones fly through the air in a cloud, then flog the ground with a force which I can only compare with that of pikes landing point-downwards.'[65] Stone-throwing mortars were soon being manufactured by gunfounders all over Europe, who gave them a larger calibre and lighter construction than their bomb-throwing ancestors. At the Valencian fortress of Denia, in 1707, one of the defenders claims that 'what most of all plagued us, and did most mischief, was the vast showers of stones sent among the garrison from their mortars. These terrible in bulk and size, did more execution than all the rest put together.'[66]

The fire of the pierriers was often supplemented by that of the diminutive coehorn mortars, which were first devised by Vauban's great rival Menno van Coehoorn. These could each be carried by two men and sited almost anywhere in the advanced siegeworks. The tiny barrel had the alarming habit of jumping high in the air when it was fired, but it hurled its fizzing grenade with considerable accuracy up to about 160 yards, and rather more wildly over greater ranges.

THE CAPTURE OF THE COVERED WAY

As soon as the besiegers struck out from the third parallel they lost much of the advantage they had hitherto enjoyed over the garrison. The approaches became narrower and more subject to enfilade than they had been before, and the batteries of the parallels behind could not lend close support without an appreciable risk of removing the heads of their own men – probably how the Duke of Berwick was killed at the siege of Philippsburg in 1734.

The defenders could now bring their countermines into action, blowing up or entombing scores of men at a time. Moreover, the infantry could stage an effective and long-drawn-out defence of the covered way, which was the outer perimeter of the fortress proper. The bloody combats at Namur in 1695, Kaiserswörth in 1702 and Freiburg in 1713 proved that the assailant could lose almost as many men in attacking this single work as in a respectable action in the open field.

The most effective defence of the covered way was therefore a question of some moment. It was debated with particular urgency by the French at Lille in 1708, when the Allies were about to storm the two hornworks on the northern fronts. The artillery commander La Frezelière writes that Boufflers, the governor, assembled his officers to discuss how they should ward off the coming assault.

> There was a mistaken opinion abroad in the army to the effect that once a covered way was assaulted it was bound to fall. Boufflers was even presented with a memorandum of the late Marshal Vauban concerning the defence of fortresses, from which it appears that he was in favour of abandoning the salient angles of the covered way, and retaining the troops only in the re-entrant places of arms, where they would be afforded more protection by the rampart.

All the officers seemed to agree with that opinion, but Boufflers remembered the heavy casualties he had inflicted when he held the whole extent of the covered ways at Namur in 1695, and he asked La Frezelière for his view. The gunner represented 'that if he abandoned the salient angles of the covered way the enemy would infallibly make lodgements there, then push their saps to right and left along the branches and rapidly gain the re-entrants'.[67] This convinced Boufflers of the correctness of his own judgement, and he arranged to have the entire covered way defended by troops.

The Allies put in the long-awaited storm on the evening of 7 September. Their leading troops were cut down as soon as they formed up, and it was immediately apparent that their engineers had made a number of serious miscalculations: the nearest trenches were two hundred yards distant from the covered ways; moreover, 'the parapets of the covered way were not sufficiently damaged, and the equipment and tools for the assault were badly designed and badly made – in particular the gabions were too bulky and heavy for the men to bring them forward'.[68] The Allies established four isolated lodgements in the covered ways at their third assault, and they paid for this modest gain in nearly 3,000 dead and wounded. One of the defenders recalled that as the sun rose on the 8th he saw that the grass of the glacis was entirely covered with bodies.[69]

After experiences like these, engineers were ready to concede by the middle of the eighteenth century that 'the taking of the covered way, when it is in a good condition and well defended, is generally the most bloody action of the siege'.[70]

The one exception was in the attack of Spanish-held fortresses, where the palisades,

> being planted on the parapet of the covered way mask half the fire from the ramparts, and facilitate the task of the workers in establishing the lodgement. Soldiers are naturally stupid – they do not know what they are doing, or where they are being taken; but in this case they simply march along behind the engineers and their officers until their heads or arms strike the palisade, at which they drop the fascines at their feet and automatically trace the lodgement.'[71]

If you shrank from the risk of an open assault, the only alternative was to approach the covered way by means of a complicated and laborious formal attack. First of all you drove a double sap from the third parallel up the capital line of each of the attacked works. About twenty-six yards short of the covered way the sap branched to right and left in half-parallels. This was where the sappers built up the 'cavalier de tranchée' – a tall parapet of several layers of gabions and sandbags. The site was cunningly chosen so as to lie just out of effective hand-grenade range of the defenders, yet near enough to deter the governor from exploding a countermine, out of fear of wrecking his own covered way.

As the dominating cavalier de tranchée was approaching completion, the garrison troops in the covered way usually abandoned the salient place of arms and retired behind the traverses and the re-entrant places of arms. This was the signal for your sappers to prolong the double sap to within a few yards of the crest of the covered way. They then split into two parties, and 'crowned' the covered way by sapping along the glacis parallel to the two branches of the covered way. They were accompanied by grenadiers or other good troops, who evicted the defenders from the traverses and the re-entrant places of arms by means of musket, bayonet and hand grenade.

Above: Assault on the covered way by grenadiers (Saint-Rémy 1702).
Opposite page: Grenadier (Mallet 1673). The characteristic grenadier cap had not yet come into universal fashion.

Occasionally the defenders would oppose the establishment of the third parallel and the progress of the double sap by impudently digging down the glacis in trenches of their own. These were called counter-approaches. Deshoulières, writing in 1675, stated that he had never seen counter-approaches practised in his own time[72] – which did not prevent the garrison of Philippsburg employing them in the very next year. They were used again at Ypres in 1678 and Landau in 1704, and in the Crimean War the Russian engineer Totleben applied them on an extensive scale in his defence of Sevastopol.

The hand grenade came into its own in the close-quarter fighting at this stage of the siege. It was a sphere of cast iron or thick glass, and weighed about two pounds, including the bursting charge of four or five ounces of powder. The Spanish seem to have been responsible for introducing this weapon into Western European warfare, employing it on a large scale in the Eighty Years War, and to the number of no less than 36,000 against the French at Valenciennes in 1656. The grenade reached the peak of its popularity in the last quarter of the seventeenth century. Thus in 1702 Baron v. Wetzel, the Austrian governor of Brescello, could express some anxiety for the safety of his otherwise well-munitioned fortress because his magazines held only 400 hand grenades, 'which are one of the best means of defence in the event of siege'.[73]

A well-thrown grenade could certainly cause great devastation. By casting one of these weapons the Chevalier de Guignard managed to burn one hundred yards of unfilled gabions in a flying sap at Lille in 1708. However, the effective use of the grenade demanded heroic strength and resolution, as well as a good sense of timing, and so the device fell into disuse after the War of the Spanish Succession. The grenadiers, the troops who had been specifically trained for the throwing of grenades, were nevertheless retained by the armies of Europe as élite soldiers who were fit for any desperate enterprise. The grenadier could still be recognised easily enough by his tall mitre cap or bearskin (less liable than the tricorn hat to get in the way of the throwing-arm), his ferocious moustaches, his height and his generally formidable bearing.

THE BREACHING OF THE REVETMENT BY CANNON-FIRE

All the effort of the siege up to the crowning of the covered way was devoted to just one object – to bring the battering guns or the miners close enough to the fortress to be able to smash a way through the ramparts for the waiting infantry.

If the siege commander decided to put his trust in the artillery method, his next step was to carve the upper part of the glacis into a number of gun positions. The forward edge of the gun pits was dug to within eighteen or twenty feet of the crest of the covered way, and the intervening thickness was cut into merlons and embrasures in a similar way to the parapets of the earlier siege batteries.

Some of the cannon were sited in counter-batteries. The counter-batteries were placed opposite the salients of the bastions, a position which gave them a clear field of fire along the ditch to the flanks of the adjacent bastions, where the defenders in all probability still had a few pieces intact. This gave rise to a brief but murderous artillery duel which almost invariably ended in the dismounting of the garrison's guns.

The breaching batteries, each comprising between four and eight 24-pounders, were positioned in pairs or trios along the branches of the covered way, so that they could batter the revetment of the ravelin or bastion face which lay directly in front of them.

The technique of cannelure cutting proved to be the best means of bringing down the masonry. Using full charges the cannon scored out a continuous line of craters as close to the floor of the ditch as possible; the fire was then concentrated against either end of the line, and two 'uprights' began to devour the masonry upwards in the direction of the cordon. The stretch of masonry between the uprights was sometimes as much as fifty yards long, and it was brought down with volleys of shot which were fired with reduced charges for the fullest shock effect.

Saint-Rémy calculated that ten or twelve pieces, each firing between 90 and 100 rounds per day, would take twelve or fifteen days to make a breach, whereas a comparable breach could be effected in only five or six days by twenty-four cannon, each firing 80 rounds a day. In other words, the greater the number of pieces in action at the same time, the more economical as well as the more speedy would be the process of opening the revetment.[14]

No one attempted to blast a hole right through the rampart from front to back. It was enough to bring down the retaining masonry so that the débris partly filled the ditch and formed a ramp that was gentle enough to be pronounced 'practicable', that is, capable of being climbed without the necessity of putting hands to ground. When the revetment collapsed it sometimes left the earthen body of the rampart standing at a disappointingly 'impracticable' slope. The remedy was to cause the earth to subside by firing howitzer or mortar bombs into it at point-blank range. Roundshot would only have rammed the earth more firmly.

The cannon of the day were capable of effecting a breach in exposed masonry at a range of two or three hundred yards, as the Allies showed at Lille in 1708, the French at Ciudad Rodrigo in 1810 and the English at Badajoz in 1811. These feats of gunnery brought very little profit, since the siegeworks were much too far away to enable the infantry to approach the breaches under cover.

THE BREACHING OF THE REVETMENT BY MINING

If the breaching of the rampart by cannon-fire promised to be difficult, the process of 'attaching the miner' offered a reasonably cheap and speedy alternative. After a few stones or bricks had been dislodged from the scarp by cannon shot, a couple of dedicated souls would dash across the ditch to the chosen spot and hack out a little cave about four feet wide and three feet high. This first lodgment was prolonged into the rampart as a small gallery. On reaching the earthen core the miners burrowed to right or left (and sometimes both directions at once) along the inner surface of the revetment, cutting passages through the counterforts as they went. All the time their mates carried timbers and other requisites across the ditch.

When the mine branch, or branches, had reached a length of about twenty feet, the ends were hollowed into chambers which were capable of holding up to 500 pounds of gunpowder each. After fuzing the charges and blocking up a good length of the branches, the miners ignited the ends of the fuzes and wormed their way out of the tunnels backwards. Two or three powerful and well-placed charges would bring down a stretch of revetment as effectively as any breaching artillery. At the siege of Antwerp in 1832, almost the last 'classic' siege of military history, the French did not shrink from using this ancient technique in their attack on the Lunette Saint-Laurent.

The defenders usually tried to smash, burn or stifle the miners in their den by dint of rolling ditch-grenades, blazing fascines or tarred wood over the edge of the revetment above the gallery entrance. Sometimes they would make a tunnel of their own inside the rampart, and advance to meet the intruders underground.

'Attaching the miner' was a simple affair compared with the weighty undertaking of what we might call a 'deep' mine, which began on the glacis or covered way and was driven beneath the ditch to the foundations of the rampart on the far side.

Work began with the sinking of a shaft to the desired depth. The bottom of the shaft was incised on the side facing the fortress with four grooves, corresponding to the dimensions of the intended gallery, and the first square wooden frame was lodged in place. The earth above the lintel was cleared away with a jemmy, and chamfered-ended planks were pushed into the slot side-by-side, then driven forward three or four feet with a maul until their ends were positioned over the place selected for the next frame. It was now safe to remove the earth for some way beneath the plank roof, and drive the plank sides forward in similar fashion. After the next frame was positioned, the second set of roofing planks was inserted between the lintel and the forward end of the first planks, and hammered forward in preparation for the next bound. Large underground boulders were broken by hammers or blasting. It was not good practice to drive the tunnel round the obstruction, for when you arrived at the far side you could not be sure of taking up the original direction.

The miners were chosen from among skilled civilian employees of coal or mineral miners. They worked in squads of four or more at a time, one cutting the earth with his pick, one scooping up the spoil and piling it on a wheelbarrow or trolley, one wheeling the container to the entrance of the tunnel, while the fourth dumped the material in a concealed spot. A carpenter and a number of mates saw to the positioning of the frames and the driving of the planks.

Experienced teams of miners and carpenters could progress between fourteen and eighteen feet in twenty-four hours, and could even drive a tight gallery beneath a water-filled ditch. Without the help of very good artificial ventilation, however, they reached the limit of their endurance at a depth of twenty-four feet, and at a length of gallery of about fifty yards. One of the expedients adopted in the seventeenth century was to sink an auxiliary shaft close to the main shaft, connect the two wells by a metal pipe, and light a fire in the bottom of the auxiliary shaft. The theory was that the rising heat in the auxiliary shaft

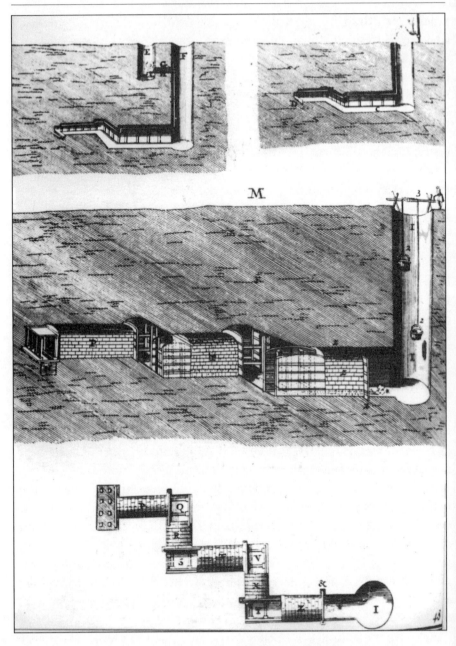

Mine shafts and galleries (Saint-Rémy 1702). Ventilation by parallel shaft and fire at top left; ventilation by windsail at top right. The centre and bottom figures show how a gallery might describe a number of right angles, to prevent the charge from blowing back up the shaft.

would suck the stale air from the gallery and induce a compensating draught of fresh air down the main shaft, if necessary with the help of a windsail. This ingenious arrangement seems to have been superseded entirely by the practice of installing a large forge-bellows at the surface and connecting the nozzle to a leather or canvas hose which ran all the way to the working face.

In contrast with the fairly neat and elegant process of blowing down the revetment after 'attaching the miner', the deep mine gained its effect by blowing the revetment (and much of the associated fortification) bodily into the air by a heavy charge placed amid the foundations.

In the breezy way of the older generation of soldiers, Montecuculi declared that thirty or forty barrels were enough to blow up a bastion.[75] Vauban investigated the subject in a more scientific manner, but he managed to saddle himself with the false doctrine that, beyond a certain weight, the charge merely threw the débris a greater distance into the air, instead of making a more spectacular crater. He believed that this 'widest possible' crater owned a diameter equivalent to double the length of the line of least resistance (the distance from the centre of the charge to the surface of the ground or fortification). It was not until the middle of the eighteenth century that Belidor established that the destructive effect of the mine continued to increase in proportion to the charge until the crater attained a diameter roughly six times the length of the line of least resistance. The shock effect of this supercharged mine (or globe of compression) travelled through the ground for a greater distance still, crushing tunnels and shaking foundations. Nineteenth-century engineers still adhered to Belidor's serviceable rule that you could find the weight in pounds of gunpowder for a supercharged mine chamber by multiplying the length of the line of least resistance (expressed in feet) by 300. A mine placed ten feet deep in moderately compact earth would therefore require about 3,000 pounds of powder – the equivalent of 90,000 musket cartridges or more than 600 charges for cannon.

The miners made the space for the charge by hollowing out a compartment in the side way at the end of one of the narrow branches. The floor was usually sunk a foot or two beneath the level of the bottom of the branch, so as to enclose the chamber by as much firm earth as possible. In Vauban's time the more old-fashioned min-

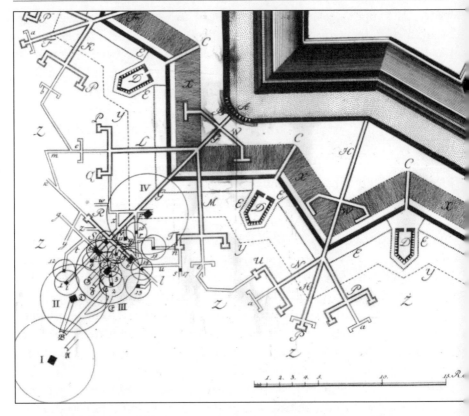

The mine battle for the Jauernicker Fort at Schweidnitz in 1762 (Tielcke 1778): A – the loopholed entrance to the countermines; C – the postern to caponnière D; E – the palisades made during the siege; I – the globe of compression, 1 September; II – the globe of compression, 16 September; III – the globe of compression, 24/5 September; IV – the globe of compression, 8/9 October. The numbered craters denote the Austrian countermines in order of succession.

ers were content to cram the compartment with barrels or sacks of powder, but it soon became the rule to deposit the powder in a specially-made square box of wood (calculating the dimensions on the rule that one cubic foot of powder weighed at least eighty pounds). A powder-filled canvas or leather 'saucisson' (hose) of one-inch diameter was jammed into a hole in the box, and the remaining space between the box and the sides of the chamber was stuffed firmly with sandbags or turf. The saucisson was led out of the chamber and along

the branch inside the 'auget' – a square-sectioned wooden channel. Taking care not to crush the auget, the miners closed the entrance to the chamber with a stout, firmly-propped door, and filled the branch all the way to its mouth with rubble or earth.

The mine chambers were usually arranged in groups of several at a time, either closely together on the same level, so that the intersecting craters would devastate a wide area, or in several storeys which would cause a number of successive explosions at the same spot.

A single saucisson was simply ignited by applying a lighted match to the end where it snaked out of the gallery. When it was vital to touch off several saucissons at the same instant, the ends of each would be fixed beneath a little wooden trap which contained a star of burning match. At the chosen moment the miner jerked a number of cords to open the floors of the traps, and the matches fell on the saucissons beneath. The 'encompassment' of the fires, as the practice was called, was invented by the French captain Boule when he was engaged on the demolition of Menin in 1744.

If the miners' arithmetic was not too badly astray, the exploding of the mine produced a gratifyingly spectacular effect on the surface. At Valenciennes in 1793 the first of the Allied globes of compression went up on 25 July with

a frightful crash, shaking the whole neighbourhood and throwing up débris like an erupting volcano. As the earth and masonry flew through the air they made a noise like a mighty hurricane, which lasted several seconds until all the material fell to earth.[76]

On such occasions the wretched defenders were hurled through the air or buried under the rubble.

When a charge was about to be exploded, the troops on the surface were usually held in readiness to exploit the confusion of the enemy and seize the crater. In the seventeenth and eighteenth centuries it was the practice for parties of grenadiers, miners and sappers to enter the actual crater and climb up the far side to make the lodgement near the rim. However, the experience of the American Civil War and World War I suggests that they would have done much better to have sent parties of troops to run round the sides of the crater first, so as to ward off counter-attack.

The employment of these 'deep' mines was tantamount to an admission by the siege commander that his attack on the surface was incapable of making further progress. This unhappy state of affairs was often caused by the existence of a network of defensive countermines. In that case the besiegers would have to engage in underground warfare beneath the glacis at the same time as the surface saps wormed forward from the third parallel.

The rival miners dug and listened by turns, hoping to detect and destroy the enemy before their own gallery was stove in by the hostile moles. The slight, sinister stirring of lice or peas on a drumhead would often give the first indication that someone else was at work below ground. The direction and nature of the sound became clearer at about thirty yards' distance, and the nearer approach could be detected by means of boring deep holes with sounding rods in the sides, roof or floor of the gallery.

If the sounding rod suddenly ceased to encounter resistance, it was high time to prepare and fire a 'camouflet' (a powder charge which was intended to cause destruction underground, but leave the surface undisturbed). In form the camouflet was a large bomb, petard or a heap of powder sacks which was supported against the chosen surface of the gallery by planks and stanchions. When exploded, the charge crushed enemy tunnels up to several yards away, and infected the earth with foul-smelling fumes for weeks. If you wished to have the use of your own tunnel immediately after the explosion, it was better to place a small charge at the end of a bore-hole.

There were several other forms of underground action. If you occupied a tunnel directly beneath the enemy's branch or gallery, you could make a hole in the roof and smoke the miners out by lighting a fire on the floor beneath. Unfortunately the enemy could retaliate by dropping grenades through the hole, or pouring boiling water on the floor of their own gallery so that the floor gave way and fell on top of you. When two rival galleries met on approximately the same level, there would ensue a ferocious fight with knives and pistols.

There was a characteristic underground battle at the great siege of Turin in 1706, when on the night of 13/14 August the Piedmontese exploded a charge beneath a French gallery. One of the defenders writes that

> this camouflet opened a large hole, through which the French let down one of their grenadiers at the end of a rope. He was killed by a pistol shot as soon as he appeared... We hastened to pile up a breastwork of woolsacks, and we brought up some grenadiers to help us to hold it.

After three further Frenchmen descended to their deaths, the besiegers finally broke into the lower gallery in force.

> Both sides opened fire, and this awful cave resounded with the reports of pistols, muskets and grenades. This fight would have continued for some time if the smoke, stench and darkness had not imposed a truce.

The discomfiture of the French was complete when the Piedmontese touched off two further charges, 'which overturned almost every cannon of the French battery above, leaving it a mass of miners, guns and gunners all intermingled and covered with earth'.[77]

For sheer technical artistry, however, one of the most remarkable episodes of mine warfare remains the Austrian defence of the Jauernicker Fort at Schweidnitz, which came under attack by the Prussians in 1762. The 'Prussian' engineer was the renegade Frenchman Simon Lefebvre, a disciple of Belidor. As soon as the Prussians had opened the third parallel, this gentleman sent a miner creeping up the glacis of the fort with a measuring cord. The miner was afraid to proceed more than a short distance, but he confidently reported back that the cord had extended to within six feet of the palisade, and Lefebvre accordingly drove a ninety-six-foot gallery from the parallel.

At nine in the evening of 1 September Lefebvre exploded the first of his charges – a globe of compression of 5,000 pounds of gunpowder, which excavated a crater ninety feet in diameter. Now begins a purgatory of frustration which would have broken harder men than Lefebvre. Because the lip of the crater fell short of the crest of the glacis by 100 feet, Lefebvre had to drive a new gallery twenty-one feet deep from the floor of the hole. The tunnel promptly filled with water. A shallower gallery was begun further to the left, and on 9 and 10 September it was systematically wrecked by the Austrian counterminers, who were directed by the Bohemian captain Pabliczek.

The Prussians drove a third gallery from the crater, and they penetrated forty-two feet before they broke into an old tunnel and were stopped short by a horrid stench. Lefebvre therefore exploded a globe of compression at the head on 16 September, and produced a crater which brought him to within sixty feet of the crest of the glacis. He dug a short tunnel from the new crater, and on the 24th he touched off another globe of compression, at the direct orders of King Frederick. This time the hole extended to within twenty feet of the covered way, which represented a total gain of thirteen yards in eight days.

Lefebvre had to dig yet another tunnel, a deep one this time, and finally on the night of 8/9 October he exploded a charge of 5,000 pounds under the covered way. A stretch of the covered way vanished, and a ramp of earth was thrown across the narrow ditch to the top of the rampart.

The Austrians were already badly shot up by the Prussian guns, and they surrendered on the following day after a resistance of sixty-three days of 'open trenches'.

On the whole, a protracted underground war strongly favoured the defensive. It was mostly in powder but very economical in manpower, and it almost always brought about a disruption of the attacks on the surface.

THE DESCENT AND PASSAGE OF THE DITCH

While the gunners or miners were breaching the bastions and ravelin, the engineers had to open the way for the infantry to pass the very considerable obstacles of the counterscarp and the ditch. The first task was to effect the 'descent of the ditch'. A number of sloping tunnels (one or more for each of the intended breaches) were opened in the glacis near the crest of the covered way, and they were continued beneath the covered way to the interior surface of the counterscarp revetment. A small hole was made in the masonry near the floor of the ditch (or close to the surface of the water in the case of a wet ditch), and numbers of fascines and sandbags were thrown through the hole until an adequate breastwork was heaped up on the side facing the most dangerous bastion flank. It was now safe to enlarge the hole and crawl a short distance into the ditch. If the ditch happened to be dry, the subsequent 'passage of the ditch' was a simple if dangerous affair of sapping across the floor of the ditch to the breach. The crossing of a wet ditch

View and section of the mines at the Jauernicker Fort (Tielcke 1778).

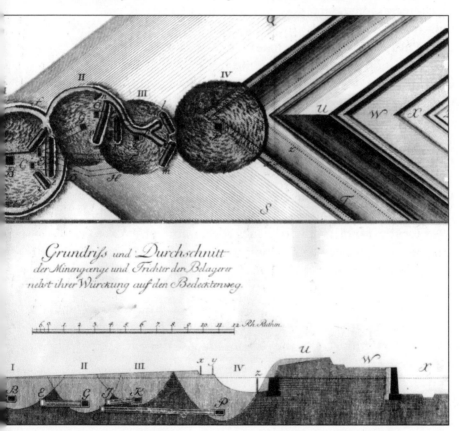

179

Right: Descent and passage of the ditch (Vauban 1704).

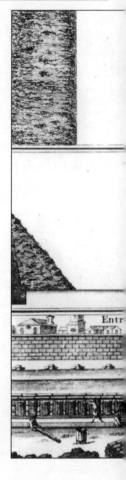

was a more complicated operation. A ditch of standing water would have to be filled with a causeway built up of successive layers of fascines and stones. This was always a lengthy process, for the fascines and the baskets of stones were passed from hand to hand by a chain of a hundred or more soldiers extending all the way from the glacis down the tunnel to the ditch.

The existence of the smallest current rendered the building of a causeway very difficult. Sometimes the only course of action was to assemble rafts of fascines or planks and barrels at the counterscarp edge of the ditch, and attach and anchor the sections one by one until they formed a continuous floating bridge. In 1710 the Allies managed to cast several wooden bridges across an outer ditch at Béthune without being detected by the garrison. The French tried to surpass the achievement by making a fascine bridge across a forty-foot-wide ditch at Philipsburg in 1734, and suffered the mortification of seeing the structure fall apart and several soldiers drown.

MORALE IN FORTRESS WARFARE

The culminating point of our siege is approaching fast, but before we consider the attack on the breaches it is important to take stock of the wear and tear of siegework upon the participants. More than geometry or fortifications, it was their state of mind that was going to determine the outcome of the siege.

The townspeople, according to their dispositions, responded to the hardships of the siege with terror, resignation or fortitude. On occasion, as at Turin in 1706, the citizens identified themselves totally with the defenders.

Everything is in troubled movement. The streets and squares near the citadel are packed. Around the esplanade

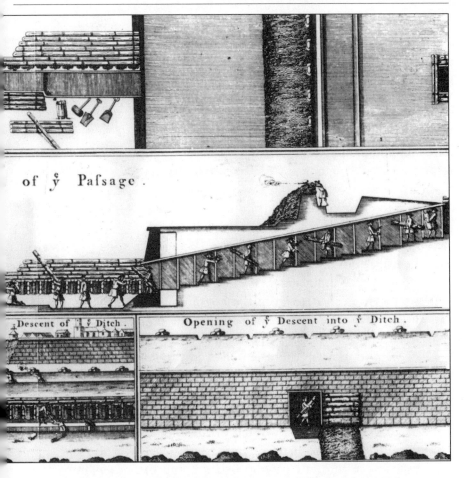

of ẙ Paſsage.

Descent of ẙ Ditch.   Opening of ẙ Descent into ẙ Ditch.

the church towers and roofs are covered with people. They hear the yells of the combatants, the reports of the muskets and cannon, and the crash of stones and mortar bombs: they see the murky clouds of dust and smoke lit up repeatedly by flashes of fire.[78]

As for the military men, they had to steel themselves against ordeals of a peculiarly taxing kind.

Until the second half of the nineteenth century nearly all battles in the open field were over and done with in a single day, and the survivors knew that they would not have to fight another action for weeks or months to come. Conditions in siege warfare, on the other hand, were much more 'modern', since the combatants stood in constant peril.

In a siege, people who are working are killed, and others who are ordered to cover them, have continually before their eyes the mouth of the cannon which may send a bullet and destruction in a moment. Others hear beneath their feet that the enemy are digging a mine.[79]

In siegework the terrors of the execution cell and the charnel-house were compounded in a way that was to remain almost unknown in field actions until soldiers entered the 'mausoleums of mud' of the Western Front in World War I. An English officer wrote in 1747 from Bergen-op-Zoom to a correspondent in London:

You express a curiosity to hear, nay, I think too, to see how matters appear among the assailants and defendants. Truly it is a sight you would very soon be sick of, for I, that have been here from the beginning, cannot without horror view the dreadful effects of one night's massacre: there you may behold the remains of a human carcass so disfigured, that all the resemblance of the divine image is lost, scorched, blackened and mangled so frightfully, that a piece of horseflesh, which has been a month sunning in a dog-kennel, cannot look more disagreeable; in another place you may see a wretch with some residue of life groaning out his tortured spirit, his bowels borne some yards from him, a leg lying by him, and the other limbs mashed to pieces, so that if conscience did not say it was a sin to do so, it would appear to be a compassion to knock him on the head; scores half-buried in the ruins of a mine, and what appears above ground horribly spread over with blood and brains and torn entrails; in short, there is never a place where nothing but the most shocking sights are the objects of amusement. War of all kinds has something sufficiently tremendous in its nature, but a siege so obstinately carried on, and so resolutely disputed, as this, is a complication of so many and such various horrors, that the most bloody engagement that I ever read of has nothing comparable to what I see every day.[80]

One of the qualifications for a successful governorship was the possession of what the Freudians would call pronounced 'anal' traits – the
mentality which Clarendon recognised in Lord Robartes, the Parlia-
mentary governor of Plymouth in the Civil War, 'a man of sour and
surly nature, a great *opiniâtre,* and one who must be overcome before
he would believe that he could be so'. [81] This fundamental obstinacy
had to be leavened by technical expertise, a dash of showmanship, and
the tact and the force of character that were needed to co-ordinate the
action of townspeople, soldiers and military technicians over a period of
weeks or months. Physical energy was desirable, but mental energy was
more important still.

It is not altogether surprising that some of the most splendidly
defiant defences in history were put up by elderly governors – men like
Vallette at Malta (1565), Livingstein at Pizzighettone (1733), Leutrum
at Cuneo (1744), Cronstrom at Bergen-op-Zoom (1747), Marschall at
Olmütz (1758), Eliot at Gibraltar (1779–83), Heintzi at Buda (1849).

Whether in the attack or the defence, the commander had to put
a great deal of trust in his engineers, the men who had made fortress
warfare their speciality. Their courage was seen to be of a different kind
from the unreflecting bravery of their comrades in the field arms.
According to Guignard,

> they need a quite extraordinary valour in order to endure
> the blows of the enemy without having any means of hitting
> back other than the eventual damage which their siege-
> works may inflict. Unlike the other warriors, they do not
> have the satisfaction of exchanging blow for blow. Not only
> that, but they have to remain cool in the midst of the most
> alarming dangers – it would be disastrous if they were pan-
> icked into mistaking one point of ground for another,
> because a blunder of that kind would lead to the trench
> being enfiladed... To sum up, the engineer must be out-
> standingly bold and outstandingly prudent.[82]

The demands of sapping and mining summed up yet a further breed of
men – materialistic, acquisitive and courageous, best compared in modern terms with people like trawlermen, oil-rig roustabouts and the
workers at the faces of deep tunnels. Having 'earned a large sum

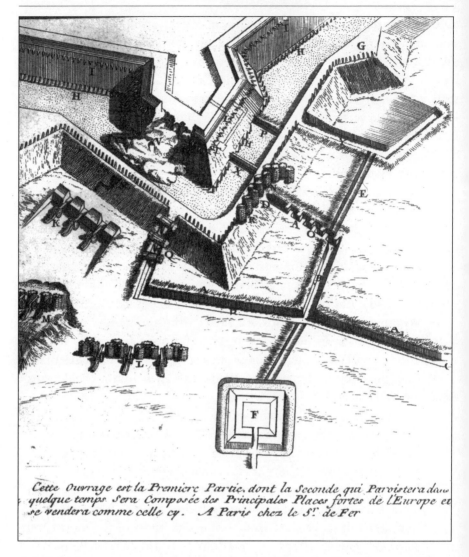

Cette Ouvrage est la Première Partie, dont la Seconde qui Paroistera dans quelque temps Sera Composée des Principales Places fortes de l'Europe et se vendera comme celle cy. A Paris chez le Sr de Fer

through the sweat, or rather the blood of their bodies, they would go and waste it in gorging, getting drunk, and playing at dice and cards'.[83]

THE STORM OF THE BREACHES

At no stage in the siege did quite so much hang upon the courage and judgement or one or two men as in the reconnaissance of the breaches. The Sieur de Pointis has left a characteristically modest record of the risks involved in his sounding-out of the breach of the Huguenot fortress of Montauban in 1621:

Opposite page: Final stages of a rather old-fashioned siege attack, with covered sap (Q), sap with bays (A, O), lodgments on the covered way (N, D, R) and breach (V) (De Fer, 1690).

I donned breastplate and helmet, stuck a pistol in my belt, ate a few mouthfuls and then presented myself to His Majesty [Louis XIII] and the army, all of whom watched me attentively. When I reached the foot of the breach I sank to my knees and offered some prayers to God behind the shelter of one of the fallen stones. I then wormed my way up as best I could, stomach to the ground. When I reached the top my first idea was to reconnoitre the ground while continuing to lie flat, so as to conceal myself and keep out of the way of the musket balls which came from all sides and whistled over me. But since I could not see what lay behind the bastion, I jumped up (exposing myself to a danger from which God alone could rescue me) and ran to the edge of the bastion, from where I could see that the enemy had made a formidable rearward retrenchment, which was held by a force which seemed to be of two thousand men or more. At the instant that I showed myself and looked over the edge they discharged such a furious volley at me that I have always regarded my salvation as a miracle.[84]

Vauban would not have dreamed of leaving this responsible task to any other engineer, let alone an officer of the field arms. He used to go to the breach himself and report back with a gruff 'cela est mûr!' or 'cela n'est pas mûr!' which settled the question beyond all argument.

In the hours immediately before the assault, the high-trajectory pieces in the third parallel and the guns in the crowning of the covered way concentrated their fire against the breaches and the areas immediately behind, so as to smash the rubble into smaller fragments and deter the defenders from building a retrenchment or 'scarping the breach' (cutting it into a steep slope). The storming parties were meanwhile formed into columns, with grenadiers or other crack troops at the head, and working parties ready to follow close behind with entrenching tools and gabions.

As for the moment of the assault, an English veteran of the Peninsular War declared that 'the most preferable time for such open advances is at the moment of daybreak. In the dark the troops are liable to imaginary terrors, and being concealed from the view of their officers, the bravest only do their duty'.[85] Most commanders would have agreed with him. The columns could assemble in secrecy during the night, while the first light enabled the troops to be kept better in hand and gave the officers and men the assurance that the generals would mark their prowess in what was, after all, the occasion of the greatest honour and danger in the course of the whole siege.

On the night of 6/7 April 1812 the British made perhaps forty separate rushes against the breaches at Badajoz

> until hundreds of brave soldiers lay in piles upon each other, weltering in blood, and trodden down by their own companions... the small groups of soldiers seeking shelter from the cart-wheels, pieces of timber, fire-balls and other missiles hurled down upon them; the wounded crawling past the fire-balls, many of them scorched and perfectly black, and covered with mud, from having fallen into the *cuvette* [a trench cut into the floor of the ditch], where three hundred were suffocated or drowned; and all this time the French on top of the parapets, jeering and cracking their jokes, and deliberately picking off those whom they chose.[86]

Such were the risks run by the storming parties.

In an unusually ambitious and successful assault the assaulting columns might rush straight over the rampart and penetrate the town beyond. More often the purpose of the assault was to gain a foothold in one or more vital works whose loss might persuade the garrison to yield the fortress by agreement. In this event, the immediate object was to establish a lodgement of gabions at the lip of the breach, from where saps could be driven forward if the garrison still did not see reason.

The defence of the breaches, particularly in the case of a general storm, was considered the 'only occasion on which the governor should fight in person, and commit all his best surviving troops'.[87] Only the existence of some fairly effective rearward defences could ever justify the governor to make a stand at the breach and thus put the lives of the garrison and townspeople at stake. His retrenchment in this case would probably be provided with storm-poles, caltrops and other obstructions, and 'thundering barrels', fire-pots, grenades, and cannon ready-loaded with grape or canister. The ground in front of the retrenchment might well be sown with fougasses, which were powder charges buried in pits and covered with beams, stones, and other injurious objects. 'Once the soldiers have seen one of these charges go up they get the impression that they are walking over volcanoes.'[88]

We have an impression of the defenders' viewpoint in the Austrian account from Freiburg in 1744, which tells of the successful defence of the Kaiser Bastion and the adjacent ravelins on the night of 2/3 November.

> Our grenadiers, who are stout Bohemians, skewer the French with their bayonets and knock them dead with their musket-butts. The excitement is tremendous, and nobody wants to give ground. As soon as a soldier has fired, he stays where he is, takes a loaded musket from his comrades behind and passes his own weapon back. The hussars and dragoons are arrayed from the Martins Gate to the ditch – they are on horseback and their sabres are drawn. The French king himself is said to be witnessing the whole storm from the Loreto Chapel. The dead are thrown into a crypt of the cathedral which has been sealed since the siege of 1713. A cloud of smoke lies over the suburb in a dense fog, and the soldiers look like charcoal-burners. A French drummer appears three times and vainly requests a truce for the burial of the dead.[89]

If the infuriated besiegers managed to fight their way over the retrenchment and into the town, the governor and his comrades could reckon themselves lucky if they escaped with their lives. Only in Russia and Spain did people ever contemplate putting up a systematic defence in the town itself. The Duke of Berwick speaks incredulously of the defence of Jativa in 1707 by the 'Habsburg' Spanish and six hundred English troops.

They could never be prevailed upon to surrender, so the breach was made, and our troops lodging themselves in it, it was necessary to bring up some cannon to destroy the retrenchments they had made behind; they were even obliged to attack street after street, and house after house; these madmen defended themselves with unparalleled bravery and firmness.[90]

CAPITULATION

There were very few defences indeed that were prolonged as far as the offering of resistance at a breach in the main ramparts. Heroic, last-ditch stands went out of fashion in the one-and-a-half centuries which intervened between the end of the Wars of Religion and the coming of the French Revolution – the temper of the times was too cool and too rational to inspire people to sacrifice themselves before the march of a siege machine which seemed to grow every year in its power and precision. Talking of the War of the Spanish Succession, Landsberg said that 'we have seen that most governors yield their fortresses as soon as the besiegers lodge on the glacis or at least on the covered way. The general opinion holds that they have no other course of action open to them'.[91]

From at least the middle period of the siege onwards, the sensible governor revolved in his mind the relative advantages of capitulation and further resistance: on the one hand he liked to see the besiegers expend a good deal of time, labour and money in trying to reduce what was left of his little domain; at the same time he performed no great service to his sovereign if he held out so long that the garrison ran the risk of being put to the sword, or forced to 'surrender at discretion' as prisoners of war at the mercy of the enemy. As the Chevalier du Theil put it: 'once a governor has defended himself sufficiently well as to leave no doubt as to the correctness of his conduct, he should allow common-sense and the good of the service and the state to prevail over a vain regard for bravery and glory'.[92]

These considerations often led the governor to indulge in what might seem to modern eyes to be face-saving haggling. In 1734 the Duke of Liria summoned old General Tattenbach, the Austrian governor of Gaeta, and was rewarded with the reply: 'It is too early. You have formed no batteries and planted no cannon which will give me any reason to capitulate. I beg you, my dear general, to be patient and wait a little longer.'[93]

Nine years later the Austrians were repaid in their own coin by the Comte de Granville, the defender of Ingolstadt, who was willing enough to surrender the place, but declared

> that he could conclude no capitulation before he had seen an army corps and a siege train brought up to attack him. However, if Bärnklau [the Austrian commander] would open the trenches and go through the siege for the sake of form, the French for their part would leave the workers in peace, keep up a lively but unaimed fire, and make no attempt to dismount the guns or launch a sortie. Six weeks after the opening of trenches he would deliver the fortress by an honourable capitulation which would leave all the fortress magazines to the Queen of Hungary.[94]

These terms were not acceptable to the Austrians, who went ahead and took the place anyway.

The governor gave notice that he wished to discuss terms by showing a white flag on the ramparts, or beating *chamade* at the breach. After the first contact had been established, it was up to the governor to propose terms of capitulation (literally 'a list of headings'), which the commander of the siege army accepted or rejected as he saw fit. A good capitulation (from the defenders' point of view) made generous provision for the life, liberties and property of the townspeople, and for the freedom and honour of the garrison. Such a document would grant the defenders a 'free evacuation' by the shortest route to their homeland or a friendly fortress, and allow them to take with them their baggage and a few pieces of artillery; they would march out by the main gate, or better still by the breach, with primed muskets and bullets in their cheeks (to show that they were still dangerous adversaries), and their music playing an enemy march (to show that they still had it in their power to pay a compliment).

There was much to be said for granting some at least of these terms. The commander of the siege army had no wish to indulge in the extravagant expenditure of powder and blood that was inseparable from the last stages of the siege, or to see the discipline of his army shattered by the experience of sacking a town after a storm. Captain John Kincaid observed after the Peninsular War that:

the moment which is most dangerous to the honour and safety of a British army is that in which they have won the place they have assaulted. While outside the walls, and linked together by the magic wand of discipline, they are heroes – but once they have forced themselves inside they become demons or lunatics.[95]

Thus, except for the few occasions when the salvation of a kingdom rested upon the resistance of a single fortress, siege warfare in the western world nearly always assumed the form of a ritual, by which the operation progressed through a prescribed number of stages, and reached a dignified end when the parties arranged the delivery of the fortress on reasonable terms.

People who stood out of cannon-shot did not always take a favourable view of such sensible dealings. On 5 April 1705 Louis XIV reminded the governors of the frontier fortresses that if they came under attack 'they are strictly forbidden to yield their places until there is a large breach on the main rampart and they have withstood at least one assault'.[96] Louis' ruling was inspired by old prohibitions, and it was in turn taken as the basis of the Republic's law on the defence of fortresses of 27 July 1792.

At the appointed hour the fortress gates opened and the garrison came out 'in the best possible order, with the veteran troops at the head and tail of the column, and the others in the middle with the baggage... The governor should station himself at the head'.[97] The municipality was often represented by a small deputation which presented the besiegers with the keys of the town and portions of bread and salt – the ancient symbols of submission.

As soon as the departing garrison had passed between the ranks of the besiegers, the most senior infantry regiment of the conquering army took over the guard of the main gate and entered the town at the head of the new garrison. The artillery and engineer officers hastened round the works and military establishments, making inventories of what artillery, ammunition and provisions were still intact, and what repairs needed to be made on the fortifications.

The rest of the army levelled the siegeworks, then held itself in readiness to assist in whatever programmes of rebuilding or demolition were determined by the commander. Entire fortifications might be destroyed by pick or shovel, or the conquerors might be satisfied with 'razing' the works – that is, cutting away the earthen parapet of the rampart to the level of the cordon. Today most surviving artillery fortifications exist in this shorn and sorry state.

THE DEFENCE AND ATTACK OF
COASTAL FORTIFICATION

SITING AND DESIGN

When it was a question of placing a work beside the sea or the estuary of a large river, all the normal complexities of fortress-designing were compounded by the additional considerations of tides, channels and maritime strategy. Even when a fortress-port met all the navigational and defensive requirements it might still prove defective in other respects, as did Brest, which had a sterile hinterland and suffered from lengthy road communications with the heart of the country.

Broadly speaking, the sites of coastal fortifications may be grouped into two categories – the coastal battery and the fortress-port.

Detached batteries and forts were positioned along shorelines in order to cover coast-hugging traffic *(cabotage)*, to deny landing-sites to enemy forces, to guard the river approaches to inland ports (eg Antwerp), or to protect towns and villages against piratical raids.

Fortress-ports were usually surrounded on the landward side by a fairly inexpensive enceinte, on the supposition that enemies who came by sea would not have the time for making a formal siege. Towards the sea, geography was sometimes obliging enough to offer islands or headlands as natural sites against naval attack, as at Sveaborg, St-Malo and Toulon. If, on the other hand, the port gave on to a straight shoreline, the engineer was frequently presented with no alternative but to go to the expense of building moles into the sea on one or both sides of the harbour entrance. Vauban was particularly proud of having completed two defensible jetties of this kind at Dunkirk in 1683.

> At the present time the port and the harbour entrance seem to be the finest and the most spacious I have ever encountered. If I were to stay on at Dunkirk for six further months,

I do not believe that I would exhaust my curiosity and admiration if I saw all the works once a day.[98]

The designer of coastal fortification had to bear in mind that these works were intended to deliver a heavy weight of fire rather than to offer resistance against prolonged siege. These considerations, taken together with the usual lack of space and earth in coastal sites, made for a characteristic architecture of simple traces, and high exposed walls executed in full revetment. The parapets and embrasures were nearly always of masonry, even though 'it had been found by experience, that nothing disheartens troops placed behind a wall so much, as the pieces of stone flying about their ears'.[99]

Given the peculiar circumstances of coastal fortification, there was still a place for isolated and tall towers of a kind that would have been considered decidedly old-fashioned in inland warfare. Such were Vauban's Tour de Camaret at Brest, and Dahlberg's tower of the Göta Lejon on the Gullberg at Göteborg. The British experienced the power of antique towers on 8 February 1794, when the seventy-four-gun ship *Fortitude* and the frigate *Juno* were badly knocked about by two 12-pounders mounted on an old Genoese-built tower at Mortella Bay on the coast of Corsica. The designs of the

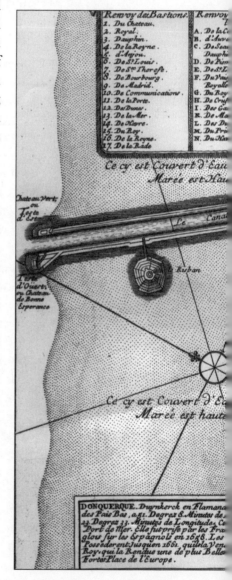

Right: Dunkirk (De Fer 1690), showing Vauban's double jetty.

tower were consulted by the British in the emergency of 1803, and between then and 1846 derivative 'Martello Towers' sprang up along the shores of England, Ireland, the Channel Islands and Canada.

SHIP AGAINST SHORE.

In the attack on coastal fortifications the 'wooden walls' of the sailing ship era seemed to stand at a decided disadvantage, being tall-

masted, thin-sided, and subject to the vagaries of wind and tide.

Writing in 1682 concerning the imminent French naval attack on the pirate lair of Algiers, Vauban argued that the ships were bound to come off the worse.

> Firstly, because the shore batteries contain many more heavy cannon than the vessels. In addition the shore cannon are better sited, and derive an immeasurable advantage from being planted on immovable ground, whereas the ships which carry the naval cannon never cease to sway about.
>
> Secondly, because earthen parapets [here Vauban makes the assumption that the parapets must have been of earth] offer far more resistance than the sides of warships . . . You can never hope to guarantee the effect of a shot which is fired from a ship's cannon – you have difficulty in aiming from a moving platform, the calibre of your gun is usually small, and the range is long, especially when the shore artillery is replying. All of this prevents you from doing much damage even to the flimsiest fortifications.[100]

Vauban might have added in support of his argument that shore batteries could employ red-hot shot, which could not be prepared on board ship without great risk, and that an ordinary cold shot from a culverin or a 24-pounder was capable of piercing the thickest timbers of any wooden warship up to a range of six hundred yards.[101]

The naval gunners by no means shared Vauban's pessimism. Indeed, while Vauban was still writing, the French marine was making ready to employ against Algiers its newest and most powerful weapon – the ship-borne mortar. The first inspiration had come from the Chevalier de Ressons, who had designed a long-barrelled naval mortar in 1680. The idea was taken up by the young Basque sailor and engineer Bernard Renau d'Eliçagaray ('Petit Renau'), who suggested that the weapon could be mounted in flat-bottomed galiots of the kind the Dutch used for commerce. Renau's patron Lieutenant-General Duquesne persuaded Colbert, as naval minister, to undertake a programme of construction, and early in 1682 six bomb vessels were ready for service. Duquesne took five of them when he sailed against Algiers in the summer of 1682.

The first bombardments – two in July, and one on 21 August – seemed to confirm Vauban's gloomy predictions, for the bomb vessels were anchored at excessive ranges, and the mortar crews were unskilled in their work. There was an exciting scene on de Pointy's *Cruelle*, when an incendiary bomb burst into flames in the muzzle, and most of the bombardiers and sailors promptly jumped overboard.

On the night of 30/31 August the bomb vessels were brought to within a hundred yards or so of the port, and this time they caused a good deal of devastation and panic. Now that the French knew what to do with their bomb vessels, they used them to spectacular effect in their further bombardments of Algiers in 1683 and 1688, and in the cannonades of Genoa in 1684 and Tripoli in 1685.

The first English bomb vessel, the *Salamander*, was built at Chatham in 1687 on the suggestion of Edmund Dummer, who had seen the French boats at practice in Toulon harbour before the Algiers expedition of 1682. In November 1693 the English employed their new bomb vessels against the French originators in a not particularly successful bombardment of St-Malo. The fleet closed in again on the French shore in 1694, and bombarded Dieppe, Le Havre and Calais. Le Havre alone was hit by about 1,100 bombs in the course of six days of fire, and suffered 300,000 livres' worth of damage.

The typical English bomb vessel of the middle of the eighteenth century was a ketch-rigged craft (a tall mast at the front, a smaller one behind), which housed two 13-inch mortars, or one howitzer and one 13-inch mortar, on oblong frames that were recessed into the single deck. The beds were set on pintles, allowing an easy traverse, and the frames as a whole were mounted on stanchions which dispersed the shock of discharge among bilge stringers and additional floors. These were versatile boats, which could be employed on cruising when they were not needed for an attack on towns or fortifications. In 1747 Captain John Jermy showed how much damage could be inflicted by a single vessel when, after a successful career of cruising, he anchored his *Carcass* behind the shelter of Cap d'Antibes and cast his bombs over the pine woods into the fortress-town of Antibes on the far side, reducing the houses to a heap of smoking rubble.

The conventional ships of the line could best attack fortifications by passing as close under the walls as possible (see the opinions of Lord Elibank concerning the attack on Cartagena in 1741, and of Admiral

Sulivan on the proposed cannonade of Bomarsund in the Crimean War).[102] The commanders stood in boldly, gambling that the guns of the high-lying shore batteries would not be able to depress sufficiently to strike the decks, and hoping that the restricted splay of the embrasures would permit each gun to get off no more than one round against every passing vessel. Once the ship came to anchor in a favourable position at close range, the naval gunners could begin to make good practice, and the marines opened a devastating fire of musketry from the fighting-tops.

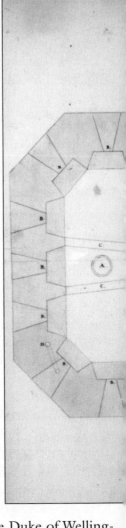

In the days of the old technology, therefore, a rough equilibrium was established in the contest between coastal fortifications and hostile naval vessels. At first sight the land batteries might have appeared to have had all the odds stacked in their favour. In practice, however, the actual duels were usually much more even, especially when the ship commanders had the nerve to lay their vessels close alongside the batteries and blast them at short range.

Even in the post-Napoleonic period naval squadrons were able to score several 'untypical' successes over land fortifications, among which we number the British and Dutch attack on Algiers in 1816, the forcing of the Tagus by the French admiral Roussin in 1831, and the British bombardment of Acre in 1840. After this last episode the Duke of Wellington duly voted the thanks of the House of Lords, but 'thought it his duty to warn their Lordships on this occasion that they must not always expect that ships, however well commanded or gallant their seamen might be, were capable of commonly engaging successfully with stone walls'.[103]

By the end of the 1850s a number of important technical developments had fundamentally altered the terms of the contest between ship and shore, and yet it was still as difficult as ever to determine which side held the upper hand.

One of Dahlberg's designs for a coastal tower

The shell cannon – a long cannon firing an explosive bomb – was gradually adopted by the leading navies of the world after the ambitious French gunner H. J. Paixhans published the first and most important of his books, the *Nouvelle Force Maritime* in 1822. Unfortunately, this flat-trajectory shell-fire came into vogue on land as well as at sea, which left Commander S. F. Dupont of the US Navy in no doubt that the result acted to the disadvantage of

197

ship-borne artillery. He wrote in 1851 that it takes solid shot to batter walls and make breaches – plenty of them, and rapidly discharged, and concentrated upon or near one spot.

On the other hand, we have only to imagine a few 8- or 10-inch shells passing through the side of a line-of-battle ship into the main or lower gun-deck, and there exploding amidst the dense crowd at the batteries, every fragment multiplying itself in countless splinters of wood or iron as destructive as itself, and if it should fail to burst, still doing all the injury a solid shot could do.[104]

From the 1820s onwards coastal fortifications, too, began to take on a more formidable shape, as engineers cast an eye back to some of

Section through an English bomb vessel. Note the stanchions under the bed and the storage racks for bombs. The coil of cable under the pintle helped to absorb some of the recoil. The mortar barrel was very long by the standards of the shore service, and the elevation was fixed at 45 degrees.

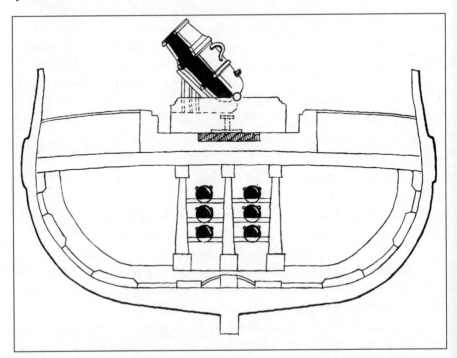

the designs in Montalembert's *Fortification Perpendiculaire* and began to build tall batteries of multiple casemated storeys. These at once produced a great concentration of artillery, and protected the gunners against shell-fire. We may cite the works at Portsmouth, Yarmouth, Cherbourg, Toulon, Genoa, Sevastopol, Kronstadt and the many fortresses of the 'Fort Sumter' type which sprang up along the coasts of the United States before the Civil War.

Less spectacular – but in the long run far more significant – was the invention of the marine mine (or 'torpedo' in the contemporary parlance). The first practicable mines were invented in Russia by 'Corporal' Bauer and his associates, and as early as the 1840s the Russians had a mine production line set up by M. Nobel, the father of the dynamite king. The Prussians sowed observer-actuated mines in Kiel harbour during the Schleswig-Holstein crisis of 1848–51 and on 20 June 1855 submarine mines claimed their first actual victims in the British steamboats *Merlin* and *Firefly*, which were damaged by the Russians off Kronstadt.

In compensation the invention of reliable marine steam engines at last gave vessels a reasonable degree of independence of winds and currents, and enabled their commanders to take greater risks, in the knowledge that they could get out of trouble more easily than before. Then again the passive resistance of warships was enhanced by iron plates, such as those that appeared on the French and British armoured batteries of the Crimean War and the monitors of the American Civil War. A French general wrote concerning the devastating performance of the floating batteries at Kinburn in 1855 that we may attribute the greatest importance to the introduction of floating batteries which are armoured with iron and capable of withstanding all the missiles at present thrown at them by coastal batteries. This development is calculated to produce a total revolution in naval armament, and, if we can endow the floating batteries with the mobility which they still lack, the advantage in combat may pass for the time being to the naval attack.[105]

The manifold experiences of the American Civil War left opinion deeply divided, though most people agreed that conventional coastal fortifications had taken a severe battering. Low-lying fortifications with exposed barbette tiers were badly shot up by ship-borne guns, while the tall new casemated works were vulnerable to attack by forces that were put ashore with the object of attacking the landward sides. Particular significance was attached to the destruction inflicted on Fort Pulaski by land-based rifled artillery in 1862.

As for mines and obstructions, Admiral Farragut successfully 'damned the torpedoes' at Mobile on 5 August 1864. Conversely it was the existence of obstructions that made it impossible for the Northerners to reduce Charleston, Mobile, Wilmington and Savannah by naval action alone.

Far-seeing people had already concluded that, deprived of the help of a land force, even a 'successful' naval attack could achieve only a partial victory. Sir Howard Douglas remarked that

> the sea defences may be silenced, guns dismounted, and habitations devastated by the cruel process of bombardment; but no substantial demolition of the defences, or material destruction of public works and property, can be effected unless the damages inflicted by the attacks of the ships can be followed up and completed, by having actual possession of the captured place for a sufficient time to ruin it entirely. No naval operation, however skilfully planned and gallantly executed, can, alone, reap the fruits of its victory.[106]

This passage deserved to have been read by the people who launched the 'naval phase' of the attack on Gallipoli in 1915.

Chapter 7
The Great Sieges

By studying siegecraft as a technical exercise we have been left with a rather fragmentary impression of what actually went on in the attack and defence of a fortress in the real world. It is important to restore the balance. For this reason we finish by following four particularly interesting attacks through from beginning to end. These operations are the sieges of Namur in 1692 and 1695, which show Vauban and Coehoorn in the process of pitting their wits against one another; the French attack on Antwerp in 1832, which demonstrates how very little siege-craft changed over the centuries; and finally the Anglo-Dutch naval bombardment of Algiers in 1816, which gives an indication of the means (and the cost) by which fortifications could be overcome by attack from the sea.

NAMUR 1692

Our two sieges of Namur are episodes taken from the War of the League of Augsburg (1688–97), a classic coalition war of the later seventeenth century, which saw a not particularly efficient alliance of Dutch, British, Spanish, Germans and Austrians pitted against the overmighty France of Louis XIV.

In 1692 the French were ready to go over to a major offensive. They decided to direct their efforts against the fortress of Namur, which stood at the junction of the Meuse and the Sambre. They reasoned that the capture of this place would open up the south-eastern flank of the Spanish Netherlands, and at the same time clear the way for future campaigning down the Meuse against the Dutch.

Vauban had already sounded out the fortifications in the course of a cheeky reconnaissance which he had conducted in 1691. He had observed that the town of Namur formed an oval on the left banks of the Sambre and the Meuse, and that it was enclosed on the landward

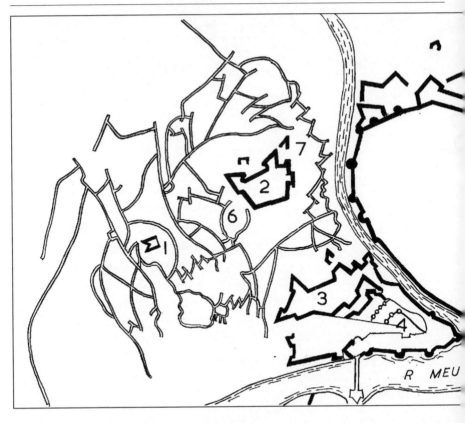

side by six bastioned fronts which ran in a gentle curve from the Sambre in the north-west to the lower Meuse in the east.

The main strength of Namur as a fortress resided, however, in the citadel complex crowning the heights of the peninsula of Entre-Sambre-et-Meuse, which lay to the west of the town and was separated from it by the Sambre. At the rear of the citadel area was the old Donjon, a small medieval castle situated on a bluff above the junction of the two rivers. On the landward (north-western) side, the Donjon was enclosed by two short bastioned fronts (La Médiane) and the extensive and irregular crownwork of Terra Nova, which had been built in 1640. Terra Nova fronted on to a deep, narrow ravine, and beyond that the ground rose to a further height, where the Spanish had commissioned Coehoorn to build a detached hornwork, called 'Fort William'. By the time of the siege of 1692 Fort William was only 'half-finished and scarcely tenable, for there were no casemates where the troops could be accommodated in cover from the bombs and incendiary missiles'.[1]

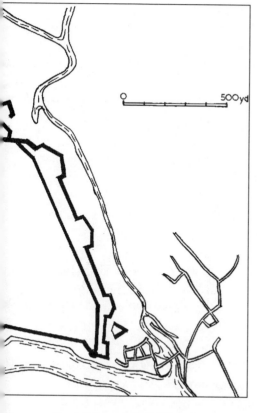

Plan of the siege of Namur, 1692, showing how Vauban embraced and surrounded Fort William by his siegeworks: 1 – Redoubt of La Cachotte; 2 – Fort William; 3 – Terra Nova; 4 – the Donjon; 5 – the town of Namur; 6 – 'High' attack; 7 – 'Low' attack.

On 25 May 1692 King Louis descended upon Namur with a siege army of about 60,000 men and a heavy train of 151 pieces. The Duke of Luxembourg and a further 60,000 men took up station on the Mehaigne to deter relief.

In the midst of these milling hordes stood the garrison of Namur – a force of some 6,000 Dutch, Spanish, Germans and English under the overall command of the Duke of Arenberg and Barbançon. Major-General Ditmar van Wijnbergen led the Dutch contingent, and under him Coehoorn had the special responsibility of defending Fort William, his own creation.

As usual, the Allies were caught unawares by the speed of the French investment, with the result that some of the garrison were stranded outside. The gossipy Marquis of Santa Cruz heard tell that one of them, Don Juan Diaz Pimenta, 'pretended to be a French sutler, and made his way to the head of the saps with a keg of brandy. He sprang from the trench and, pursued by some musket balls, he

203

reached the fortress, where he served for the rest of the siege'.[2]

Vauban at once addressed himself to the capture of the town, and he began by making an attack on an unusually narrow front against the sector where the town enceinte met the Meuse. The French, according to one of their officers, 'constructed several of the best manned and equipped batteries that were ever seen; the presence of the king excited such emulation that all ranks sought to surpass themselves in their duties'.[3] These batteries occupied almost as wide a front as the trenches themselves, and their covering fire enabled Vauban within four days to fill in a number of ditches and establish a lodgement in the lunette immediately beside the Meuse.

The royal historian Racine was at pains to explain to his friend Boileau that the besiegers were not dealing with cowards.

> Our troops in the siegeworks were astonished at the courage of the defenders. But you may form some impression of the dreadful effect of the cannon and the bombs when I tell you that a Spanish officer, who was captured yesterday in the outworks, said that our artillery had killed two hundred of their men in just two days. Imagine three batteries keeping up a ceaseless fire against the wretched troops of the garrison, who cannot find a single corner where they are safe! Our men say that they found the outworks full of headless bodies which had been decapitated by the cannon balls as neatly as if they had been severed by swords.[4]

On 5 June the battered garrison yielded up the town on condition that they would be allowed to retreat to the citadel and that the French would renounce any idea of attacking the citadel from the direction of the town.

The French now had to win ground for a wide-based attack on the citadel complex. On Louis' urging, Vauban first turned his attention to the redoubt of La Cachotte, which stood on a broad stony plateau to the west of the citadel. The trenches were opened on 8 June, and by the morning of the 13th the approaches were close enough to justify an assault. With characteristic foresight Vauban planted pickets on the trench parapet, so that each unit would know its frontage, and he advised the soldiers:

My children, we do not forbid you to chase the enemy when they are on the run, but I don't want to see you get yourselves killed to no purpose when you come up against the covered way of their rearward works. I shall keep five drummers by me who will call you back when it is time. As soon as you hear the drums beat, don't lose any time in falling back to your positions.[5]

The redoubt was stormed according to plan.

The siege of the citadel could now begin. A 'High Attack' with spacious parallels was developed over the Cachotte plateau against Terra Nova and the left, or western branch of Fort William. A simultaneous 'Low Attack' snaked forward from the Abbey of Salsinnes against the right (north-eastern) salient of the Fort.

From now until the end of the siege, said Saint-Hilaire,

the weather was ... so wet and appalling that I truly believe that there never has been seen worse at this time of year. Since the trenches were running uphill, all the water flowed into them and flooded them out. Added to that, the bluish-grey subsoil formed a heavy mud from which you could not drag yourself free.[6]

La Colonie comments that

the fields had become so sodden with rain as to render cartage impossible, and all that could be done was to carry a few bombs and cannon balls on the backs of pack-horses and mules. Even these animals had the greatest labour in extricating themselves from the bad places, and had con-stantly to make fresh tracks.[7]

This painfully transported ammunition was fired to no great effect, for several days' battering effected only a narrow breach in the left branch of Fort William and failed to break a single stake in the palisade. The secret of the fort's resistance lay in the clever way in which Coehoorn had sited the rampart just behind the crest of the hill, so that the further the besiegers advanced, the more the works seemed to retreat and diminish.

Vauban eventually surmounted every difficulty by dint of vigorous sapping, and by 22 June the trenches had closed to the distance that he usually demanded before he could bring himself to risk an assault – the High Attack was a matter of yards from the left branch of Fort William and its breach, while the Low Attack had embraced the north-eastern salient of the fort, and was worming towards the ravine that separated the fort from Terra Nova behind. Thus Coehoorn found himself almost cut off from the main fortress, and, thinking it time to make a melo-dramatic gesture, he had his own grave dug in Fort William as a sign of his determination.

At nine in the evening of 22 June the French troops swarmed out of the trenches and came close to converting Coehoorn's gesture into something more than rhetoric. Coehoorn for a time managed to check the enemy who were emerging from the trenches of the Low Attack, but the French from the High Attack streamed in through the breach and attacked the defenders from the rear. Coehoorn was in no condi-tion to stem the new flood, for a mortar bomb had exploded right next to him, wounding him in the head and killing his faithful valet. The 1,280 survivors hastened to beat *chamade* (a drum-beat indicating a desire to parley), and were granted an honourable evacuation to friendly territory.

The garrison of Fort William and their wounded chief came out on 23 June.

> Vauban was curious to see Coehoorn, and after heaping praises upon him he asked him whether his attack could have been improved upon. Coehoorn replied that if the fort had been attacked in the ordinary way, by a trench directed against the curtain and two demi-bastions, he could have held out at least fifteen days more and inflicted heavy casu-alties on the French. As things were, he had been sur-rounded on all sides, and forced to give himself up.[8]

Thus the French account.

Coehoorn's son records the interview in rather different terms:

> Vauban, amongst other pretty compliments about the defence, told Coehoorn that he could console himself for

his capitulation with the thought that he had had the honour of being attacked by the greatest king in the world. Coehoorn replied that he was sensible of the distinction, but went on to say that he was particularly honoured to have compelled Vauban, the greatest of all men in siege warfare, to have changed the sites of his batteries seven times before he could force the fort to surrender.[9]

This certainly sounds more like Coehoorn's tart manner of speaking.

There remained the attack on Terra Nova and the Donjon. On the night of 24/25 June the High and Low Attacks were joined in a broad parallel which embraced the whole extent of Terra Nova. A brave Parisian soldier then crept forward and discovered that there were 'practicable' gaps in the double covered way, and on the 28th the counterscarps were taken by assault while Louis looked on from the covered way of Fort William. The soldier was rewarded with twenty louis, of which he gave two to his captain, spent two more on drinking the king's health, and sent the remainder back to his wife.

On the following night a French reconnaissance party penetrated Terra Nova, and roamed the interior under the guidance of a captured enemy sentry, who had a knife at his throat. Daylight on the 29th showed that the defenders had abandoned Terra Nova altogether and were now crammed into the Donjon, from where they sounded bugles and ran up a white flag. The capitulation was concluded on the same day, and the garrison marched out to its freedom on the 30th.

Vauban had just put forth one of the most accomplished of his technical performances. The difficult terrain at Namur did not lend itself to any startling innovations, but Vauban had chosen the targets of his attacks with boldness and judgement, and he had managed to cover every yard of the progress of his trenches by effective artillery fire. Particularly skilful was the way in which he contrived to avoid a frontal attack on Fort William.

The French launched altogether four assaults, but Vauban made sure on every occasion that the way was well-reconnoitred, that the battalions were thoroughly conversant with their tasks, and that the troops had to cover only the shortest possible stretch of open ground before they reached their objectives.

The comparatively modest butcher's bill of 6,966 casualties was the best indication of the value of Vauban's cautious proceedings. When you took a fortress as strong as Namur it was a rare achievement to have lost scarcely 300 men more than the defenders.

NAMUR 1695

By 1695 the Allies were ready for an attempt to win back Namur for its Spanish owners. Unfortunately the place was, if possible, still more formidable than it had been three years earlier. The garrison of about 13,000 troops was commanded by the resolute governor Boufflers, and Vauban had been hard at work for three years now, adding a ravelin and two demi-lunes to Fort William and encircling the whole perimeter of the fortress with a line of lunettes – eleven of them defended the access to the citadel complex, while eight more were disposed in front of the town.

La Colonie does not hesitate to describe the Allied siege as

a bold stroke, and more brilliantly conducted than in our own case. It is true that we were at a disadvantage [in 1692], as we were ignorant as to the best point of attack, but at that time it had an inferior garrison. They, on the other hand, had to contend with excellent fortifications and a complete little army of fine troops commanded by a marshal of France... But what a scourge is war! Human life counts for nothing when such an enterprise is determined on![10]

The Dutch authorities were only too well aware that the operation was going to be 'extremely costly', and that 'much artillery and ammunition would thereby be consumed or destroyed by the enemy gunfire'.[11] King William III of England and his allies lacked any experience of sieges on this scale, but they did their best to 'play the Louvois', bringing together an ill-assorted army of Dutch, Spanish, English, Brandenburgers, Hessians and Hanoverians, and assembling a siege train of about 170 pieces. A hundred boats were acquired to ship the guns and ammunition upstream from Maastricht, and river transport also had to be provided to convey the wounded to the hospitals which were being set up at Huy, Maeseyck and Roermond. The area round Namur was by now eaten out of green fodder, and so the vast number of cavalry and train horses had to be fed at some expense from the magazines which were accumulated by the civilian contractors Machado and Pereyra.

The first Allied forces arrived before Namur on 2 July 1695. Their commander was the Earl of Athlone, better known to us as Godert de Ginkel. Another veteran of William's Irish wars was the Dutch Grand Master of Artillery, Julius v. Tettau, who, in common with du Puy de l'Espinasse, the Director-General of Fortifications, could think of nothing better to do than repeat the pattern of Vauban's siege of 1692. Thus the first attacks were once more directed against the southernmost front of the town – an operation which was bound to be attended with heavy casualties, now that the besiegers had to overcome the new lunettes which had been built by Vauban.

On the night of 17/18 July Major-General v. Salisch stormed the lunettes of Saint-Fiacre, Coquelet and Balard just at the moment when the night guard was taking over from the day guard. The garrison of the Coquelet lunette gave way after offering some resistance, and the French lost about 1,000 men before they could reach the safety of the St Nicholas Gate, for 'the English had cut off the enemy in their retreat to the counterscarp, and in the bitterness of the fighting they were in no mood to give quarter. [12]

Allied casualties were, however, at least as great as those of the French, and the besiegers did not complete their task of breaking through the line of lunettes until they reduced the Balard work by mining on 26 July. On the next day King William in person directed a successful attack on the outer covered way of the town by 400 English and Dutch grenadiers, who

> disregarded the heavy enemy fire and, sword in hand, established themselves on the glacis of the covered way. They were supported by the ordinary infantry, who shortly afterwards made a lodgment there and dug themselves in. The fire was unspeakable in its intensity. [13]

The French remained in possession of the inner covered way, and they abandoned it only when Major Lindeboom advanced to make a new assault on 2 August. This final stroke put the French in 'such a state of

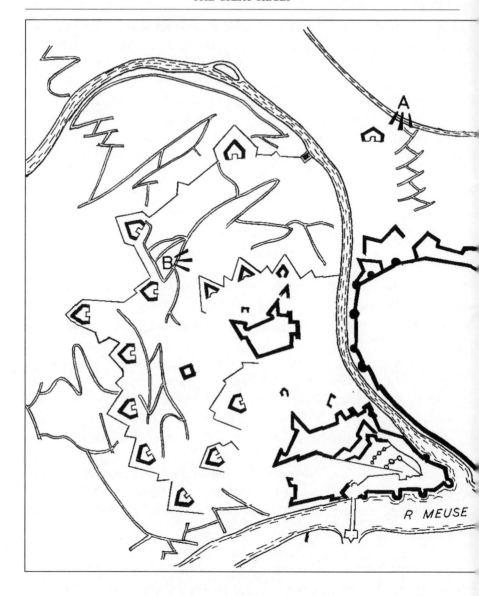

panic that they rapidly made up their minds to show the white flag and talk about surrender'.[14] Two days later the garrison agreed to abandon the town and retreat to the citadel complex.

During all this heroic corpse-making, Coehoorn argued with his superiors that they would never take the whole of Namur by such a manner of proceeding. At length King William was prevailed upon to assemble a council of war, at which Coehoorn

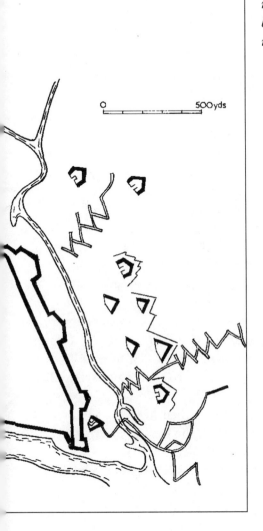

Plan of the siege of Namur, 1695, showing how Vauban's new lunettes forced the Allies to begin their siegeworks well out into the country.

O _____ 500yds

spoke out against all the other members of the council, who had proposed the old method. He argued that it was essential to avoid a long and very difficult siege, which would cost many officers and soldiers their lives. He knew the fortress well and had made some works there himself, and he was confident that he could wipe out the powerful garrison by a continuous fire of cannon and mortars.[15]

The Elector of Bavaria (the new Governor of the Spanish Netherlands) was mightily impressed, and he made sure that the protesting gunner Tettau fell in with every one of Coehoorn's directions.

Coehoorn at once showed what he had in mind. He planted the greater number of his batteries in the gardens of the town beside the Sambre, so that they bore on the right (eastern) branches of Fort William and Terra Nova. According to Saint-Hilaire, this was the one side which Vauban had left out of account when he was building his elaborate new works, 'for he had succumbed to the besetting French sin of believing that other nations must of necessity follow our ideas and judge them the best. In this persuasion he neglected to make new fortifications on that flank'.[16]

From 20 August the Allies thundered against the citadel complex with breaching fire from seventy-four cannon, enfilading fire from twenty-five more, and high-trajectory fire from thirty mortars and twenty-two howitzers. Within a few days five practicable breaches had been effected in the works, and Marshal Boufflers jokingly offered the command of battered Fort William to his boastful subordinate, the Sieur de Vigouroux. This gentleman chose to decline the invitation. In reality Boufflers was putting the best face on a serious situation, for there were too few casemates to shelter the garrison from the incessant cannonade, and the French had no picks with which to hack from the rocky earth the materials that were needed to repair and retrench the breaches.

The effect of the artillery fire more than lived up to the Allies' expectations, but by the end of the month the trenches were still five or six hundred yards short of the citadel works. These delays were occasioned by the lack of cash for the labourers, who were 'unwilling to serve at the risk of their lives when they are unpaid'.[17]

The end for Namur came in a violent and altogether unexpected manner, and one which contrasts sharply with the steady march of Vauban's siege in 1692.

At one in the afternoon of 30 August a soldier touched off a powder keg, and the explosion was the signal for the best battalions of the Allied army to climb out of the trenches and advance against the citadel complex – the French themselves were struck with admiration at the sight of Lord Cutts's English grenadiers and fusiliers, as they moved steadily across six hundred yards of fire-swept ground with drums beating and colours flying. To all appearances the assault met with disaster. The English were flung back from their assigned breach in Terra Nova, and all that the Allies had to show for the loss of about 2,000 lives was four lodgements in the covered ways of the citadel.

All the same, Coehoorn had his vindication soon enough. The French, too, had been severely mauled in the fighting, and rather than undergo a further storm Boufflers capitulated in return for an evacuation on the afternoon of 1 September,

> which inspired Monsieur Mesgrigny [Bouffler's engineer] to declare that by this one siege of Namur Coehoorn had acquired more glory than had Vauban when he took such a number of fortresses on behalf of the king, his master. Thus fell the famous stronghold of Namur, over the gate of which the French had set these striking words: *Reddi quidem, sed vinci non potest,* which means: 'This fortress may be surrendered, but never taken'. But the recapture of Namur proves the contrary.[18]

The news of the stirring events at Namur reached Vauban while he was on a tour of inspection in Brittany. The response was predictably sour. He wrote in a reproving tone to Le Peletier concerning the assault of 30 August:

> You seem to regard this action as a prodigy of valour. As for me, I see it as one of the most stupid mistakes that has ever been made in siege warfare. We should be very fortunate if God puts it into the heads of our enemies to keep on attacking us in this way.[19]

It is not surprising that Vauban was unappreciative of a method which was so different from his own. Coehoorn's first struggle in the siege was not his artillery duels with the French, but his effort to break through the 'middle management' of his own military hierarchy and convince the Allied sovereigns that he was proposing the right course of action. He had done the same at the siege of Bonn in 1689.

Coehoorn then had to design a plan of attack that would not overtax the capacity of an impoverished army of seven national contingents, who could bring nothing to the siege except a mass of artillery and their own courage in an assault – an army of this kind would have gone to pieces if Coehoorn had imitated Vauban's method of systematic approach. Coehoorn therefore abridged the siege by opening up the weak eastern side of the citadel complex, by pelting the French with shot, bombs and howitzer shells, and last of all by draining their final resources of morale by his assault of 30 August.

Vauban rendered an unwitting tribute to Coehoorn's tactics when he tried to explain how Boufflers could have surrendered the citadel as easily as he did:

> I cannot impute this decision to any lack of will or courage. Perhaps the garrison was exhausted and ruined in the process of defending bad positions at the beginning of the siege; perhaps some essential requisites were lacking; or perhaps it was because the great quantity of bombs and the horrid cannon-fire succeeded in decimating the defenders, and opening up every sector of the ramparts.[20]

ANTWERP 1832

After centuries of bearing other people's rule with reasonable equanimity, the Catholic southern Netherlands found themselves unable to tolerate the Dutch regime that was imposed upon them after the defeat of Napoleon. The Belgians were angered by the refusal of the Dutch to take them into anything resembling an equal partnership, and so the example of the Paris revolt of July 1830 ignited a rebellion which spread throughout the southern Netherlands.

The Dutch garrisons fled from most of the strongholds, rather than be stranded in a hostile countryside, and the authority of the new government was finally assured late in 1832 when the French Armée du Nord of Marshal Gérard came over the border in support of the Belgians.

By November the last foothold that the King of Holland owned in the southern Netherlands was the citadel of Antwerp, which he was determined to hold both as a symbol of his claim to Belgium and as a means of pinning down the French without having to engage in a general war. The French duly retaliated by undertaking one of the last great sieges of the classic age of artillery fortification.

The citadel of Antwerp was an accretion of various styles and periods. The core of the work was formed by the original pentagonal brick citadel, which Pacciotto of Urbino had designed for the Spaniards in 1567. At the turn of the seventeenth and eighteenth centuries five large new bastions were built round the old ones, which now served as redoubts, and finally after 1815 the Dutch surrounded the place with a circuit of five strong lunettes, the salients of which projected three hundred yards into the country.

In November 1832 the citadel was held by a strong garrison of 4,500 men, who stood under the command of Baron Chassé ('Général Bayonette'). This old war-horse had earned his laurels under Napoleon, though he had gone over to the Dutch in time to appear on their side at Waterloo. 'The French spoke with respect of an ancient and well-approved comrade, and perhaps only the *canaille,* or off-scourings of the city, who had tasted of the old man's discipline on some former occasion, were ever heard heartily to abuse him.'[21]

Against the citadel the French brought 16,000 infantry and a curious but effective assortment of officers – ex-Napoleonic *vieilles moustaches* who were good at dealing with the troops, as well as a younger generation of keen and well-connected staff officers. The 1,900 gunners and the eight companies of sappers and miners represented the pick of the French technical arms, and they were ably directed by General Haxo, a man who was 'tall and somewhat corpulent, with features strongly but handsomely marked, and developing thought and intellect'.[22]

The French seemed to be taking their time about their preparations, and so on Sunday 25 November the townspeople of Antwerp came streaming out in all their finery.

> Groups of both sexes and all ages strolled over ground that was soon to be crossed at the peril of life: the day was mild and beautiful, and the laughing, chattering, reckless crowds appeared as near to the devoted citadel as the garrison would permit, and within short range of its guns. The horizontally tricoloured flag of the Dutch was hoisted on Chassé's house and hung listlessly in the air: a sentry, and

occasionally an officer or soldier, was seen on the parapet, but there was nothing else to denote that the place was tenanted by upwards of four thousand spirits, hourly awaiting the commencement of a fearful contest.[23]

Without any warning at all, 4,500 French workers appeared before the southern side of the citadel on the night of 29/30 November and opened a first parallel against the Lunette Saint-Laurent and the adjacent Toledo Bastion. The French went on to establish four dismounting and ricochet batteries in the parallel, and three batteries of mortars behind it, and with this artillery they opened fire at ten on the hazy morning of 4 December.

The brick scarps of the citadel rang under the hammering of the shot, but it soon transpired that the French had sited their artillery at too great a range to silence the bravely served Dutch guns by low-trajectory fire alone. What really did the damage was the French mortar fire, which wrecked the interior establishments of the citadel, turned the ground into a maze of overlapping craters, and drove most of the garrison into the crowded and airless casemates.

Meanwhile the Belgian armourers hastened to deliver a seven-and-a-half-ton present to their French friends. This was the 600 mm monster mortar *Leopold,* which had been cast in Liège to the designs of the French colonel Paixhans. *Leopold* arrived in time to open fire on 21 December. The first of the 1,000-pound shells burst dangerously near the main magazine, and General Chassé gave a segment-shaped splinter to a lieutenant and asked him to work out the dimensions and weight of the whole missile. The results were frightening.

The trench attack continued to make relentless progress according to the most elaborate rules of late seventeenth-century siegecraft. The French sappers 'descended' the wet ditch of the Lunette Saint-Laurent; they made the 'passage' on rafts, then blew up the salient of the work on the night of 13/14 December and effected a lodgement. The gunners could now establish their heavy cannon in batteries on the captured lunette, and at eleven on the morning of 21 December they opened a breaching fire against the left face of the Toledo Bastion. Fragments of earth and brick were thrown up by the impact of every shot, and the débris began to fill the ditch.

By the evening of 22 December the defence was *in extremis*. Forty-four guns had been dismounted, and the remainder could not be transported to the threatened front across the shell-pitted interior of the citadel. The garrison was shocked and enfeebled, and it already counted 478 casualties. Chassé accordingly decided to capitulate, and on the 23rd the rival commanders proclaimed a truce. The pallid Dutch soldiers took the opportunity to emerge from the casemates and promenade on the ramparts, where they were applauded by the French.

By the terms of capitulation the Dutch were to be made prisoner after having been accorded the honours of war. The garrison duly marched out on Christmas Eve to lay down its arms on the glacis. Many of the old soldiers hated to part with their favourite weapons, and rather than give them up to the French they smashed the stocks and trampled the cartridges underfoot. One warrior heaved his musket into the muddy ditch, where it remained with the stock projecting from the water like a symbol of defiance.

The French were agreed that the place could not have been held for a day longer than it was, and an English observer wrote that it was

> impossible to give the reader an accurate idea of the appearance of the interior of the citadel, but when I say that there was not a foot's space of ground or building that was not shattered or pierced by shot or shell, I am confident I speak within bounds. The only remains of the buildings were a few bare walls, and, occasionally, a part of the roof, perforated with innumerable holes. The church, the barrack, the general's and officers' houses, were all heaps of ruins. Cannon balls and splinters were strewed and scattered among the broken earth, which had been everywhere ploughed up by the explosion of the shells. On the right, as we entered, we saw a place where the *monstre bombe* had fallen. It had made an immense excavation, having the appearance of a place from whence an enormous tree had been uprooted.[24]

In one of the holes the French discovered the remains of seven gun carriages, which told of the price the Dutch had paid for keeping a single cannon in action nearby.

It is pleasant to record that the French and Dutch observed all the old-fashioned codes of chivalrous conduct as well as the conventions of siegecraft – they reserved all their animosity for the Belgians. The Chevalier de Richemont was wandering over the fortifications on 26 December when he encountered a townswoman who was covering a mysterious object with a cloth. She asked half a franc to uncover what was beneath, and when she drew the cloth aside Richemont was confronted with the decaying head of a sapper, who had been buried up to his neck. Such was the birth of the sovereign state of Belgium.

ALGIERS 1816

For our attack against coastal fortifications we take a short sea voyage in the company of Edward Pellew, Lord Exmouth, who on 27 August 1816 led a combined British and Dutch fleet against the Barbary corsair port of Algiers.

The Dey of Algiers had hoped to check the advance of the Allies with a swarm of small boats, but the five British battleships swept down in line abreast, and Lord Exmouth's flagship the *Queen Charlotte* came to anchor in an enfilading position about eighty yards from the head of the casemated mole which covered the port. Rear-Admiral Milne's *Impregnable* (74 guns) anchored further off, fifteen hundred yards from the town.

The Algerines had not reckoned on such boldness, and they were ill-prepared to meet the massed broadsides. Their desperate gunners had to scoop up their powder in open ladles, and the cannon barrels were so long that they had to clamber outside the casemates in order to carry out the operations of loading. They had no ovens to heat red-hot shot, and they were encumbered by crowds of townspeople who swarmed over the mole to view the firework display.

Exmouth motioned the spectators to stand out of the way, then at about three in the afternoon he opened fire. Manoeuvring about her two cables, the *Queen Charlotte* engaged successive targets – first of all the mole, which was silenced by 3.35 pm, and then the Algerine ships and the town. However, the surviving shore batteries fought back most effectively. The *Queen Charlotte* escaped comparatively lightly, with 8 dead and 131 wounded, but the *Impregnable* fought at a disadvantage on account of the greater range and she had to be rescued by a frigate which provided a sorely needed diversion. She lost 50 dead and 138 wounded, and after the action it was found that she had been holed 233 times.

After nine hours of fire the British and Dutch had discharged 60,000 solid shot, 960 shells from the four British bomb vessels, and a large quantity of Congreve rockets and further bombs from the smaller craft. The ships' magazines were now almost totally exhausted, and Exmouth was grateful to a land breeze which enabled him to draw out of range and open talks with the Dey. The Algerines, too, had had enough of the fight, and they agreed to release the Christian slaves in their captivity and abide by the terms of their treaties with the western powers.

A British squadron had to pay Algiers a return visit in 1824, after the corsairs resumed their evil ways, and these incorrigible pirates were not finally subdued until the French conquered the town and the hinterland in 1830.

These circumstances in no way detract from the achievement of Exmouth and his men, and his biographer concludes that 'regarded as a naval operation, the Battle of Algiers was the hottest engagement and one of the most brilliant victories of the classic age of English naval history'.[25]

A few statistics serve to illustrate the typical severity of a ship-to-shore combat. There were at least 3,000 guns on board the French and Spanish ships at Trafalgar in 1805, and they inflicted 1,587 casualties, whereas in 1816 the 225-odd Algerine guns accounted for the proportionately much higher butcher's bill of 883 men killed or wounded.

Appendix 1
Glossary

ABATIS A defence made of felled trees.

APPROACHES Trenches dug towards a fortress to enable the besieger to approach under cover from fire.

ASSAULT A storm made against a fortification.

ATTACK 1 An operation (usually by formal siege) aiming at the reduction of a fortress.

2 A body of trench approaches, directed against one of the fronts of a fortress.

AUGET A square-sectioned wooden channel which protects a length of fuze in a mine.

BANQUETTE An infantry fire-step, built behind the parapet of a rampart, a covered way or a trench.

BARBETTE A cannon is positioned *en barbette* when the carriage is high enough (or the parapet low enough) to permit the barrel to point over the top of the parapet without the necessity of cutting an embrasure.

BASTION A four-sided work which projects from the main rampart, and consists of two faces and two flanks.

BATARDEAU A dam which retains water in a ditch.

BATTER The slope given to the outer face of a revetment.

BATTERY 1 An emplacement for cannon or mortars.

2 A group of cannon or mortars.

BERM A space left between the edge of a ditch (or trench) and the foot of the slope of the rampart (or parapet).

BODY OF THE PLACE *see* ENCEINTE

BOMB 1 A shell fired from a mortar or howitzer.

2 A mortar boat.

BOMBARDMENT A generalised cannonade of a fortress town.

BONNET A triangular work placed in front of the salient angle of a ravelin.

BOYAU A communication trench.

BRANCH 1 A small mine gallery.

2 A long straight stretch of a work of fortification.

BREACH An opening made in a rampart or wall by artillery-fire or mining.

BREASTWORK *see* EPAULEMENT

BRICOLE A cannon fires *en bricole* when the ball strikes a revetment on a horizontal plane which departs markedly from the perpendicular.

CALTROP An obstruction consisting of a small iron tetrahedron with pointed ends.

CAMOUFLET A mine charge which is intended to take all its effect against enemy mineworkings underground.

CANNELURE CUTTING A technique for breaching a wall by cannon fire.

CAPITAL An imaginary centre-line, running through the salient angle, which divides a work into two equal parts.

CAPITULATION An agreement to give up a fortress on terms.

CAPONNIERE 1 A covered communication, usually in the form of a trench with raised sides, running from the enceinte to a detached work.

2 A powerful casemated work, projecting perpendicularly across a ditch for the purpose of delivering flanking fire.

CARCASS An incendiary shell.

CASEMATE A covered chamber, usually of masonry. A defensive casemate is one which is pierced with loopholes or embrasures for musketry or artillery. *See also* HAXO CASEMATE.

CAVALIER A raised interior battery, usually in the centre of a bastion..

CHAMBER (FOURNEAU) A space made in a mine for the housing of an explosive charge.

CHEMIN DES RONDES A sentry walk running round the top of the masonry of a revetment.

CHEVAL DE FRISE (FRIZZY HORSE) An obstruction made of a squared beam to which are attached wooden stakes.

CIRCUMVALLATION A line of siege works which faces the open country so as to hold off the army of relief.

CITADEL A compact, independent and very strong work of four or five sides. It is usually sited next to a town enceinte.

CORDON A continuous, rounded coping stone which surmounts the

221

revetment of a masonry rampart.

COUNTER-APPROACH A trench dug from the fortress against the siegeworks.

COUNTERFORT An interior buttress.

COUNTERGUARD A detached bastion, standing in front of a bastion of the enceinte.

COUNTERSCARP The slope or retaining wall on the outer side of the ditch.

COUNTERVALLATION A line of earthworks made at the beginning of the siege and facing the fortress under attack.

COVERED WAY An infantry position, running along the rim of the counterscarp.

CREMAILLERE A work *en crémaillère* is in saw-toothed form.

CREST The innermost edge of a glacis or parapet.

CROCHET A miniature parallel in the approach trenches.

CROWNWORK A kind of hornwork, composed of two long branches on either side and two small bastioned fronts at the head.

CURTAIN A stretch of rampart running between two bastions.

CUVETTE (or CUNETTE) A narrow ditch sunk in the floor of the main ditch.

DEBLAI Material excavated in the digging of the ditch.

DEFILEMENT The science of aligning the summits of fortifications in a vertical plane, so as to evade gunfire from a height outside the fortress.

DEMI-LUNE *see* HALF-MOON *and* RAVELIN

DESCENT OF THE DITCH The process of advancing siegeworks from the crest of the glacis to the floor of the ditch.

DISCRETION A garrison surrenders at discretion when it delivers itself to the mercy of the besieger without terms.

DOUBLE CROWNWORK A kind of crownwork with three bastioned fronts at the head.

ECLUSE DE CHASSE An entry sluice.

ECLUSE DE FUITE An exit sluice.

ECOUTE A small mine gallery.

EMBRASURE An opening made through a parapet or wall, to enable a cannon to fire through the thickness.

ENCEINTE (BODY OF THE PLACE) The main, continuous perimeter of a fortress.

ENFILADE Fire coming from the flank in such a way that the effect is felt along the length of a fortification or a body of troops.

ENVELOPE (COUVREFACE GENERALE) A continuous outer enceinte.

EPAULEMENT (BREASTWORK) A parapet which protects troops or guns against enfilade fire.

ESCALADE The climbing of a work by means of ladders.

ESPLANADE The open space left between a citadel and the buildings of a town.

EXPENSE MAGAZINE A small magazine placed close to a battery.

EXTERIOR SIDE OF FORTIFICATION An imaginary line drawn from the salient of one bastion to the salient of the next.

FACES Outer sides of a work which converge to form a salient angle.

FASCINE A bundle of branches used in sieges.

FAUSSE-BRAYE A low outer rampart, usually built of earth.

FLANK The side of a work, more particularly the part of a bastion which connects one of the faces with the curtain.

FORT D'ARRET (SPERRFORT) An isolated fort guarding a pass or passage.

FOUGASSE A small mine placed a short distance below ground to take effect against troops.

FRAISES *see* STORM-POLES

GABION A basket of woven brushwood which is filled with earth and used extensively in siegework and as a supplement to fortifications.

GABION FARCI *see* SAP ROLLER

GALLERY The largest kind of mine tunnel.

GARDE-FOU A free-standing tablette, running along the outer rim of the chemin des rondes.

GLACIS The open slope descending from the crest of the covered way to the open country.

GORGE The side or neck of a bastion or detached work which faces towards the centre of the fortress.

GUERITE A sentry box which is sited on the ramparts.

HALF-MOON (DEMI-LUNE) A ravelin.

HAXO CASEMATE A vaulted defensive casemate, sited on the terreplein.

HORNWORK An outwork composed of two branches at the sides and a small bastioned front at the head. *See also* CROWNWORK.

INSULT The taking of a fortress by surprise or storm, without recourse to formal siege.

LINE OF DEFENCE An imaginary line, extending from the salient of a bastion along a face and thence to the curtain or flank of an adjacent bastion.

LUNETTE 1 A detached triangular work standing on or beyond the glacis.

2 A small work sited to the side of a ravelin.

MANTLET A wheeled timber screen, employed to protect the head of a sap.

MERLON The solid portion of a parapet between two embrasures.

ORILLON A projecting shoulder of the bastion, which partially screens a retired flank from fire.

PALANKA A small fortification made of logs or palisades, more particularly on the Turkish theatre of war.

PALISADE A fence of close-set, pointed wooden stakes.

PARADOS *see* PARAPET

PARALLEL A wide and deep siege trench, describing an arc roughly equidistant along all its length from the covered way of the fortress.

PARAPET A stout wall or bank of earth, placed along the forward edge of fortifications or siegeworks, and giving protection to the troops behind. A rearward parapet is called a 'parados'.

PAS DE SOURIS A narrow flight of steps, set in the counterscarp revetment.

PETARD A bell-like device, used for blowing in a gate.

PLACE OF ARMS An enlargement of the covered way, at the re-entrant or salient angles, where troops are assembled for sorties or for the obstinate defence of the covered way.

PROFILE A cross-section of fortification.

RAMEAU A medium-sized mine tunnel.

RAMPART A thick wall of earth, masonry, or both, which forms the main defence of the fortress.

RAVELIN A triangular detached work, placed in front of a curtain and usually between two bastions. NB in French the ravelin is termed the *demi-lune*.

REDAN A V-shaped work, open to the rear.

REDOUBT 1 A detached work, enclosed on all sides.

    2 A small, powerful work, usually in the form of a redan, which is placed inside a bastion or a re-entrant place of arms.

RE-ENTRANT An angle facing inwards from the field.

REMBLAI The material (usually from the excavation of the ditch), which is piled up to form the body of the rampart.

RETIRED FLANK A recessed portion of a bastion flank.

RETRENCHMENT An interior defence.

REVETMENT A retaining wall. In works in demi-revetment, the masonry covers only the lower part of the rampart.

RICOCHET FIRE The firing of cannon shot or howitzer shells at high trajectory and low charges, so that the missile drops over the parapet of a work and bounces along its length.

SALIENT An angle pointing outwards towards the field.

SALLY-PORT A small gate, usually set in a curtain, which permits troops to leave on a sortie.

SAP A narrow siege trench which is established by the planting of gabions or sandbags. In a flying sap, a row of gabions is planted simultaneously, and not (as is usual) in succession.

SAP ROLLER (French GABION FARCI) A stout gabion which is rolled horizontally in front of the head of a sap.

SAUCISSON A fuze made of a powder-filled hose of canvas or leather.

SCARP The outer slope of a rampart.

SHOULDER ANGLE The angle of a bastion which is formed by the meeting of a face and a flank.

SPERRFORT *see* FORT D'ARRET

STORM-POLES (French FRAISES) A palisade planted in the scarp of a work, and projecting horizontally or slightly downwards.

TABLETTE A low wall crowning the cordon of a rampart.

TAIL The entrance to the siege trenches.

TALUS 1 The rearward slope of a rampart.

    2 Any earthen slope.

TAMBOUR A small palisaded perimeter.

TENAILLE A low work stationed in the ditch in front of a curtain.

TENAILLE FORTIFICATION A fortification on a zigzag trace.

TENAILLON A small work standing to one side of a ravelin.

TERREPLEIN The wide upper part of a rampart (or covered way), stretching from the banquette to the edge of the talus (or counterscarp).

TRACE Ground plan.

TRAVERSE A bank or wall, usually set at right-angles to the main alignment of the work, which protects the defenders from enfilade.

WALL-PIECE (French MOUSQUET A CHEVALET) A very long and heavy musket used in sieges.

ZIGZAGS Approach trenches.

ZONE OF SERVITUDE An area beyond the glacis on which civil building is restricted or forbidden.

Appendix 2
Schools and Systems of Fortification

THE ITALIAN SCHOOL

CHARACTERISTICS

Massive ramparts of masonry and earth, blunt-angled hammerhead bastions, supplemented later by ravelins and covered way.

REPRESENTATIVES

Giuliano di Francesco Giamberti da Sangallo – made probably the first plans for a bastioned fortress (1487); invented orillons for his fort at Nettuno (1501).

Genoese engineers built the first ravelin – Sarzanello 1497.

Michele di Sanmicheli – built the first elaborate bastioned fortress town at Verona from 1530; the Porta Nuova at Verona had a fundamental influence on the design of fortress gates.

Niccolo Tartaglia invented the covered way (1556).

Pacciotto of Urbino designed influential citadels at Turin (1564) and Antwerp (1567).

Floriani evolved the tenaille from the fausse-braye (1630).

THE NETHERLANDISH SCHOOL

CHARACTERISTICS

Low-lying ramparts of earth or in demi-revetment, acute-angled salients, multiple wet ditches, proliferation of outworks – demilunes, hornworks and the like.

REPRESENTATIVES

Simon Stevin (1594), Marolois (1614), Adam Freitag (1630), Hendrik Hondius (1634), Andreas Cellarius (1645), Menno van Coehoorn (1685). Coehoorn's three 'systems' placed emphasis on separate features of the defence: the 'first' on a combined bastion and fausse-braye; the 'second' on a continuous fausse-braye; the 'third' on huge ravelins and lunettes. Otherwise a general reliance on alternate wet and dry ditches, narrow orillons, and protracted defence from concealed redoubts.

THE GERMAN SCHOOL

CHARACTERISTICS
Immense proliferation of largely theoretical designs, and a general distortion of features borrowed from the Italians and Dutch: multiple bastion flanks, lavish use of demi-lunes, curtains broken inwards into shallow 'V's; many styles are based on the star-shaped tenaille trace.

REPRESENTATIVES (AMONG VERY MANY OTHERS)
Daniel Speckle (1589), J. H. Sattler (1619), Wilhelm and Johann Dilich (1640), Matthias Dögen (1647), C. Neubauer (1679), Georg Rimpler (1673, 1674, 1678 and interpreted by C. L. Sturm 1729).

THE FRENCH SCHOOL

CHARACTERISTICS
Motifs from the Italian and Dutch styles were developed into a bastioned fortification of classic simplicity by the time of Vauban. Thereafter increasing elaboration and stultification until fresh ideas were introduced by Montalembert and later writers of heretical tendencies.

REPRESENTATIVES
Jean Errard de Bar-le-Duc (1594). Strong Italian influence, with bastions with right-angled shoulders. Antoine de Ville (1629). Simplified Italian-style enceinte without orillons or casemates; powerful hornworks borrowed from Dutch.
Blaise de Pagan (1640). Evolved a simple and harmonious style that was identical with the so-called 'first system' of Sébastien le Prestre de

Vauban. Vauban evolved a 'second system' in 1687 (Besançon, Belfort and Landau) by which the main bastion became a detached counterguard and was commanded from the rear by a casemated 'bastion tower' that was incorporated in the curtain. The 'third system' of 1698 (Neuf-Brisach) was simply an elaboration of the second.

The French 'corrected trace'. Evolved in the middle and later eighteenth century by Louis de Cormontaigne and his disciple Fourcroy, and characterised by long ravelins and retrenchments in the bastion gorges. Consecrated as the 'corrected trace' in the nineteenth century, and survived with modifications until the 1860s.

Marc-René de Montalembert. His *Fortification Perpendiculaire* (1776–96) advocated powerful artillery defence from casemates, and the replacement of the bastion by the caponnière. Condemned by official circles in France, but highly influential elsewhere in Europe.

Lazare Carnot (1810). Loopholed free-standing scarps, gently sloping counterscarps, mortar casemates. Also influential outside France.

General Rogniat (1816). Retrenched camps with detached forts.

Captain Choumara (1827). High casemated traverses in bastions and ravelins. Earthen parapets independent of scarp walls.

Appendix 3
Considerations in Fortress Wargaming

Wargaming originated as a princely pastime in seventeenth- and eighteenth-century Europe. In the nineteenth century the staffs of leading armies considered wargames to be an excellent means of developing an officer's military sense – and in modern times wargaming techniques have been elaborated and computerised as a basis for Operational Planning.

Recreational wargaming has introduced many people to a serious study of military history, and at the time of writing three forms hold the field: wargaming by computer programme, supported by realistic graphics; board wargaming, using printed boards and symbols – this, like computer wargaming, is normally a commercial product; and tabletop wargaming, with terrain, equipment and figures represented in miniature.

The last of these three, the tabletop variety, still has considerable merits. For its purposes you can represent a fortress or a front of fortification very easily by making successive photocopy enlargements of any suitable plan, such as those which appear in this book. If necessary, the crest of the covered way and the scarps of the works may be emphasised by sticking strips of dowelling to the paper.

The 'scientific' progress of a siege lends itself particularly well to wargaming, and the following comments are intended not to set up a new set of rules, but to underline the considerations which ought to he given weight when adapting programmes of field wargaming to siege warfare.

MOVES
These should be of two types:

The 24-hour move, to represent the course of the attack and the defence over a day and a night. This would subsume, for example, the digging of an entire siege parallel, and the progress of the zig-zag saps. The maximum rate of advance of the saps must diminish the closer they approach the covered way, and, depending on the fall of the dice or the generation of random numbers, the advance of the trench attack may be retarded or halted altogether. Allowance should be made for the besieger failing to achieve surprise when he attempts to dig a parallel.

The tactical move, representing one or more episodes within a 24-hour move, such as a sortie or the storm of a breach. Here the normal rules for field wargaming will do service with no essential alterations.

COVER

Casualties and losses will be reduced for personnel and ordnance sheltered by parallels, zig-zags, covered ways, and ramparts of all kinds, as long as they are secure against enfilade by cannon fire. However enfilade fire by cannon will exact penalties over and above nullifying cover. Mortar and howitzer fire nullify all except casemated cover.

BREACHING THE SCARP BY ARTILLERY

This is a cumulative process, assessed by 24-hour rules, unless it is interrupted by sorties; the requisite number of such moves will depend on the number of designated 24-pounder cannon which can be brought into action against the target; the breaching batteries must have an uninterrupted view of the scarp, normally from the covered way.

PASSAGE OF THE SCARP

An intact scarp may be assaulted only by escalade, and thus in the unlikely event of the besieger achieving surprise. Practical breaches in the scarp are climbed at a greatly reduced rate of the normal infantry move.

MINING

Mine warfare is best entrusted to separate teams of players; otherwise it should be omitted altogether, so as not to slow down the progress of the game.

In tabletop gaming, at least, mining demands the presence of an umpire. The defender submits a copy of his countermines to the umpire, who enters it on a master-plan. The umpire plots the progress (at an agreed rate) of the siege galleries on his master-plan, and when one or more of the galleries approach within a certain distance of a countermine he informs the parties that someone else is working nearby, but gives no clue as to the direction.

The miners in each mine gallery or individual countermine are allowed to explode one camouflet in every 24-hour move, and one full mine charge in every three moves. The miner must tell the referee of the direction in which he intends to explode his camouflet, and the effect will be represented as a cone radiating over an angle of forty-five degrees and for a set distance from the seat of the charge. The camouflet destroys all underground workings within the indicated zone. To avoid unnecessary complications, in all except computerised wargames the countermines and galleries will be assumed to be on the same horizontal plane.

The effect of a full mine charge is expended upwards in a crater of set diameter on the surface, wrecking any fortifications or siegeworks which repose thereon. The umpire must consult his master-map very carefully to determine just what surface works have been destroyed by the miners.

In general, good siege wargaming rules will offer a good representation of siege warfare in our period. Experience shows that, just as in real life, any pronounced departure from Vauban's principles will bring about a disaster. Siege parallels in particular seem to be almost indispensable for the success of an attack.

The wargamer may add as many complications as he wishes – he may choose to limit the garrison's food or ammunition, or stuff the town with mutinous citizens or inflammable buildings. The advance of an army of relief will lend interest to the proceedings.

Appendix 4
Touring a Fortress

The amateur of military history knows few experiences that promise more reward and frustration than a visit to a fortress of the artillery period. It is in an attempt to spare my readers some time and effort that I ask them to stay with me a little longer.

Artillery fortifications are sprawling affairs which are carried out on a scale which is somewhat inhuman. It is not easy to distinguish the lie of the curtains, bastions and ravelins at the best of times, and nowadays the glacis and parapets are frequently obstructed with such a growth of trees and bushes as would succeed in mystifying Vauban himself.

A fortress (like a church) should first be toured from the outside. The circuit may well be immense, and the sensible or slow-moving pilgrim will soon appreciate that he will be able to investigate the works most comfortably with the help of a car – perhaps Vauban would have invented some machine of the sort, if he had lived just a little longer. He once expressed the wish that fortifications would move round *him*, instead of leaving it to him to walk round *them*.

The extreme horizontal emphasis of artillery fortification militates against good photography from the ground level. With ordinary lenses a bastion or ravelin taken at close range tends to appear on the print as an uninteresting and modern-looking stretch of wall, while at longer distances the ramparts are liable to be lost among trees and outlying buildings. A 23 mm or other wide-angle lens gives rather better results.

A modern town map, however simple, is an invaluable help in taking up the trace of the surviving fortifications. The maps in the *Guides Michelin* are quite adequate in this respect. However, normal road maps have ceased to represent contours and do little to bring out the strategic importance of a given fortress in a theatre of war.

England has some good specimens of transitional sixteenth-century fortifications in the Henry VIII forts which are scattered along the south and west coasts. Deal Castle is the largest of the kind, though nearby Walmer is more picturesque. Out of the host of continental transitional fortifications it is worth mentioning the strongholds of Salses (in Roussillon) and Sarzanello (above Sarzana on the Riviera di Levante), which lie hard by the routes to the respective pleasures of the Costa Brava and Viareggio.

As for the early bastion fortifications, the least adventurous tourist need not go far out of his way to see the Borgo enceinte at Rome, or the Citadel da Basso (under restoration) at Florence. Only slightly more remote are the compact and complete Citadel of Santa Barbara at Siena (a more pleasant town anyway than Florence). and the fortress town of Bergamo on its impressive hill site. In northern Europe the enceinte of Berwick-upon-Tweed is possibly the most complete surviving essay in the Italian style, even if the atmosphere is unmistakably British, what with the golf course outside the walls and the allotments immediately inside.

The Dutch-style fortifications in earth have not survived the passage of time very well, but Naarden (near Amsterdam) retains its clearly defined star trace. At Newark there are still fairly extensive traces of both the Royalist fortifications and the Parliamentarian siege lines which, by a rare chance, were left unrazed in 1646 out of fear of plague among the labour force.

The work of Vauban is still well represented by the fortifications which he built or restored at Bergues, Gravelines, Le Quesnoy, Maubeuge, Rocroi, Belfort town, Neuf-Brisach (under restoration), Mont-Louis (in the Pyrenees) and Blaye. The citadel of Lille is reasonably intact, but the citadel at Belfort is difficult of access, and the one at Strasbourg is represented by a single front of two bastions and one ravelin which stands in a remote and unprepossessing corner of the city.

A number of fortresses deserve special mention. On the whole, North America's heritage of fortification is carefully preserved, brilliantly displayed, and well written up in publications like the *American Forts* series and the guides of the National Parks. We have one of the finest examples of a Spanish colonial fort in the seventeenth-century Castello de San Marcos at St Augustine in Florida, while Ticonderoga presents an essay in a later and less pretentious style. The nineteenth-century Fort Henry at Kingston in Canada is periodically brought to life by the drills of its Guard, while Louisbourg on Cape Breton Island is in an advanced stage of restoration.

Returning to Europe we encounter another outstandingly successful restoration in Fort George, near Inverness, where the mid eighteenth-century banquettes and covered ways have been brought back to their pristine state.

Strategically important islands almost always repay a visit. We need only call to mind the spectacular showpiece of Valletta on Malta, or the heavily defended shores of the Channel Islands where German bunkers of World War II jostle for space alongside Napoleonic-period forts and martello towers.

Würzburg in West Germany is remarkable for the onion-skin effect of layer upon layer of outworks surrounding a medieval heart. As you climb the citadel hill from the river Main you penetrate the outer circuits that were planned by Gustavus Adolphus of Sweden in the Thirty Years War, and finished off by the Schönborn prince-bishops in the seventeenth and eighteenth centuries. Then you turn into a courtyard and on the left you see the sandstone sixteenth-century Echtertor and the little bastions on either side. Finally the passage leads over a deep ditch and into the medieval core of the fortress complex.

For dignity and beauty the palm must surely go to the Italian fortress of Lucca, where the spacious ramparts of warm brown brick cast a protective girdle round a town of great interest, and are crowned by the leafy rampart walks that have been famous for centuries.

For a complete bastioned fortress-town, set in an unspoilt environment, there is nothing to compare with Almeida, near the eastern frontier of Portugal. Coming from the west you travel over a vast granite tableland, where you see large and unidentifiable birds of prey wheeling over slabs of rock. You come over a little hill, and there is Almeida, sitting in the middle of an empty green plain. The roofs and the church towers are still packed into a tight perimeter, and the grey walls and grassy outworks seem ready to do battle not just with any potential enemy but with the whole of the outside world.

Notes

The place of publication is London unless otherwise stated.

Prologue

1 Muller, J. A *Treatise of Artillery (1757)*, 10
2 Straith, H. *A Treatise on Fortification* (Croydon, 1833), 24

1. Why Fortresses Were Built

1 *Système Militaire de la Prusse* (1788), 194
2 *Traité des Sièges* ([1704]; Paris, 1829), 9
3 *De la Défense des Places Fortes*, 3rd ed (Paris, 1812), ix
4 Muller, J. *A Treatise Containing the Practical Part of Fortification* (1755), l20
5 *Traité*, wording from Eng trans. *A Treatise on the Safety and Maintenance of States by Means of Fortification* (1747), 13
6 To Dejean, *Correspondance de Napoléon*, 32 vols (Paris, 1858–70), XIII, 131
7 *Political Discourse*, Book II, Chapter 24

8 Vieilleville. *Mémoires*, in *Nouvelle Collection des Mémoires*, 1st series, IX (Paris, 1850), 239
9 Maigret, 94
10 To the National Assembly 1792. *Mémoires sur Carnot, par son Fils*, 2 vols (Paris, 1861), 1, 197

2. Where Fortresses Were Built

1 Maigret, 102–6
2 *De l'Architecture des Fortresses* (Paris, 1801), 227
3 *Vom Kriege (c* 1831), Book VI, Chapter 9
4 Kinsky, Count. *Ueber Emplacement der Festungen* (Vienna, 1790), 18
5 'Marengo' in *Correspondance de Napoléon*, XXX, 373
6 Ibid
7 Eg, A. H. Jomini. *Précis de l'art de la Guerre* (1837), 2nd ed (Paris, 1855), 347
8 *Rêveries* (The Hague, 1756), 117
9 Muller. *Practical Fortification*, 145
10 Maigret, 195–6
11 *De la Fortification depuis*

Vauban, 2 vols (Paris, 1861), I, 131

12 *Tratado de la Artilleria* (1613), French trans (Zutphen, 1621), 52

13 Maigret, 145

14 Sieur de Ville. *Fortifications* (Amsterdam ed of 1679), 14

15 *Essai Général de Fortification*, 2 vols (Berlin, 1797–8), II, 257

16 Muller. *Practical Fortification*, 128

3. How Fortresses Were Built

1 The French royal foot stood in relation to the English foot at about 16:15, and to the Rhineland foot (used in Holland and Germany) at about 29:30. Twelve Rhineland feet made up one Rhineland rod *(Ruthe)*, or approximately two toises. French engineering regulations mention scales of 1:3,600 (one inch to 300 feet) in 1727, and 1:1,800 (four inches to 600 feet) in 1744. John Muller talks of 'fair plans' on the scale of 1:2,160 (one inch to 180 feet).

2 Chotard, K. *Louis XIV, Louvois, Vauban et les Fortifications du Nord de la France* (Paris, 1890), 45

3 Vauban. *Le Directeur-Général des Fortifications*, 32; printed as appendix to Goulon, *Mémoires pour l'Attaque et la Défense d'une Place* (The Hague, 1730)

4 Vauban to Louis XIV, 18 November 1681, in Rochas d'Aiglun. *Vauban, sa Famille et ses Ecrits*, 2 vols (Paris, 1910), II, 201–2

5 Maigret, 312

6 Ricolfi, H. *Vauban et le Génie Militaire dans les Alpes-Maritimes* (Nice, 1935), 27

7 Mendoza, B. de. *Theorica y Practica de Guerra* (Madrid, 1577), Eng trans by E. Hoby, *Théorique and Practise of Warre* (1597), 87

8 Vauban to Le Peletier, 17 February 1693, in Rochas d'Aiglun, II, 379

9 To Louvois; M. Sautai, *L'Oeuvre de Vauban à Lille* (Paris, 1911), 15

10 To Louvois 14 January 1673, in Rochas d'Aiglun, II, 88

4. The Parts of a Fortress

1 Maigret, 309–10

2 *A Journey from London to Vienna and so to Buda*, British Museum, Stowe MSS 447

3 Mallet, A. Manesson. *Les Travaux de Mars*, 3 vols (Paris, 1673), I, 54

4 *Mémorial pour la Fortif-*

ication Permanente, Oeuvres Posthumes, 3 vols (Paris, 1806–9), I, 113

5 *Traité de la Défense* ([1706]; Paris, 1829), 20

6 *Memorie*, Book I, Chapter 5

7 *Traité de la Défense*, 22

8 Ibid, 25

9 Anon. *An Authentic Journal of the Siege of Bergen-op-Zoom* (London, 1747), 9–10

10 Ville, 162

11 Favé, M. *Mémoires Militaires de Vauban et des Ingénieurs Hué de Caligny*, 2 vols (Paris, 1854), II, 221

12 *A Description of Bombay Town's Fortification* 1756, British Museum, King's Topographical Collection CXV

13 Muller. *Practical Fortification*, 222

14 *De la Fortification depuis Vauban*, 2 vols (Paris, 1861), II, 784

5. The Service of a Fortress

1 *Mémoires de Frederick Baron de Trenck*, 3 vols (Strasbourg and Paris, 1789), I, 119

2 Pajol, Count. *Les Guerres sous Louis XV*, 7 vols (Paris, 1881–91), VII, 505

3 *De la Défense des Places Fortes*, 609

4 *Traité de la Défense*, 92

5 Ville, 336–7

6 *Traité de la Défense des Places Fortes* ([1723]; Paris, 1846), 169–87

7 *Generalsreglement* (Vienna, 1769), 192

8 Ibid, 183

9 Ville, 310

10 Vauban to Dupuy–Vauban, 2 October 1704, in Rochas d'Aiglun, II, 549–50

11 *Mémoires de Saint-Hilaire*, 6 vols (Paris, 1903–11), IV, 178

12 Boyvin, J. *Le Siège de la Ville de Dole* (Antwerp, 1638), 101

13 Du Boys de Riocour. *Histoire de la Ville et des Deux Sièges de La Mothe* (Neufchâteau, 1841), 30

14 Ibid, 98

6. The March of the Siege

1 *Generalsreglement*, 163

2 Miethen, M. *Artileriae Recentior Praxis* (Frankfurt and Leipzig, 1683), 2

3 *Treatise of Artillery*, 284–5

4 *Generalsreglement*, 200

5 *Memoirs of the Duke of Berwick*, 2 vols (1779), I, 84

6 *Traité des Sièges*, 253

7 Bousmard, I, 145

8 Santa Cruz. *Réflexions Militaires*, French trans, 10 vols (The Hague, 1736–40), X, 162

9 Quincy, Marquis de. *Histoire*

Militaire du Règne de Louis le Grand, 8 vols (Paris, 1726), IV, 317

10 Sully, Duc de. *Mémoires des Sages et Royales Oeconomies d'Estat de Henry le Grand*, in *Nouvelle Collection des Mémoires*, 2nd series (Paris, 1850), II, Chapter 11, 29

11 *Ecole de Mars*, 2 vols (Paris, 1725), II, 223

12 *Mémoires d'Artillerie*, 2 vols (Amsterdam, 1702), I, 271

13 *The Relation of Sydnam Poyntz, Camden Society*, 3rd series (1908), XIV, 115

14 Bonneville's commentary on Marshal de Saxe's *Esprit des Loix de la Tactique*, 2 vols (The Hague, 1762), 458

15 Pajol, II, 121–2

16 Du Boys de Riocour, 109

17 Dolleczek, A. *Geschichte der Österreichischen Artillerie* (Vienna, 1887), 307

18 Miethen, 11

19 Guignard, II, 212

20 De Vigny, quoted in Saint-Hilaire, II, n364

21 Saluces, A. de. *Histoire Militaire du Piémont*, 5 vols (Turin, 1817–18), V, 487–8

22 Landmann, I. (quoting Mouze). *A Treatise on Mines* (1815), 148–9

23 Porter, W. *History of the Corps of Royal Engineers* (1889), 182

24 Henrard, P. *Histoire du Siège d'Ostende* (*1601–1604*) (Brussels and Leipzig, 1890), 27

25 Cormontaigne, L. de. *Mémorial pour la Défense, Oeuvres Posthumes*, III, 171

26 *Erik Dahlberghs Dagbok*, ed H. Lungström (Stockholm, 1912), 127–8

27 Lazard, P. *Vauban 1633–1707* (Paris, 1934), 229–30

28 Tielcke, J. G. *An Account of the Most Remarkable Events of the War*, Eng trans, 3 vols (London, 1787), II, 318–19

29 Santa Cruz, X, 195

30 Sautai, 145

31 *La Fortification Perpendiculaire*, 11 vols (Paris, 1776–96), VII, 43–4

32 Bousmard, I, 75

33 *Oeuvres Complètes*, 2 vols (Maastricht, 1778), I, 21

34 Colin, J. *Les Campagnes du Maréchal de Saxe* (Paris, 1901–4), I, 225–6

35 *Memorias Militares*, 2 vols (Madrid, 1898), I, 193

36 *Generalsreglement*, 167

37 31 January 1672. Anon. *Campagne de Hollande, en MDCLXII, sous les Ordres de Mr le Duc de Luxembourg* (The Hague, 1759), 14

38 *Réflexions Militaires*, VIII, 7

39 *Fantaisies Militaires* (Dresden, 1795), II, 131–2

40 *Treatise*, 331

41 Quoted in E. S. Kite. *Brigadier-General Duportail* (Baltimore, 1933), 47

42 *Rélation des Sièges et Défenses de Badajoz, d'Olivenca etc*, 2nd ed (Paris, 1837), 241

43 *Adventures with the Connaught Rangers 1809–1814* (1902), 91–2

44 *Mémoires pour l'Attaque et la Défense d'une Place* (The Hague, 1730), 24

45 *Mémoires d'Artillerie*, I, 258

46 *L'Ecole de Mars*, II, 213

47 Saint-Hilaire, IV, 30

48 *Mémoires d'Artillerie*, I, 264

49 *A Treatise on Naval Gunnery*, 5th ed (1860), 232

50 La Pommeraye, A. Texier de. *Rélation du Siège et Bombardement de Valenciennes, en . . . 1793* (Douai, 1839), 116

51 Malthus, T. *A Treatise of Artificial Fire Works* (1629), 28

52 Colin, I, 56

53 Anon. 'Die Hessen vor Belgrad und auf Sicilien 1717', in *Beihefte zum Militar-Wochenblatt* (Berlin, 1887), 267–8

54 La Marguerite, Solar de. *Journal Historique du Siège de la Ville et de la Citadelle de Turin en 1706* (Turin, 1838), 15

55 *Mémorial pour la Défense*, 1923

56 Carnot, 43

57 *Traité des Sièges*, 81

58 Guignard, II, 444

59 Müller, H. *Geschichte des Festungskrieges*, 2nd ed (Berlin, 1892), 75

60 *Rêveries*, 118

61 *Les Fortifications*, 341

62 *Instructions Militaires*, in *Les Mémoires de Messire Jacques de Chastenet, Chevalier, Seigneur de Puységur*, 2 vols (Paris, 1690), II, 562

63 *Traité de la Défense*, 106

64 Bousmard, I, 102

65 Rochas d'Aiglun, II, 85

66 *Memoirs of Captain George Carleton* (Edinburgh, 1808), 310

67 Augoyat, M. *Aperçu Historique sur les Fortifications, les Ingénieurs et le Corps du Génie en France*, 2nd ed, 3 vols (Paris, 1860–4), I, 333–4

68 General Schulenburg, in Austrian General Staff, *Feldzüge des Prinzen Eugen von Savoyen*, 22 vols (Vienna, 1876–81), X, 420

69 Guignard, II, 439

70 Muller, J. *A Treatise Containing the Elementary Part of Fortification* (1746), 41–2

71 Goulon, 33–4

72 *Discours sur la Défense des Places,* printed with Vauban's *Traité de la Défense,* 285–6

73 *Feldzüge,* IV, 173

74 *Mémoires d'Artillerie,* I, 264

75 Montecuculi, Book I, Chapter 5

76 Unterberger, L. *Tagebuch der Belagerung und Bombardirung der französischen Festung Valenciennes . . . 1793,* 2nd ed (Vienna, 1815), 70

77 La Marguerite, Solar de, 117

78 Ibid, 90–1

79 Cooper, T. H. *Military Cabinet,* 2 vols (London, 1809), I, 85

80 *An Authentic . . . Journal,* 2

81 *The History of the Rebellion,* 8 vols (Oxford, 1826), VIII, 562

82 *L'Ecole de Mars,* II, 235

83 Baudart, G. B. *Les Guerres de Nassau,* 2 vols (Amsterdam, 1616), II, 330

84 *Mémoires,* in *Nouvelle Collection des Mémoires,* 2nd series, VI (Paris, 1850), Book VII, 479–80

85 Jones, J. T. *Journals of Sieges Carried On by the Army under the Duke of Wellington in Spain,* 3rd ed, 3 vols (1846), I, 400

86 'An Officer of the Seventy-Seventh', in *Peninsular Sketches,* ed. W. Maxwell, 2 vols (1845), I, 281

87 Quincy, VIII, 228

88 Dufour, G. H. *Mémorial pour les Travaux de Guerre* (Geneva and Paris, 1820), 130

89 Kriegsarchiv (Vienna). *Oesterreichischer Erbfolge-Krieg 1740–1748,* 9 vols (Vienna, 1896–1914), VI, 569

90 *Memoirs,* I, 365

91 *Herrn Obristen von Landsbergs Neue Grund-Risse und Entwürffe der Kriegs-Bau-Kunst* (Dresden and Leipzig, 1737), 53

92 *De l'Usage de l'Artillerie Nouvelle* (Metz, 1778), 233

93 *Feldzüge,* XIX, 451

94 *Erbfolge-Krieg,* VI, 21.

95 Kincaid, J. *Random Shots from a Rifleman* (1835), 261–2

96 Augoyat, I, 290

97 Puységur, II, 670

98 Augoyat, I, 98

99 Muller. *Elementary Fortification,* 207

100 Vauban to Louvois, 19 May 1682, in Rochas d'Aiglun, II, 212–13

101 Douglas. *Gunnery,* 67

102 Richmond, H. *Amphibious Warfare in British History* (Exeter, 1941), 29–30

103 Douglas. *Gunnery,* 356

104 House of Representatives, 37th Congress, 2nd Session,

Permanent Fortification and Sea-Coast Defences (Washington, 1862), 439

105 Auger, General. *Guerre d'Orient*, 2 vols (Paris, 1859), I, 534

106 Douglas. *Gunnery*, 372

7. The Great Sieges

1 Coehoorn, G. T. van. *Het Leven van Menno Baron van Coehoorn* (Leeuwarden, 1860), 8

2 *Réflexions Militaires*, X, 167

3 La Colonie. *Chronicles of an Old Campaigner*, ed C. Horsley (1904), 16

4 Rochas d'Aiglun, II, 344–5

5 Ibid, II, 346

6 *Mémoires*, II, 218

7 *Chronicles*, 19

8 Rochas d'Aiglun, II, 348

9 Coehoorn, 11

10 Chronicles, 39–40

11 Quoted in F. Ten Raa and F. de Bas, *Het Staatsche Leger 1568–1795* (The Hague and Breda, 1911 etc), VII, 99

12 Quoted in Ibid, VII, loo

13 Loc cit

14 Loc cit

15 Coehoorn, 12

16 *Mémoires*. II, 367

17 Quoted in *Staatsche Leger*, VII, 102

18 Coehoorn, 15

19 Rochas d'Aiglun, II, 439

20 Loc cit

21 Wortley, C. S. *Journal of an Excursion to Antwerp during the Siege of the Citadel in December 1832* (1833), 50–1

22 Ibid, 70

23 Ibid, 45

24 Ibid, 190

25 Parkinson, C. N. *Edward Pellew, Viscount Exmouth* (1934), 468

Select Bibliography

BIOGRAPHICAL STUDIES

Augoyat, M. *Notice Historique sur le Lieutenant Général Lapara de Fieux*, Paris 1839. Lapara de Fieux was one of the most gifted of Vauban's fellow engineers

Blomfield, R. *Sébastien le Prestre de Vauban 1633–1707*, London 1938. Blomfield was a practising architect

Chotard, K. *Louis XIV, Louvois, Vauban et les Fortifications du Nord de la France*, Paris 1890

Coehoorn, G. T. van. *Het Leven van Menno Baron van Coehoorn*, ed J. W. Van Sypesteyn, Leeuwarden 1860. By Coehoorn's son

Ericsson, E., and Vennberg, E. *Erik Dahlbergh*, Uppsala and Stockholm 1925

Erik Dahlbergh's Dagbok, ed H. Lundström, Stockholm 1912

Guerlac, H. 'Vauban. The Impact of Science on War', in *Makers of Modern Strategy*, ed E. M. Earle, Princeton 1944 and later reprints

Halevy, D. *Vauban*, Paris 1923

Lazard, P. *Vauban 1633–1707*, Paris 1934. Still the best of the Vauban biographies

Lloyd, E. M. *Vauban, Montalembert, Carnot. Engineer Studies*, London 1887

Michel, G. *Histoire de Vauban*, Paris 1879

Parent, M., and Verroust, J. *Vauban*, Paris 1971. With some remarkable modern photographs of Vauban's fortifications

Pujo, B. *Vauban*, Paris 1991

Rebelliau, A. *Vauban*, Paris 1962

Rochas d'Aiglun. *Vauban, sa Famille et ses Ecrits*, 2 vols, Paris 1910. A mass of important material

Sauliol, R. *Le Maréchal de Vauban*, Paris 1924. The best short study

Toudouze, G. G. *Monsieur de Vauban*, Paris 1954

HISTORIES OF FORTIFICATION, SIEGECRAFT AND RELATED SUBJECTS

Alderwerelt, J. K. H. de Roo van. *De Vestingoorlog en de Vestingbouw in hunne Ontwikkeling Beschouwd*, The Hague 1862

Allent, A. *Histoire du Corps Impériale du Génie*, Paris 1805

Anon [Aparici y Garcia?]. 'Resumen Historico del Arma de Ingenieros', in *Memorial de Ingenieros*, I, Madrid 1846

Augoyat, M. *Aperçu Historique sur les Fortifications, les Ingénieurs et le Corps du Génie en France*, 2nd ed, 3 vols, Paris 1860–4. Very important

Blois, E. de. *De la Fortification en Présence de l'Artillerie Nouvelle*, 2 vols, Paris 1865

Bonaparte, L.-N. *Etudes sur le Passé et l'Avenir de l'Artillerie*, Vol. II, Paris 1851, for the section on fortress warfare

Bonin, U. v. *Geschichte des Ingenieurkorps und der Pioniere in Preussen*, 2 pts, Berlin 1877–8

Centre Pro Civitate. *Plans en Relief de Villes Belges Levés par des Ingénieurs Militaires Français XVIIe–XIXe*, Brussels 1965

Centro Internazionale per lo Studio delle Cerchia Urbane [at Lucca]. This organisation produces a number of useful monographs, most notably the *Quaderni* associated with its annual exhibitions

Cockle, M. J. *A Bibliography of Military Works up to 1642*, London 1900, 2nd ed 1957

Dolleczek, A. *Geschichte der Österreichischen Artillerie*, Vienna 1887. A much wider survey than the title suggests

Duffy, C. J. *Siege Warfare I: The Fortress in the Early Modern World, 1494–1660*, London 1979

Duffy, C. J. *Siege Warfare I: The Fortress in the Age of Vauban and Frederick the Great, 1660–1789*, London 1985

Hall, A. R. *Ballistics in the Seventeenth Century*, Cambridge 1952

Hughes, Q. *Military Architecture. The Art of Defence from the Earliest Times to the Atlantic Wall*, Liphook 1991. The most comprehensive and scholarly overview of fortification. Finely illustrated.

Jähns, M. *Geschichte der Kriegswissenschaften*, 3 vols, Munich 1889–91

Lavallée, T. *Les Frontières de France*, Paris 1864

Maggiorotti, L. A. *L'Opera del Genio Italiano al l'Estero. Gli Architetti Militari*, 3 vols, Rome 1933–9

Mayern, F. F. v. *Ueber den Geist der Befestigungskunst in den Verschiedenen Geschichtsepochen*, Vienna 1848

Müller, H. *Geschichte des Festungskrieges seit Allgemeiner Einführung der Feuerrwaffen bis zum Jahre 1892*, 2nd ed, Berlin 1892

Robertson, F. L. *The Evolution of Naval Armament*, London 1921

Seydel, F. S. *Nachrichten über Vaterländische Festungen und Festungskriege*, 4 vols, Leipzig and Züllichau 1818–24

Tripier, J. *La Fortification Déduite de son Histoire*, Paris 1866

Tychsen, V. E. *Krigsbygningskunstens og Faestningskrigen Udvikling fra de Aeldeste Tider indtil Vore Dage*, 2 vols, Copenhagen 1863

Vauvilliers, L. H. *Recherches Historiques sur le Rôle et l'influence de la Fortification*, Paris 1845. By an opponent of fortification

Vernois, General Prévost de. *De la Fortification depuis Vauban*, 2 vols, Paris 1861

Villenoisy, Cosseron de. *Essai Historique sur la Fortification*, Paris 1869

Viollet-le-Duc, E. *Histoire d'une Forteresse*, Paris undated. Illustrates the history of fortification through a history of the fictional fortress of La Roche-Point.

Zastrow, H. v. *Geschichte der Beständigen Befestigung*, 3rd ed, Leipzig 1854

Zeller, G. *L'Organisation Défensive des Frontières du Nord et de l'Est au XVIIe Siècle*, Paris 1928

INFORMATIVE CONTEMPORARY TEXTS

Belidor, B. F. de. *La Science des Ingénieurs dans la Conduite des Travaux de Fortification et d'Architecture Civile*, Paris 1729. Especially on the practical details of fortress-building

Blondel, N. F. de. *Nouvelle Manière de Fortifier les Places*, The Hague 1684

Bousmard. *Essai Général de Fortification, et d'Attaque et Défense des Places*, 2 vols, Berlin 1797–8

Caligny, L.-R. Hué de. *Traité de la Défense des Places Fortes avec Application à la Place de Landau* (1723), Paris 1846

Carnot, L. *De la Défense des Places Fortes*, 3rd ed, Paris 1812

Coehoorn, M. van. *Nouvelle Fortification* (1685), new ed, The Hague 1741

Cormontaigne, L. de. *Architecture Militaire ou l'Art de Fortifier par un Officier de Distinction sous le Règne de Louis XIV*, 2 vols, The Hague 1742

— *Oeuvres Posthumes de Cormontaigne*, 3 vols, Paris 1806–9, comprising: I *Mémorial pour la Fortification Permanente et Passagère;* II *Mémorial pour l'Attaque des Places;* III *Mémorial pour la Défense des Places*

Deidier, l'Abbé. *Le Parfait Ingénieur Français*, new ed, Paris 1757

Douglas, H. *A Treatise on Naval Gunnery*, 5th ed, London 1860

Dufour, G. H. *Mémorial pour les Travaux de Guerre*, Geneva and Paris 1820

Fer, N. de. *Introduction à la Fortification*, 2 vols, Paris 1690–5

Goulon. *Mémoires pour l'Attaque et la Défense d'une Place*, The Hague 1730. With an appendix containing Vauban's *Le Directeur-Général des Fortifications*

Guignard, Chevalier de. *L'Ecole de Mars*, 2 vols, Paris 1725

Kinsky, Count. *Ueber Emplacement der Festungen*, Wiener Neustadt 1790

Landmann, I. *A Treatise on Mines*, London 1815

Maigret, P. *Traité de la Sûreté et Conservation des Etats par le Moyen des Forteresses*, Paris 1727. Eng trans, *A Treatise*, London 1747

Mallet, A. Manesson. *Les Travaux de Mars*, 3 vols, Paris 1673

Mandar, C. F. *De l'Architecture des Forteresses*, Paris 1801

Muller, J. *A Treatise Containing the Elementary Part of Fortification*, London 1746; *A Treatise containing the Practical Part of Fortification*, London 1755; *The Attac* [sic] *and Defence of Fortified Places*, 2nd ed, London 1757; *A Treatise of Artillery*, London 1757. John Muller was a lecturer at the Royal Academy of Artillery, Woolwich

Noizet, General. *Principes de Fortification*, 2 vols, Paris 1859

Quincy, De. *Maximes et Instructions sur l'Art Militaire*, Paris 1726 (vol VIII of his *Histoire Militaire*)

Saint-Rémy, S. de. *Mémoires d'Artillerie*, 2 vols, Amsterdam 1702

Straith, H. *A Treatise on Fortification*, Croydon 1833

Struensee, K. A. *Anfangsgründe der Kriegsbaukunst*, 2nd ed, 2 vols, Liegnitz and Leipzig 1786–9

The works of Vauban:

Abrégé des Services du Maréchal de Vauban (1703), ed M. Augoyat, Paris 1839

Le Directeur-Général des Fortifications, printed as appendix to Goulon's *Mémoires* (above)

Mémoires Inédites du Maréchal de Vauban, ed M. Augoyat, Paris 1841

Mémoires Militaires de Vauban et des Ingénieurs Hué de Caligny, 2 pts, Paris 1847–54

Mémoire pour Servir d'Instruction dans la Conduite des Sièges et dans la Défense des Places (1667–1672, published 1740), trans and ed G. A. Rothrock as *A Manual of Siegecraft and Fortification,* Ann Arbor 1968

Traité des Sièges et de l'Attaque des Places (1704), ed M. Augoyat, Paris I 829

Traité de la Défense des Places (1706), ed de Valazé, Paris 1829. Also contains *Discours sur la Défense des Places, Présenté à Louis XIV en 1675, par Deshoulières*

Thematic Index

Artillery
evolution, 9, 16–17
fortress artillery, 11, 30, 56–9,
  99–103, 138
mortars, 11, 31–2, 35, 122–5,
  151–6, 162–3, 216, 217
siege artillery, 11, 12, 16,
  110–11, 122–5, 140–56,
  162–4, 168–70,

Engineers as a corps 12, 13,
  136–7, 183–4

**Engineers (as individuals),
  practitioners of engineering
  and fortress warfare**
d'Arçon, M., 24
Aristotle, 19
Belidor, B. F., 52, 173, 177
Bell, Schall von, 30
Belle-Isle, Marshal, 154–5
Brialmont, H., 80
Carnot, L., 15, 20, 24, 98–9, 229
Chasseloup de Laubat, General,
  80
Choumara, Captain, 229
Clausewitz, C., 25
Coehoorn, M., 13, 61, 71,
  163–4, 202–14, 228–9
Cormontaigne, L., 65, 71, 74,
  166, 229

Dahlberg, E., 12–13, 39, 44,
  127, 192, 197
Dilich, J., 17, 228
Dilich, W., 228
Errard de Bar-le-Duc, J., 65, 22
Floriani, 75, 228
Fourcroy, C.-R., 229
Frederick the Great, 13, 32, 33,
  68. 79
Freitag, A., 22
Guignard, Chevalier, 119
Lefèbvre. S. D., 177–8
Machiavelli, N., 23
Maigret, P., 19, 20, 24, 25, 53
Mandar, C. F., 25
Mesgrigny, Comte de., 106
Montalembert. 13, 15, 198–9,
  229
Montecuculi, R., 67, 173
Muller, J., 16–17
Napoleon Bonaparte, 14, 22–3,
  26, 80
Neubauer, C., 228
Noizet, General, 16
Pacciotto of Urbino, 78, 215,
  228
Pagan, B., 12, 65, 228–9
Paixhans, H. J., 197
Pinto, Colonel, 33
Plato, 19
Prévost de Vernois, General, 31

Richards, J., 59–60
Rimpler, G., 228
Rüsensteen, H., 52
Sangallo, G. F. G., 227
Sanmicheli, M., 227
Santa Cruz, A. N., 116, 128, 135
Sattler, J., 228
Saxe, Marshal, 27–8, 115, 121–2
Speckle, D., 228
Stevin, S., 228
Sturm, C. I., 228
Tartaglia, N., 10, 228
Ufano, D.,31
Vauban, S. Le P.
  character, 11–12, 105–6
  defensive techniques, 156, 164
  and the engineering corps, 12
  fortress construction, 30, 31, 32–3, 36, 40–1, 43, 45–6, 191–2
  fortress designs, 12, 228
  legacy, 17
  siege techniques, 12, 32, 114–5, 124, 128, 129–30, 137, 149, 159–60, 162–3, 173, 185, 194, 201–08
  strategy, 12, 20, 25
Vieilleville, Sieur de, 23
Ville, A., 33, 65, 161

Fortification, evolution of:
sixteenth-century Italian and the evolution of the bastion system, 10–11, 66, 227
sixteenth- and seventeenth-century Dutch, 11, 65, 227–8
seventeenth- and eighteenth-century French, 12, 13–14, 74, 228–9
seventeenth- and eighteenth-century German, 228
nineteenth-century German, 79

Fortification, parts and features of (see also Appendix I, Glossary, 220–6)
abatis, 80,
banquette, 56–8
barracks, 92–6
bastion, 10, 30, 55, 62–7
bastion flank, 63–6
batardeau, 68
berm, 61
bonnet, 74–5
bridge, 88–9
caltrop, 80
caponnière, 79, 89
casemate, 48
cavalier, 64–5, 66
cheval de frise, 81
cistern, 44
citadel, 23–4, 77–8, 108, 129
construction, 29–52
cordon, 49, 50
counterfort, 50
counterguard, 75
countermine (permament), 48–9, 82–4
counterscarp, 10, 69
couvreface-generale, 75
covered way, 10, 69–71
crémaillère, 71
crownwork, 77
cuvette (cunette), 68
déblai, 46, 67

defilement, 32
demi-lune, 67–8, 74
disease, 17–18, 29–30, 34–5,
  81–2, 107
ditch, 35, 46, 59, 178–80
embrasure, 50, 58–9
envelope, 75
fausse-braye, 61–2
fort, 32, 78–80
fort d'arret (Sperrfort), 27
garde-fou, 61
garrison, 28, 97–8
gate, 84–8, 116–117,
glacis, 11, 71–2
gorge, 89
governor, 105–8, 130, 183
guérite, 58–9
hornwork, 76–7, 150
inundation, 181–2
latrine, 96
lunette, 79
magazine, 91–2
maison forte, 33
Martello Tower, 192–3
orillon, 63– 4
palisade, 11, 69–70, 165
parapet, 58–9
pas de souris, 90
place of arms, 70–1
postern, 89
provisions, 28, 29, 62, 98–9,
  125–6
rampart, 48–52, 55–63
ravelin, 10, 72–4, 88
remblai, 66
retrenchment, 30, 66–7
revetment, 50–5, 56; demi-revetment, 60–1

sally-port, 89
scarp, 48–52, 62; Carnot scarp,
  63
sluice, 81
storm poles, 61
strategy, 12, 13, l5, 19–27
tablette, 60–1
talus, 56–7, 89
tenaille, 75–6, 228
tenaillon, 74
terreplein, 56, 57
traverse, 32, 71
trees, 59–60
urbanism, 17–18
zone of servitude, 72

**Fortresses, forts and defensive
  positions** (with year of siege):
Acre (1840), 196
Alessandria, 80; (1746), 126
Algiers (1682), 194–5; (1816),
  218–19
Alicante (1709), 32
Almeida, 235; (1809), 155
Amiens (1597), 117
Antibes, 41, 43; (1747), 195
Antwerp, 25, 60, 78, 228;
  (1832), 170, 214–18
Arras, 22; (1654), 114
Ath (1697), 32, 76, 150; (1745),
  32
Ayut'ia, 34
Azov (1737), 155
Badajoz (1811), 138, 170;
  (1812), 16, 120, 186
Batavia, 22
Bayonne, 35
Belfort, 43, 228, 234

Belgrade (1690), 155; (1717), 155–6; (1789), 125, 155

Bergen-op-Zoom, 81–2, 84, 120; (1747), 182, 183; (1814), 120

Bergues, 234

Berwick-upon-Tweed, 66, 68, 234

Besançon, 228

Béthune, 81

Blaye, 234

Bouchain (1712), 79

Breda (1590), 116

Breisach (1704), 117–18

Breslau (1757), 155

Briançon, 26, 32

Brussels (1695), 124–5

Buda (1849), 183

Burgos (1812), 149–50

Cahors (1584), 118

Calais (1694), 195

Tour de Camaret (Brest), 192

Candia (1667–9), 115

Fort Carillon (Ticonderoga), 80, Cartagena (1741), 195

Casale, 26

Charleroi (1693),

Château-Queyras, 44

Cherbourg, 199

Ciudad Rodrigo (1810), 170

Coblenz, 26

Coevorden, 34

Condé, 35

Copenhagen (1658), 127

Cremona, 36; (1702), 116

Cuneo, 36; (1744), 183

Deal, 233

Delhi (1857), 120

Denia (1709), 163

Dieppe (1694), 195

Dunkirk, 22, 192–3

Entrevaux, 22

Evora, 30

Exilles, 26, 33

Fort Bard (1800), 26–7

Fort Carillon (Ticonderoga), 80

Fort Fuentes, 22

Fort Pulaski (1862), 199–200

Frederiksborg, 22

Fredriksten (1718), 130

Freiburg (1713), 25, 29, 32; (1744), 187

Gaeta (1734), 188

Geneva, 35

Genoa, 32

Ghent, 23

Gibraltar, 22; (1779–83), 31–2, 151, 153, 183

Glatz, 33

Glückstadt, 22

Göta Lejon Tower (Goteborg), 192

Grave (1677), 89

Gravelines, 234

Grosswardein, 22

Haarlem (1573), 116

Havana, 22

Hesdin (1637), 66

Ingolstadt (1743), 189

Jativa (1707), 187–8

Kaisersworth (1702), 164

Kinburn (1855), 199

Kolberg (Colberg) (1758), 128

La Fère, 34

La Mothe (1634), 122

Landau, 34, 79, 228; (1702), 79

Le Havre (1694), 195
Le Quesnoy, 234; (1712), 79
Lille, 23, 29, 41, 43; (1708), 70, 77, 164, 168, 170
Louisbourg, 44, 234
Lucca, 60, 235
Luxembourg (1684), 66
Maastricht, 59–60
Mainz, 25, 26; (1688), 70
Malta, 22; (1565), 183
Mannhe im, 25
Mantua, 22, 29, 34
Maubeuge, 35, 234
Menin, 35
Metz, 23
Milan (1522), 113
Mobile (1864), 200
Mons (1691), 114
Montauban (1621), 184–5
Mont-Louis, 32–3, 234
Mortella Bay (1794), 192–3
Naarden, 2 34
Namur, 26, 79; (1692), 201–8; (1695), 164, 165, 208–14
Narva (1700), 115
Neisse (1741), 68
Neuf-Brisach, 35, 234
Nice (1691), 155
Ochakov (1737), 155
Ofen (1686), 155
Olmütz (1758), 183
Ostend (1601–4), 67, 75
Oudenarde (1677), 81
Palmanova, 26
Paris, 16, 35, 80
Péronne, 34,
Perpignan,, 22, 36
Peschiera, 22

Philippsburg, 25, 34; (1676), 168; (1688), 34 (1734); 164
Pinerolo, 26
Pizzighettone (1733), 35, 183
Poltava (1709), 116
Portsmouth, 199
Prague, 30; (1741), 120–22; (1757), 81
The Quadrilateral (Verona–Mantua–Peschiera–Legnago), 22
Raab (1598), 119
Rochefort, 29
Rocroi, 234
St Augustine, 234
St-Malo, 191; (1693), 195
Sarrelouis, 35
Sarzanello Castle, 234
Schweidnitz, 79; (1762), 155, 174–5, 177–8
Sevastopol, 168, 1 99
Siena, 234
Strasbourg, 29, 35, 36, 41, 234
Sveaborg, 191
Ticonderoga (Fort Carillon), 80
Toulon, 191
Tour de Camaret (Brest), 192
Tournai, 30, 33, 35; (1709), 106; (1745), 138
Turin, 83, 228; (1706), 67, 79, 115, 177, 180–1; (1799), 125
Utrecht, 23
Valenciennes, 23, 29, 35; (1656), 114, 168; (1677), 128; (1793), 143, 175
Verdun (1792), 84
Verona, 22, 26
Verrua (1704–5), 148
Vieux-Brisach, 32

Villefranche, 33
Wachtendonck (1588), 122
Wesel, 25
West Point, 22
Würzburg, 235; (1866), 33
Yarmouth, 199
Ypres, 77; (1598), 117; (1678), 168

Fortress warfare (stages, techniques and weapons; see also Appendix 1, Glossary, 220–6),
artillery attack, 16, 31, 33, 110, 122–5, 140–56, 162–4, 168–70
artillery defence, 31, 99–103, 156–7, 160–1
blockade, 32, 125–6
bombardment, 122–5
breaches and breaching, 12, 28, 148, 168–70
camouflet, 176
cannelure cutting, 169
capitulation, 12, 28, 188–91
cavalier de tranchée, 166
circumvallation, 113–15
countervallation, 112–13

covered way, capture of, 164–8
escalade, 119–21
fascine, 131, 134
gabion, 133–4, 158–60
grenade, 166 – 8
insult, 103–5
investment, 112–16
mantlet, 155
mine, 32, 170–8, 193–100, 218–19; marine, 199
parallel, 12, 137–9, 141, 157, 161, 162–3
passage of ditch, 178–80
petard, 117–19
plans and preparations, 109–12, 126–31
reconnaissance, 126–9
ricochet fire, 149–51
sandbag, 134
sap, 157–60
saucisson, 174–5
shrapnel, 151
siege train, 109–11, 131–4
sortie, 31, 68, 70, 161–2
storm of breaches, 184–8
surprise, 103–5, 116–22
zig-zag, 139